Telepathy and Literature

Telepathy and Literature

Essays on the Reading Mind

Nicholas Royle

Basil Blackwell

Copyright © Nicholas Royle 1990
First published 1991
First published in USA 1991

Basil Blackwell Ltd
108 Cowley Road, Oxford, OX4 1JF, UK

Basil Blackwell, Inc.
3 Cambridge Center
Cambridge, Massachusetts 02142, USA

British Library Cataloguing in Publication Data

A CIP catalogue record for this book is available from the British Library.

Library of Congress Cataloging in Publication Data

Royle, Nicholas.
Telepathy and literature: essays on the reading mind/Nicholas Royle.
p. cm.
Includes bibliographical references and index.
ISBN 0–631–16311–5: $70.00 — ISBN 0–631–17691–8 (pbk.): $19.90
1. English literature — History and criticism. 2. American literature —
History and criticism. 3. Psychoanalysis and literature.
4. Reader-response criticism. 5. Telepathy in literature. I. Title.
PR99.R68 1991
820.9′353–dc20   90–36377
CIP

Typeset in 11 on 13 pt Garamond
by Graphicraft Typesetters Ltd., Hong Kong
Printed in Great Britain

For my parents

Contents

Acknowledgements

I am grateful to the following publishers who are owners of copyright material:

Quotation from Salman Rushdie: *Midnight's Children* reproduced by permission of Jonathan Cape Ltd and Alfred A. Knopf Inc.; quotation from Jacques Derrida: 'The time of a thesis: punctuations' (in *Philosophy in France Today*, ed. Alan Montefiore) by permission of Cambridge University Press; quotation from Virginia Woolf: *The Waves* by permission of the Hogarth Press and Harcourt Brace Jovanovich; quotations from Virginia Woolf: 'Kew Gardens' (in *The Complete Shorter Fiction*, ed. Susan Dick) by permission of Triad Grafton; quotation from Raymond Chandler: *The Little Sister* (in *The Chandler Collection*, vol. 1; London, 1983) by permission of Hamish Hamilton Ltd and Houghton Mifflin.

In the course of working on this work I have been especially indebted to the suggestions, advice and support of Jacqueline Hall, Minnamarja Rasi and Ann Wordsworth. In an inevitably less determinable way, I would also like to thank all those others the imprint of whose intellectual friendship may be recognizable in these pages. Finally I would like to express my gratitude to the staff of the Bodleian Library, in Oxford, of the Attila and Pyynikki libraries, in Tampere, and at the Society for Physical Research, in London.

1

Introduction

If therefore the whole church be come together in one place, and all speak with tongues, and there come in those that are unlearned, or unbelievers, will they not say that ye are mad?

But if all prophesy, and there come in one that believeth not, or one unlearned, he is convinced of all, he is judged of all:

And thus are the secrets of his heart made manifest ...

(I Corinthians 14, 23–5)

By sunrise, I had discovered that the voices could be controlled – I was a radio receiver, and could turn the volume down or up; I could select individual voices; I could even, by an effort of will, switch off my newly-discovered inner ear.

(Salman Rushdie, *Midnight's Children*)

Every conceptual breakthrough amounts to transforming, that is to deforming, an accredited, authorized relationship between a word and a concept, between a trope and what one had every interest to consider to be an unshiftable primary sense, a proper, literal or current usage.

(Jacques Derrida, 'The Time of a Thesis')

What is telepathy? What happens to the question of telepathy when it is brought into relation with literature? Conversely, how might our understanding of 'literature' be modified by an analysis and fundamental reconsideration of the question of telepathy?

No doubt many people would suppose that the concept of

telepathy is as old as the hills. But 'telepathy' is a comparatively recent word, little more than a hundred years old. *The Oxford English Dictionary (OED)* traces its first use to F. W. H. Myers, in 1882. Let us turn back, then, and begin with the first appearance and first definition of the word 'telepathy', as provided by Frederic Myers at a meeting of the Society for Psychical Research in London, in December 1882:

> *we venture to introduce the words* Telesthesia *and* Telepathy *to cover all cases of impression received at a distance without the normal operation of the recognised sense organs. These general terms may, we think, be found of permanent service; but as regards what is for the present included under them, we must limit and arrange our material rather with an eye to convenience, than with any belief that our classification will ultimately prove a fundamental one. No true demarcation, in fact, can as yet be made between one class of those experiences and another; we need the record of as many and as diverse phenomena as we can get, if we are to be in a position to deal satisfactorily with any one of them.*[1]

Two immediate observations regarding this definition. First, Myers is not offering 'Telepathy' in isolation but alongside 'Telesthesia'. It is striking how differently these two words have fared: the former is very much in everyday use, while the latter is apparently now obsolete.[2] The present study will venture, among other things, a reintroduction of the word 'telesthesia'. Second, Myers's definition is remarkably indefinite. The Index of Volume I of the SPR *Proceedings* reiterates the very general description of 'Telepathy' and 'Telesthesia' as 'Impressions transferred otherwise than through the recognised channels of sense.'[3] Myers's concern is evidently to keep all 'classification' and 'demarcation' as flexible as possible; and to emphasize the importance of multiplicity and diversity.

The following pages bear a certain fidelity to Myers's original definition, specifically by taking up the question of 'telepathy' in relation to literature. 'Telepathy', then, is being consigned to a process of conceptual elaboration and possible transformation. Accordingly, I offer analyses of various kinds of writing – the novel, novella, short story, poetry, drama. But the readings which appear here are tentative and highly provisional; they are necessarily exploratory and experimental. They are not confined to literary texts published since 1882; nor are chapters arranged in accordance with a rectilinear 'literary history'. This is not intended as an anti-historical gesture (whatever that might mean). Rather, it is part of the more general attempt at a fundamental reconsideration of the very notion of telepathy. As I hope to suggest, such an analysis does not stop short of the question of history 'itself'.

To submit 'telepathy' in an effective manner to a work of conceptual elaboration is unavoidably to acknowledge the primary and prerequisite importance of historical considerations. The present study is thus, in crucial respects, historical. 'Telepathy' did not just appear from nowhere. It is closely bound up with the more general emergence of spiritualism and psychical research in the second half of the nineteenth century. In some ways it is peculiarly 'English', even if in others it remains inseparable from a more general context of nineteenth-century American and European culture.[4] The emergence of 'telepathy' is linked to the crisis of Christianity in the Victorian age. As Janet Oppenheim observes in her excellent book *The Other World: Spiritualism and Psychical Research in England, 1850–1914*: 'In an effort to counter [their] insecurity, to calm their fears, and to seek answers where contemporary churches were ambiguous, thousands of British men and women in the Victorian and Edwardian eras turned to spiritualism and psychical research.'[5] If people were no longer able to believe in God, contends Oppenheim, they could at any rate try 'to believe in *something*' (p. 4). 'Telepathy' here would seem to be a substitute for 'God'.

'Do you believe in God?' 'Do you believe in telepathy?' Nowadays the question of belief in the latter at least is powerfully enmeshed with psychiatry and institutions of mental health. DSM-III, the *Diagnostic and Statistical Manual of Mental Disorders* (3rd edn.), for example, published by the American Psychiatric Association, provides what it calls 'Diagnostic Criteria for Schizotypal Personality Disorder'. Top of the list of eight criteria comes 'magical thinking, e.g., superstitiousness, clairvoyance, telepathy, "6th sense", "others can feel my feelings"'.[6] This is 'telepathy' in one of its most highly determined forms. No need to have any uncertainty about the meaning of the word: belief in 'telepathy' is a definite symptom, a sure sign of the 'schizotypal'. Yet such a psychiatric or psychologistic representation has its underside. Oppenheim's *The Other World* performs another service, in fact, by showing the extent to which the history of spiritualism and psychical research is interwoven with that of psychology. Emphasis is given to the overlapping, and even the synonymity, of the terms 'spiritualist' and 'psychological', especially in the later years of the nineteenth century.[7]

Oppenheim also touches on the links between spiritualism, psychical research and psychoanalysis, noting for example Freud's affiliation with the Society for Psychical Research, based in London, and the fact that it was Myers – the man credited with the introduction of the word 'telepathy' – 'who had first publicized in England the Breuer–Freud studies of hysteria' (p. 245). Other writers, however, have provided a more specific and more important focus. The writings of Nicolas Abraham and Maria Torok, and Jacques Derrida, in particular, can be seen as offering a radically different understanding of the historical and conceptual relations between psychoanalysis and telepathy.[8] The present study is, in part, an attempt to explore these relations further.

The emergence of 'telepathy' is bound up not only with the crisis or failure of Christian belief and with the forms of modern psychology. At least two further factors should be taken into account. Firstly, the history of the term 'telepathy' is intimately related to that of the concept of sympathy. This relation could be traced through the work of David Hume and Adam Smith or, in poetry, through Wordsworth and Coleridge.[9] Liddell and Scott give συμπαθεια as 1. *fellow-feeling, sympathy*; 2. In the philosophy of Epicurus, *corresponding 'affection' or quality, affinity.*[10] The classical conception is legible in the Argument to Book X of *Paradise Lost*, when Milton writes: 'Sin and Death sitting till then at the gates of hell, by wondrous sympathy feeling the success of Satan in this new world, and the sin by man there committed, resolve to sit no longer confined in hell, but to follow Satan their sire up to the place of man.' Today we might translate or paraphrase Milton's 'wondrous sympathy' as 'telepathy'. The emergence of Romanticism, however, in the second half of the eighteenth and through the early nineteenth centuries, seems to be directly linked to an intensified, even unprecedented preoccupation with notions of sympathy. In some ways the historical appearance of 'telepathy' could be viewed as the inevitable outcome, or hyperbolization, of the importance accorded to 'sympathy' in Romanticism. In the later nineteenth century there is a kind of sliding, whereby the term 'telepathy' comes to stand in for what a few years earlier had been designated as 'sympathetic clairvoyance': as I hope to show, this is especially dramatized in the context of the work of George Eliot.

Secondly, it should be clear that 'telepathy' is historically linked to numerous other tele-phenomena: it is part of the establishment of tele-culture in general. It is necessarily related to other nineteenth-century forms of communication from a distance through new and often invisible channels, including the railway, telegraphy, photography, the telephone and gramophone. It is thus part of a culture which is still in the process of being articulated, and in this respect perhaps the question 'Do you believe in telepathy?' need not be regarded as categorically or essentially distinguishable from questions such as, 'Do you believe in the telephone?' or 'Do you believe in television?'

As well as engaging with the question of telepathy in relation to the more general everyday world of tele-phenomena, the readings assembled here will perhaps also address the interests of parapsychologists. In this respect, however, a note of caution may be sounded. In an essay entitled 'Parapsychology and Literature', Joseph M. Backus observes that 'there has been little application of parapsychology to the study of literature, or of the findings of literary study to the interests of parapsychology'; and he hopes that 'discussion will eventually lead to the formulation of a parapsychological approach to literature'.[11] The present study, it should be stressed, is in no way concerned with the formulation of such an approach. If anything, it may serve to indicate something of the opposite, namely a literary approach to parapsychology. At any rate, it seeks to open up the possibilities of thinking about parapsychology *differently*.

The central concern here is, strictly speaking, an impossible one. It is to write *on behalf of* literature. No doubt this involves a certain divergence from the work of Jacques Derrida: insofar as he represents his work as being 'true to philosophy', the present pieces seek to be true to literature. In a talk at the Institute of Contemporary Arts in London, in 1985, Derrida responded to a question about the use of the word 'philosophy' in the title of the Collège International de Philosophie (in Paris):

> *I never said a word against philosophy.... As soon as you give up philosophy, or the word philosophy, what happens is not something new or beyond philosophy, what happens is that some old hidden philosophies under other names – for instance the name of literary theory or psychology or anthropology and so on – go on dominating the research in a dogmatic or implicit way. And when you want to make this implicit philosophy as clear and as explicit as possible, you have to go on philosophising. And even if you deconstruct philosophy or if you want to think of the limits of philosophy, of the special kind of limits of philosophy, you have not only to philosophise in a general and a historical way but to be trained in the history of philosophy and to go on learning and teaching philosophy. That's why I am true to philosophy.*[12]

This is not to suggest that Derrida's work can or should be regarded chiefly in a philosophical context: indeed it is important to acknowledge that one of his avowed initial concerns was specifically with the question of literature.[13] It is also clear that his work is an attempt to perform and represent the mutual contamination of the 'literary' and the 'philosophical'.[14] But this is done, in general terms, from the side of philosophy, under the name of 'philosophy'. The present study is not against philosophy; nor is it making any crude claim to an escape from metaphysics. It is rather an involvement with 'literature'. Perhaps in some ways reminiscent of Michel Foucault's *Madness and Civilization*, such an involvement is necessarily dangerous and impossible at the same time.[15]

Yet the essays gathered here hope to have learned a little from the texts of Derrida and Foucault. They are offered as an uncertain and preliminary effort to mark something minuscule and unnamable. For it is tempting, though no doubt precipitous, to speak in terms of the 'minute displacement or interval' evoked by Philippe Lacoue-Labarthe and Jean-Luc Nancy in their study *The Literary Absolute: The Theory of Literature in German Romanticism*.[16] Lacoue-Labarthe and Nancy are concerned with the moment or space of 'the inauguration of the *theoretical* project in literature', with 'the *theoretical* institutionalization of the *literary genre* (or, if you like, of literature *itself*, of *literature* as absolute)' (pp. 2–3). They argue that 'romanticism is neither mere "literature" (they [i.e., the romantics] invent the concept) nor simply a "theory of literature" (ancient and modern). Rather, it is *theory itself as literature* or, in other words, literature producing itself as it produces its own theory' (p. 12). Lacoue-Labarthe and Nancy warn against the inevitable and widespread tendency to repeat the moves or gestures by which it becomes possible to speak of what Madame de Staël called '"philosophical systems applied to literature"' (p. 13).

The present work is an attempt to mark, in a slightly different way, the space or moment of literature, specifically in terms of 'telepathy'. 'Telepathy' may be the site of a certain fold, of a cutting or interruption. It may appear, on occasion, as some uncanny reading-machine, a sort of reader-response criticism in reverse. Elsewhere it will be linked with questions of divination and fortune-telling, androgyny and sexual difference, proper names and cryptonymy, doors and thresholds, poetry, hysteria and hypnosis, apocalypse and the so-called death drive, silence, ghosts and writing. Just as it may become impossible to conceive psychoanalysis, or a theory of the unconscious, without telepathy, so telepathy will be seen as interdependent with literature, as well as with literary criticism or theory: this is partly the position reached in the following chapter.[17] But there is no desire to limit 'telepathy' (or 'literature') to what Paul de Man calls 'the teleology of controlled meaning'.[18]

Finally, the following pages are preoccupied, even if in a silent manner, with notions of 'collective hallucination'. This was a topic to which one of the founding members of the Society for Psychical Research, Edmund Gurney, devoted considerable attention.[19] A more contemporary and political version might be seen in the work of Louis Althusser, in which it is argued that the experience of being a subject is in effect a matter of collective hallucination.[20] As Paul Hirst puts it,

Althusser argues contrary to the empiricist conception that there are not given subjects with an experience of the real. Subjects are not essential but are constituted. There is no 'social reality' which can be present to experience. Men's [sic] conditions of existence cannot

be manifest to them and in consequence they live their relation to these (absent) conditions in an imaginary mode. They live them in an imaginary presence, 'as if' they were given.[21]

That Althusser's work no longer carries the persuasive and influential weight it once did illustrates a further complexity, namely the relation of collective hallucination to questions of reading and interpretation.[22] Who is reading? What is being read and how? What effects can texts generate, even (or especially) in spite of themselves, or in spite of their readers? To what extent might a notion of collective hallucination be productive for an account of the strange 'event' of reading? Such questions are explored below, particularly in the pieces on George Eliot, Wordsworth and Coleridge, and Raymond Chandler.

2

Telepathy: from Jane Austen and Henry James

Here I should like to consider at least three texts.[1] In focusing on them and in showing various ways in which they are interrelated, I wish to try to suggest the productive and generative consequences of thinking about literature, and the novel in particular, in terms of the telepathic. Telepathy will be my subject.

The first text is Jane Austen's *Emma*, published in 1816.[2] This is the novel about Emma Woodhouse and the small world of Highbury in which she lives with her father, Mr Woodhouse. Her friend and former governess, Miss Taylor, has married a Mr Weston. Mr Knightley is the neighbour and the gentleman whom Emma finally marries: this is, on an initial reading of the novel, one of the two chief 'surprises'. Although Emma and Knightley seem very well suited to one another, it is not until the closing chapters of the novel that – contrary to repeated references to Emma's unwillingness to marry – she and Knightley are united. In the meantime there is much in the way of Emma's match-making (for example on behalf of the orphan Harriet Smith and the local Reverend Mr Elton) and in the way of possible intrigue (in particular, Frank Churchill's relation to Emma and Jane Fair-fax). Mr Weston is the true father of Churchill, whose visits (promised or actual) always cause local excitement. The main surprise of the novel, the governing secret of the narrative, is the revelation, in the closing pages, that Churchill has been secretly engaged to Jane Fairfax. It is this secret which is very much in danger of being revealed during the celebrated game of Alphabets, played between Frank Churchill, Emma, Jane and Harriet. And it is principally the concealment of this secret liaison which has led critics, at least since Robert Liddell in 1963, to regard the novel as a detective story.[3]

The second text is Henry James's short horror novel *The Turn*

of the Screw, published in 1898.[4] The narrative largely comprises
the contents of a manuscript relayed to and by a man called
Douglas, then relayed again to and by the author Henry James.
The manuscript was written by a governess, who remains nameless – though we are informed that she was 'a fluttered, anxious
girl out of a Hampshire vicarage' (p. 11): that Jane Austen was
also a girl out of a Hampshire vicarage might for the moment be
registered as merely a coincidence. The governess takes up a post,
in an old house in Essex, looking after two exceptionally beautiful
children, Miles and Flora. The tale concerns her attempts to
shield these children from the apparent 'ghosts' of two former
servants, the steward Peter Quint and the previous governess
Miss Jessel. These 'ghosts' seem to appear only to her. The
governess's attempts have the effect of reducing Flora to terror
and in the final scene Miles dies in her arms while the ghost of
Peter Quint looks on through the window. Many fascinating
aspects of James's text have been elucidated by Shoshana Felman,
in her now famous essay 'Turning the Screw of Interpretation'.[5]
Although I shall concentrate more on *Emma*, *The Turn of the
Screw* (including Felman's account of it) may perhaps be glimpsed
in what follows, operating silently, a little like a ghost-text. In
these terms, Felman's essay is particularly important for its stress
on how we as readers *'are forced to participate'* in what we read
of in the James story. Felman draws decisive attention to what she
calls the 'uncanny trapping power of Henry James's text as an
inescapable *reading-effect'*.[6]

The third text is by Jacques Derrida, entitled 'Telepathy' and
first published in 1981.[7] Derrida cannot see very clearly in 'Telepathy'. The form and syntax, even the putative authorship of this
text – not an essay but rather fragments inadvertently detached,
split off from the 'Envois' in *La Carte postale* (1980)[8] – fragments
of love letters, sentences, tracks and passages which apparently
trail off, arrested, written (at least in part, but what part, how in
the end would one fix the boundaries?) by Freud ... All of this
belongs to an exploration of 'telepathy' as 'communication between mind and mind otherwise than through the known channels
of the senses' (*Chambers*) – communication or feeling ($\pi\alpha\Theta o\varsigma$) at
a distance ($\tau\epsilon\lambda\epsilon$). Derrida communicates with Freud's writings on
telepathy.[9] This strange communication or correspondence oper-

ates on a number of levels and takes many directions. One doesn't know, any more with Derrida than with Freud, whether or not he 'believes' in 'telepathy'. But any supposedly 'ordinary usage' sense of 'telepathy' is unsettled, displaced. Thus, for example, Derrida follows and elaborates upon Freud's linking thought-transference and telepathy with fortune-telling and clairvoyance. He also considers the contemporary roles of computers and tele-media, together for example with the implications of the fact that Freud uses the metaphor of the telephone (literally, voice at a distance) in order to convey the idea of telepathy.[10] Derrida investigates, most generally, relations between telepathy and writing, especially telepathy and the epistolary, and between telepathy and concepts of time. Finally, he is examining telepathy in relation to the psychoanalytic concept of the unconscious. Derrida writes: 'Difficult to imagine a theory of what they still call the unconscious without a theory of telepathy. They can be neither confused nor dissociated' (p. 14).

How might thinking be thought *without* a concept of the unconscious or rather, according to some other formulation and an other logic? Derrida's work – and not only such texts as those dealing with Freud and scenes of writing or Nicolas Abraham and the anasemic[11] – could be read as a consistent confrontation with this question. Derrida says that he feels like laughing every time he uses the word 'unconscious' – 'especially with a possessive mark' (*T*, p. 16): 'Freud's unconscious', 'Derrida's unconscious', characteristics *of* the unconscious … What kind of logic, what conceptual network is in operation if we stand at the very edge, thinking the limit, the boundary of confusion and/or dissociation by which 'telepathy' is brought into relation with psychoanalysis and science? Derrida suggests that we attend to 'our immediate apprehensions, our pathies, our receptions, our apprehensions because we are letting ourselves be approached without taking or comprehending anything and because we are afraid' (p. 13).

It is frightening. Reading Derrida is frightening. As he says in 'Telepathy', he scares other people and he scares himself. In a sense this is a form of seduction: as he observes elsewhere, 'in saying in a certain tone, "I am in the act of seducing you," I do not suspend, I can even increase, the seductive power'.[12] Telepathy is a frightening thought, perhaps, and especially if (to adopt

Derrida's allusion to telemedia) 'one could not be sure of being able to cut ... or to isolate the lines' (*T*, p. 19). This may be frightening, but so is the other, as he also observes: 'The truth, what I always have difficulty getting used to: that non-telepathy is possible. Always difficult to imagine that one can think something to oneself, deep down inside, without being surprised by the other, without the other being immediately informed' (p. 13).

It may be a question of the name – or of 'something nasty', 'like a word', something 'which poisons life'. That is how Derrida's 'Telepathy' begins: 'I felt, from a distance and confusedly, that I was searching for a word, perhaps a proper name ... it had the initiative, according to me' (p. 3).

Suppose we were to transpose all of this to an analysis of a text such as Jane Austen's *Emma*? There is nothing frightening about *Emma*. What could be less frightening than this delightful novel, this (as Ronald Blythe describes it) 'the climax of Jane Austen's genius and the Parthenon of fiction' (*E*, p. 7)? Strange name, 'Parthenon' – a foreign monument, in a foreign language, deriving from the Greek word παρθενος, meaning 'virgin' – but leave that: perhaps a step sideways

Thank you for your letter. Freud writes to Wilhelm Knöpfmacher, in August 1878, enclosing copies of his first two publications, 'On the Origin of the Posterior Nerve Roots in the Spinal Cords of Amnocoetes' and 'Observation on the Formation and Finer Structure of the Lobed Organs in Eels described as Testes', both published in 1877. He writes:

> *I am also sending you herewith my collected works, not my complete ones as I have reason to suspect, for I am awaiting the correction of a third ['On the Spinal Ganglia and Spinal Cord of the Petromyzon' (1878)], and a fourth and fifth keep appearing in my prescient mind which is startled by them like Macbeth by the ghosts of the English Kings: "What! Will the line stretch out to the crack of doom?"*[13]

What would it mean for a text to be a ghost? Or for a text to have prescience, foresight, foreknowledge? Or, since I have just quoted a letter, for such so-called 'psychic phenomena' to be somehow essentially textual? Why is it that, reading *Emma*, I should think, find myself thinking of Henry James's *The Turn of the Screw* and, in particular, of those two small children, Miles and Flora? 'There was no occasion to press the matter farther. The conviction seemed real; he looked as if he felt it' (*E*, p. 228). 'I can no longer see very clearly' (*T*, p. 5), writes Derrida.

Roots, cords, lines. A 'discursive formation': this is the term Michel Foucault introduces for the purpose of 'general' historical or 'archaeological' analyses which seek, from the outset, to suspend the notions of tradition, the oeuvre, the book, the author and even 'history' itself.[14] It is especially provoking in the cases, for example, of Marxism and Freudianism, since Marx and Freud are regarded also as what Foucault calls 'founders of discursivity'.[15] They stretch out, almost as entities one might call by singular proper names, but monsters that seize on that calling, and absorb that call into the appearance of all the other calls which constitute their own identity and singularity. 'We are absolutely unable to know, forecast, / foresee, foretell, fortune-tell /' (*T*, p. 3), observes Derrida. And if in the failing light of that I foresee the following hypothesis, it is necessary to think that it also foresees me: literature is a discursive formation. This is one of the things I wished to introduce as a hypothesis here, and also to try to establish some of the grounds, or absence of grounds, according to which such a hypothesis might be thinkable. How could such a hypothesis be demonstrated, especially when 'literature' so manifestly lacks identification and cohesion by way of the proper name of an individual (Freud, Marx and so on)? How and where, in the name of who or what, would literature, as discursive formation, operate?

We may suppose or imagine things, Derrida suggests, 'as if we were late with respect to that which has already happened to us in the future, / the one which foresees us / and by which I sense us predicted, anticipated, snapped up, called, summoned from a single casting, a single coming' (*T*, pp. 3–4). This is the time of *Emma*, the novel which, because of what it conceals and ultimately reveals about the relations between characters, in a sense only becomes legible once a 'first' reading has been completed. It is not merely that the time of this text, and perhaps of its name as well, is split, doubled, destines itself always to the time of another reading, defers itself and ultimately enforces a reading that makes it always differ from itself. This is not untrue; but it is also that *Emma* situates subjectivity itself in this way. Everything is staged within the sense of a certain *après-coup* of anticipation, and in the constitutive necessity of a certain foreseeing of the past. For example, there is the account of Emma's response to seeing Harriet and Frank Churchill together. Their being together is just what we have been led to believe Emma herself has foreseen. It is in the aftermath of the encounter with the 'party of gypsies' (p. 330):

> *Could a linguist, could a grammarian, could even a mathematician have seen what she did, have witnessed their appearance together, and heard their history of it, without feeling that circumstances had been at work to make them peculiarly interesting to each other? – How much more must an imaginist, like herself, be on fire with speculation and foresight! – especially with such a ground-work of anticipation as her mind had already made. (p. 331)*

Emma's delusion here nevertheless bears a structure corresponding to that of the experience of Mr Weston when, at the 'end' of the novel, he is informed of Emma's and Knightley's marriage: 'the wonder of it was very soon nothing; and by the end of an hour he was not far from believing that he had always foreseen it' (p. 450). Here, at the end of the novel, 'there was nothing to be shifted off in a wild speculation on the future' (p. 450); but when speculation and the narrative itself ends, it begins. Or more, we are called upon to locate a decisive aporia, a kind of death sentence in which the text has finished but has not properly begun, an arrest that is rather the undecidability of a dance frozen in 'the felicities of rapid motion' which may, or may not, 'be its own reward' (*E*, pp. 253, 262).

Called by a single coming: everything in *Emma*, including the very possibility and structure of its narrative, is a matter of foreseeing, of anticipation, of coming. Most explicitly, at the level of thematic description, this may be figured in the anticipation of the coming, not coming or coming again, of Frank Churchill to the little community of Highbury. But, more generally and more crucially, it is a question of the epistolary and of letters, of all the letters which come, right up to the final letter (pp. 423–8), the revealing letter from Churchill which finally comes to reveal the truth, including the truth of the letter.

In 'Telepathy' Derrida reads what he calls Freud's three 'fake lectures' on telepathy, and suggests that there is a non-coincidental relation between the fact that these lectures were never delivered, although supposedly written for oral delivery, and the fact that the material which Freud uses in the context of the question of telepathy is 'almost always written, literal, or even solely epistolary (letters, postcards, telegrams, visiting cards)' (p. 18). Derrida implies that a theory of telepathy, especially insofar as his 'own' text promotes the possibility of such a theory, is inextricably linked to the question of writing.

'Telepathy', as we noted, is hardly an essay, but rather a fragmentary series of fragmentary love letters. And a theory of the epistolary is something Derrida explores here, as in *La Carte postale*. Among other things, in 'Telepathy', he explores the putatively familiar experience whereby the addressee of a letter 'is determined . . . on receipt of the letter' (p. 5). Derrida is not concerned with 'a letter which would be the external occasion, in some sense, of an encounter between two identifiable subjects – and who would already be determined' (p. 5). Rather he focuses on what he describes as the 'gentle and terrible decision' by which the addressee says 'It was me', '"me" the unique addressee' (p. 6). He focuses, that is, on the fact and some of the extraordinary implications of the fact that 'one cannot say of the addressee that s/he exists before the letter'. And the addressor or sender too. Derrida quotes, with evident delight, a letter from Flaubert to Louise for example: 'it is now ten o'clock, I have just received your letter and sent mine, the one I wrote last night. – Only just up, I am writing to you without knowing what I am going to say to you' (p. 12). Derrida is careful to stipulate that the gesture or movement by which one says 'It was me' has nothing to do with 'identifying with the hero [or heroine] of a novel' (p. 6). But what we may ask ourselves, and ask ourselves who it is we are asking when we ask ourselves, is whether there is or can be such a categorical exclusion of the literary as such; or at least, we may ask, what is happening in the case of a text, such as *Emma*, which specifically and quite systematically elaborates, on the one hand, questions of the epistolary, of the determinacy of addressor and addressee and, on the other hand, questions of whether 'It was me', it is 'me', the unique addressee and so on?

A letter may not reach its destination and no letter is ever single, nor is it ever reducible to the time – whatever that might be – of a single reading. *Emma* is profoundly a novel about the post office and telecommunications. It stages the constitutive necessity of a doubling and redoubling of the reading of a letter at numerous points; but nowhere more explicitly than in the final, multiple and disseminatory appearance of the letter from Frank Churchill – a letter addressed to Mrs Weston, and read by her but (on its 'initial' appearance or presentation) framed by another letter, from herself to Emma, read then by Emma, and then again, in the following chapter, by Knightley. It is in this context of the disseminatory time of a letter, and of the constitutive indeterminacy of its addressee, that we find ourselves perhaps, and find ourselves determining, or failing to determine precisely, the equivocality of its opening sentence: 'If I made myself intelligible yesterday, this letter will be expected; but expected or not, I know it will be read with candour and indulgence' (p. 423).

Read by whom?

Churchill's letter goes on to offer a formidable emplacement of the indeterminacy of addressor and addressee, specifically in relation to the unforeseen. For instance: 'Since I began this letter, which will be longer than I foresaw, I have heard from her [i.e., Jane Fairfax]' (p. 425). And again, following the syntactic rupture of a dash: ' – I have been walking over the country, and am now, I hope, rational enough to make the rest of my letter *what it ought to be*' (p. 426, my emphasis). Finally, the uncanny return; the disruption of letters within the letter – when, Churchill reports, Jane Fairfax writes announcing that their engagement has been '*dissolved*':

> *This letter reached me on the very morning of my poor aunt's death. I answered it within an hour; but from the confusion of my mind, and the multiplicity of business falling on me at once, my answer, instead of being sent with all the many other letters of that day, was locked up in my writing-desk; and I, trusting that I had written enough [!], though but a few lines, to satisfy her, remained*

without any uneasiness. – I was rather disappointed that I did not
hear from her again speedily; but I made excuses for her, and was
too busy, and – may I add? – too cheerful in my views to be
captious. – We removed to Windsor; and two days afterwards I
received a parcel from her, my own letters all returned! (p. 427)

Emma's response to Frank Churchill's letter is unexpected, but
foreseen. She is determined by it, despite what may have been her
own determination: 'This letter must make its way to Emma's
feelings. She was obliged, in spite of her previous determination
to the contrary, to do it all the justice that Mrs Weston foretold.
As soon as she came to her own name, it was irresistible.' (p.
429). Caught up in a dissemination of possible addressees, one is
determined by the letter. 'You say "me" the unique addressee and
everything starts' (p. 6), observes Derrida.

Does this mean me? Is this a discussion about 'me'?

This question of whether it is 'me', the unique addressee, is at
play throughout the novel, and figured at various moments in
terms of erotic or romantic misidentification. For example:
'"Me!" [Harriet] replied with a smile of astonishment, "are you
imagining me to be Mr Elton's object?"' (p. 133). Or Emma: '"I
am very much astonished, Mr Elton. This to *me*! you forget
yourself"' (p. 149). Or again: '"Me!" cried Emma, shaking her
head. – "Ah! poor Harriet!"' (p. 456).

Me? No. I cannot see very clearly, for example what is meant
by 'me'. It is an issue of identification, naturally enough, by way
of the name, the transferential or ostensible auto-affective appeal
of its appealing, its appearing and, above all perhaps, of the
strange materiality of its inscription: 'As soon as she came to her
own name, it was irresistible.' Difficult to imagine a theory of
fiction, a theory of the novel, without a theory of telepathy.
Starting perhaps from the hypothesis that fiction is, in some
radical sense, incapable of non-telepathic representation; starting
from the thought that the telepathic founds the very possibility of
character, characterization, etc. – from the 'omniscient narrator'
onwards, 'Jane Austen' and 'her' heroine, and so on. Like *The
Turn of the Screw*, the novel *Emma* is pervaded by the telepathic.
I would suggest, above all, that these two texts correspond with
one another, in a doubling and ineluctably uncanny way, at the

level of style. Both texts are radically *tele*-texts: narratorially and stylistically, they are at a distance, a distance which cannot be measured, and in the case of both it is a matter of an inhabiting of distance which is at the same time an irremediable disturbance of any experience of distance. This is inscribed, perhaps, in the name of Miles, and in his final terrifying word, '*Where?*'

At narrative and thematic levels it is perhaps unnecessary to enumerate the telepathic characteristics of James's text. Appearing to put it into the distance, I will continue to try to follow Austen's. *Emma* is, at these levels, also pervaded by the telepathic – in particular by what might be conventionally moralized as the dangers of speculation and 'reading thoughts'. Communication or interpretation would occupy a domain analogous to that de- scribed by Freud in *Totem and Taboo* – the domain where 'the element of distance is disregarded; in other words, telepathy is taken for granted'.[16] A few familiar instances may suffice: when Emma 'had no doubt of what Mr Weston was often thinking about' (p. 205); or when it seemed to Emma that Frank Churchill 'looked as if he fully understood and honoured such a sentiment' (p. 212); when, a little later, she challenges him with, '"You may *say* what you chuse – but your countenance testifies that your *thoughts* on this subject are very much like mine"' (p. 226); or when Churchill 'looked at her, as if wanting to read her thoughts. She hardly knew what to say. It seemed like the forerunner of something absolutely serious, which she did not wish' (p. 265). And this dimension of the relation between Frank Churchill and Emma will be most disturbingly staged in the Box-Hill episode in which, like something in the novel which is *showing* and (to adapt Henry James's words) 'not quite right', Churchill announces to her: 'You order me, whether you speak or not. And you can be always with me. You are always with me' (p. 362).

But in this domain, attention seems to fall, most of all, on the idea of the name. Emma finds her own name irresistibly impor- tant – for example, the day after having dinner with them, she feels that 'She must have delighted the Coles ... And left a name behind her that would not soon die away' (p. 239). Or in her perusal of a letter from Frank Churchill to Mrs Weston: 'The charm of her own name was not wanting. *Miss Woodhouse* appeared more than once' (p. 269). Emma assumes that the name has irresistible power for others too, for example when she tells Harriet: 'At this moment, perhaps, Mr Elton is shewing your picture to his mother and sisters, telling how much more beautiful is the original, and after being asked for it five or six times, allowing them to hear your name, your own dear name' (p. 82).

Everything in the text depends on the foreseeing or anticipation of the name, of saying or hearing it, of misreading the silence apparently surrounding it. For instance:

> 'Me!' cried Harriet, colouring, and astonished. 'Why should you caution me? – You do not think I care about Mr Frank Churchill.'
> . . . [Emma] could not speak another word. – Her voice was lost; and she sat down, waiting in great terror till Harriet should answer
> . . .
> 'Harriet!' cried Emma, collecting herself resolutely – 'Let us understand each other now, without the possibility of farther mistake. Are you speaking of – Mr Knightley? . . . I could almost assert that you had named Mr Frank Churchill'. (pp. 395–6)

Here, like a little later on when waiting for the truth from Knightley, voice is arrested, strange silence: 'Emma could say no more. They seemed to be within half a sentence of Harriet' (p. 416). As in *The Turn of the Screw*, everything seems repeatedly to lead to the point of the 'surrender of the name' (*TS*, p. 121).

It is politic, and politically sound, to avoid naming names. As Mrs Elton says: 'I mentioned no *names*, you will observe. Oh! no; cautious as a minister of state. I managed it extremely well' (p. 437). And yet everything depends on it, it engages a singular and extraordinary fervour. This may be one way of considering the game of Alphabets in the novel. I try to get in touch with it, but somehow sense that every attempt to determine the meaning of this game, and of the first word that appears in it, can be shown to be a blunder. One cannot see very clearly, or *simultaneously* one may see very clearly but without the slightest comprehension. The game of Alphabets, with the box of letters (each of these letters 'beautifully' written in Emma's hand), seems not too distant from a séance, clairvoyance, playing with a ouija-board, or, perhaps, the scene described by Coleridge in the Preface to 'Kubla Khan', in which the words rise up before him 'as *things*':[17]

Frank Churchill placed a word before Miss Fairfax. She gave a
slight glance round the table, and applied herself to it. Frank was
next to Emma, Jane opposite to them – and Mr Knightley so placed
as to see them all; and it was his object to see as much as he could,
with as little apparent observation. The word was discovered, and
with a faint smile pushed away. If meant to be immediately mixed
with the others, and buried from sight, she should have looked on
the table instead of looking just across, for it was not mixed; and
Harriet, eager after every fresh word, and finding out none, direct-
ly took it up, and fell to work. She was sitting by Mr Knightley,
and turned to him for help. The word was blunder; *and as Harriet*
exultingly proclaimed it, there was a blush on Jane's cheek which
gave it a meaning not otherwise ostensible. Mr Knightley connected
it with the dream; but how it could all be, was beyond his compre-
hension. (p. 344)

Then there is a word which remains nameless and unspoken, and
the next word in the game is '*Dixon*' – at which Jane Fairfax
'was evidently displeased; looked up, and seeing herself watched,
blushed more deeply than [Knightley] had ever perceived her, and
saying only, "I did not know that proper names were allowed",
pushed away the letters' (p. 345).

Blunder: doesn't this word itself take on something of a proper
name effect? It recurs at various moments in the text, but invariably in contexts also involving the materiality of writing. For
example, there is the moment at the end of the novel where Frank
Churchill is explaining to Emma the circumstances of the letter in
which Jane informs him of the doctor Mr Perry's acquisition of
a new carriage, inadvertently revealing the knowledge of which
forces Churchill to invent the 'dream'-excuse mentioned, just
before the game of Alphabets. With Jane present, 'though trying
to seem deaf', Churchill then tells Emma: 'Do not you see that, at
this instant, the very passage of her own letter, which sent me the
report, is passing under her eye – that the whole blunder is spread
before her' (p. 460). Or perhaps a more complex and provocative
example, which comes in a conversation between Jane Fairfax and
Mr Knightley's brother John, concerning the post office, telecommunications and the singularity of handwriting:

'The post-office is a wonderful establishment!' said she. – 'The
regularity and dispatch of it! If one thinks of all that it has to do,
and all that it does so well, it is really astonishing!'

> '*It is certainly very well regulated.*'
> '*So seldom that any negligence or blunder appears! So seldom that a letter, among the thousands that are constantly passing about the kingdom, is even carried wrong – and not one in a million, I suppose, actually lost! And when one considers the variety of hands, and of bad hands too, that are to be deciphered, it increases the wonder!*' (p. 296)

The deep irony of this is of course that, for Jane Fairfax and Frank Churchill, there is at least one crucial letter which does not arrive; and that this blunder is not made by the post office but by Churchill. As he will point out in his letter towards the end of the novel, 'imagine how, till I had actually detected my own blunder, I raved at the blunders of the post' (p. 428). There is always the chance of a blunder. Blunders do happen and no text perhaps illustrates this in a finer or more rigorously sustained way than Jane Austen's *Emma*. Would it necessarily be a blunder to name names?

In the conversation between Jane Fairfax and John Knightley, the idea of the singularity of one's handwriting is linked with the saying of a name. For Emma interrupts:

> '*I never saw any gentleman's handwriting*' – *Emma began, looking also at Mrs Weston; but stopped, on perceiving that Mrs Weston was attending to someone else – and the pause gave her time to reflect,* '*Now, how am I going to introduce him? – Am I unequal to speaking his name at once before all these people? Is it necessary for me to use any roundabout phrase? – Your Yorkshire friend – your correspondent in Yorkshire; – that would be the way, I suppose, if I were very bad. – No, I can pronounce his name without the smallest distress. I certainly get better and better. – Now for it.*'
>   *Mrs Weston was disengaged and Emma began again –* '*Mr Frank Churchill writes one of the best gentlemen's hands I ever saw.*' (p. 297)

Mr Knightley, who is also present, immediately responds. '"I do not admire it," said Mr Knightley. "It is too small – wants strength. It is like a woman's writing"' (p. 297). This response signals attention to at least two things. First, that Mr Knightley's perceptions and judgements – critical, romantic, aesthetic or otherwise – are not exempt from the distortions and delusions affecting Emma herself. If Knightley is, from its supposed 'inside', the novel's best reader and critic, he mimes here what might be termed the jealousy of the critic in relation to the original text. Second, that handwriting – and especially 'a woman's writing' – is something (it can scarcely be called a theme or motif, or even a concept or metaphor) which haunts the text of *Emma*, not least in the assumed entelechy of so many handwritten letters throughout.

Letters of the alphabet and epistolary letters: *Emma* allows for a strangely productive homonymy.

Let us try this hypothesis: everything in the text works in the direction of the name of Jane Austen. It is me, 'Jane Austen'. 'Jane Austen' must be said; 'Jane Austen' cannot be said. It is a question, for example, of the impossible, or telepathic, identification between 'Jane Austen' and 'Emma' – the necessity *and* impossibility of saying the name *in* the name of 'her' heroine. Propriety and nomination concerning the title of the text for instance; and the difficulties here are not merely Austen's but those of her editors, critics, readers. Jane Austen noted: 'The name of the work *not* to be *Emma* – but of the same sort as S & S, and P & P.'[18] A curious negation perhaps; at any rate, a critic such as Frank Bradbrook will hardly be thought controversial in remarking that '*Emma* is the only major novel of Jane Austen that takes its title from the name of its heroine.'[19] And this can be juxtaposed to Austen's celebrated observation, while planning the novel: 'I am going to take a heroine whom no one but myself will much like.'

Mr Weston says:

> 'What two letters of the alphabet are there, that express perfection?
> ... Ah! you will never guess ... – I will tell you. – M. and A. –
> Em-ma. – Do you understand?'
> Understanding and gratification came together. (pp. 364–5)

This is a wedding, the marriage, the hymen; and what also haunts the closing pages of the novel. How to say the name, what name to say, the name of Emma's husband for example:

> '"Mr Knightley." – You always called me, "Mr Knightley;" and, from habit, it has not so very formal a sound. – And yet it is

formal. I want you to call me something else, but I do not know what."

'I remember once calling you "George" ...'

'And cannot you call me "George" now?'

'Impossible!' (p. 445)

Impossible; but then Emma changes her mind: "'I will promise to call you once by your Christian name. I do not say when, but perhaps you may guess where; – in the building in which N. takes M. for better, for worse"' (p. 445). What is this building, and what are 'N' and 'M'? Knightley and Emma being married in church, no doubt. But isn't there also the thought of a play here between the names of 'Jane Austen' and 'Emma'?

Saying the name is deadly, as it is at the end of *The Turn of the Screw*: everything in James's text leads up to it, and Miles's more or less enforced act of naming, when he says '"Peter Quint, you devil!"' (p. 121), is enough to kill him. As a common noun, 'quint' is a musical term – 'an organ-stop a fifth above the foundation stops' or 'the E string of a violin' (*Chambers*) – and it would be possible to read the whole of James's text in terms of naming and of the phantasmagoric sounds of silence. Jane Austen cannot say her name, in the name of 'Emma', and yet ... It is a question of sound, perhaps, of the sound of that name, absent from the title-page of the first edition of the novel, 'Jane Austen', the phonetic scattering of the name that would be a kind of monstrous birth, and death, the impropriety of giving birth to one's name and monumentalizing it. I could not foresee this on 'first' reading *Emma*; could not foresee why I should have been thinking of *The Turn of the Screw* and Miles and Flora. But then, on the same closing page as the discussion about the name 'George' – the name, as it happens, of Jane Austen's father – there is perhaps a signature-effect, there is a child, and the naming of a child, a mute character, bearing the name of 'Anna Weston' ... 'Jane Austen'. But this is unspeakable.[20]

Jane Austen's *Emma* is a building, a monument, 'the Parthenon of fiction'. How should it speak its name, to say the letters 'M' and 'A'? It is a question, in part, of how the text – the title and the name of its singular 'heroine' – should be self-identical. This is Emma, I am Emma, I am me, I am mama, the mother, my mother, my mother's mother ... Irreducible fictionality and otherness of a parthenon. Whose blunder is all this? 'Emma' has its etymological derivation in the Germanic word meaning 'whole', 'universal'. The revelation of the secret, the concealment never entirely concealed within the word 'blunder', is 'the whole blunder' (p. 460) spread out in writing, referred to by Churchill in one of the last sentences of the novel. There still remains the fear, perhaps, described by Derrida at the end of 'Telepathy', the fear 'of not finding (or of finding) all alone' (p. 38).

Then one must say 'me': *Emma* asks us to agree, to agree to be the addressee who is determined by the text, determined by a foreseeing of the past and by the function of the unforeseen in that determination. When *Emma*, the text, its reading and its blunders end, then they (and we) begin. This would seem, among other things, to corroborate Paul de Man's observation that 'there is never enough knowledge available to account for the delusion of knowing'.[21]

If this is where everything starts between us, between me and you, myself and myself, me and the others, I would like to conclude by suggesting one or two of the implications of this reading of *Emma* and 'Telepathy'. I cannot see very clearly, and the light is going ... In 'Telepathy', Derrida explores the idea that 'one cannot say of the addressee that s/he exists before the letter'. It is not simply a matter of saying that *Emma* in various ways supplies illustrations or analyses of this; it would be a question rather of saying that *Emma*, like *The Turn of the Screw*, *is* a letter, and also of course more than one, it is the dissemination of the epistolary. Derrida's proposition concerning the letter and the determination of the addressee need not, in principle, be confined to 'the letter' in the narrow epistolary sense, but may be extended to constitute a necessary theorization of texts in general, and of literature in particular. As its name indicates, 'literature' would be the domain of *letters* in the most radical sense. And, in the context of what has been suggested here regarding the proper name, and the *saying* of the name, it need not be the case that, as Derrida speculates in *La Carte postale*, the telephone and 'a certain technological regime of telecommunications' threatens the death of literature.[22] Rather it may be where – through a reinscribed concept of the epistolary and of the telephone – literature begins, however differently. This is partly what I had in mind

when I spoke, near the outset, of literature as a discursive formation: engaged as the letter and the telephonic, literature would be,
among other things, the addressing of oneself, and the impossibility of giving the name.

I am not hypothesizing so much another way of thinking about
a pre-given body of texts designated as literary, but rather about
another space of 'literature'. Perhaps it is not coincidental that in
1981 both Jacques Derrida and Maria Torok separately propose
that 'telepathy' is 'the name Freud unwittingly gave to a foreign
body within the corpus of psychoanalysis'.[23] Maria Torok's elaboration of this is now published in the Afterword to *The Wolf
Man's Magic Word* (1986). She writes:

> *Telepathy could thus be seen as the precursor to a type of research
> that dares the imagination as regards oneself and others, that
> refuses to be imprisoned in systems, mythologies, and universal
> symbolic equivalents. Telepathy would be the name of an ongoing
> and groping research that – at the moment of its emergence and in
> the area of its relevance – had not yet grasped either the true scope
> of its own inquiry or the conceptual rigor necessary for its elabora-
> tion.* (p. 86)

I would like to modify and supplement this by proposing 'Telepathy' as a name for literature as discursive formation. This proposal should be taken as, by its very nature, highly provisional and
exploratory.

There might appear to be two areas, two discourses. First, on
the side of literature, an intransigent, isolated but intertextual
space, in which literary texts uncannily correspond with one
another. Harold Bloom's work on relations between poetic texts
might serve as one point of critical departure for conceiving such
a mode of correspondence. But, in accordance with Foucault's
emphasis on the discursive formation as a 'system of dispersion'
and discontinuity, this would from the outset entail a displacement and reinscription of the place of the subject, of addressor
and addressee, and of the role of history. It would be a kind of
correspondence necessarily governed also by the logic of what
Derrida has called 'destinerrance'.[24] As he has warned: 'The ultimate naïvety would be to allow oneself to think that Telepathy

guarantees a destination which "posts and telecommunications" fail to provide' (*T*, p. 16).

Second, there would be the putatively critical discourse – philosophical, psychoanalytical, political and so on – attendant on the discourse of literature. This critical discourse would, in itself, bear a number of the characteristics of 'Telepathy' as Maria Torok formulates it, or of critical writing as it is suggestively worked over by the effects of 'taking chances'.[25] It may be daring and frightening, but also hesitant, uncomprehending and scared.

However, it should be clear that these two areas or discourses cannot be merely discrete. Literature – or Telepathy, as I'd like to call it – would not be distinct from what has operated under the name of criticism.[26] The two discourses would themselves be in telepathic correspondence. One would then be thinking of an expansion of what Roland Barthes put forward in 1970 as 'The Theory of the Text', where he advocates, for example, that *the commentary be itself a text*.[27] One would be envisaging, then, a discourse which would be neither literary nor critical, and both at once. It would engage, no doubt, with the thought of the literary text as reading-machine, as reading-effect, that is as always in advance including, foreseeing, its addressee – this would be the telepathic structure – but without knowing where it is going, who is speaking or who is listening, or at what distance.

POST-SCRIPT

Derrida writes of what 'I'd told you on the telephone the day that you put your hand on the phone in order to call me at the same moment that my own call started to ring through' (*T*, p. 19). Who makes contact with whom? Or what makes contact? Derrida cites a Zen text on the art of archery: 'Something shoots! Something hits the target! Is it me who hits the target or the target which shoots me?' (*T*, p. 12) This might be compared with the 'handshake' in Jane Austen's novel, between Knightley and Emma. This is the locus also of a blunder that scarcely conceals itself; and of a desire made more articulate, more eloquent, by the concealment of its expression: 'He took her hand; – whether she had not herself made the first motion, she could not say – she might, perhaps, have rather offered it – but he took her hand, pressed it, and certainly was on the point of carrying it to his lips – when ...' (p. 377). I leave you to remind yourself of how all that goes on. And as a post-script to this post-script I would only like to mention a postcard, which I had no reason to expect or foresee, posted in the United States on the day, as it happens, I began writing this. It arrived in the middle, and is a photograph of the Parthenon – at night – in Centennial Park, Nashville, Tennessee.

3

Cryptaesthesia:
the Case of Wuthering Heights

I

The following reading focuses on three texts: *The Wolf Man's Magic Word: A Cryptonymy*, by Nicolas Abraham and Maria Torok; 'Fors', the essay by Jacques Derrida which precedes the *Cryptonymy* and provides such an exemplary exposition of it; and, finally, Emily Brontë's *Wuthering Heights*.[1] These are some of the questions I wish to consider here: What is cryptonymy? What is a crypt? What is a ghost? How might these be related to literature and to the notion of telepathy which we have been elaborating?

The Wolf Man's Magic Word, with its Foreword by Derrida and an Introduction by the translator, Nicholas Rand, was published in 1986. The blurb on the back cover includes some very positive, and provoking, praise from the late Paul de Man: '*The Wolf Man's Magic Word* succeeds', he writes, 'because of its very specific lexical interpretations coupled with a demonstration of how a genuine link between psycho-analysis and literary analysis can be established.' Even greater claims are made by the translator, who proposes that Abraham and Torok's text is 'not only a revolutionary approach to psychoanalysis but also a turning point in the history of literary criticism and the many other disciplines dealing with issues of interpretation' (p. li). Rand goes on to provide a section on 'The Literary Uses of Cryptonymy' in which he attempts to illustrate, by way of an analysis of Stendhal's *The Red and the Black*, 'the general value and impact of *The Wolf Man's Magic Word* as a critical tool' (p. lx). I do not wish to take issue with the overall efficacy of Rand's illustration, but would wonder about the appropriateness of determining

Abraham and Torok's work as a 'critical tool' – as a critical text being brought to bear, in a clinical and instrumental way, on a 'literary' text. This is a significant question for at least two reasons. First, because what we are engaged with here is the attempt precisely to question and displace such notions – of 'criticism' as an instrument, as something by definition outside, as categorically discrete from literature 'itself'. Second, and more generally, because Abraham and Torok's work is at present becoming increasingly widely read, both in the United States and elsewhere, and the problems and dangers of institutionalization (in the style, for example, of so-called American deconstruction) should not be ignored. The present essay seeks to mark a necessary hesitation in this respect.[2]

The Wolf Man's Magic Word is an astonishing re-reading of Freud's case history, of the Wolf Man's own writings, and of other writings contributed by various psychoanalysts to this highly complex and strange case. The re-reading is centred on a theory of the crypt. Everything in the traumatic history of Sergei Pankeiev, the Wolf Man, can be traced back to a crypt. Abraham and Torok note that 'The crypt works in the heart of the Ego as a special kind of Unconscious' (p. 80). The crypt is an effect of mourning. Following on from Freud's important essay 'Mourning and Melancholia' (in *PFL*, 11: 245–68), Abraham and Torok elaborate a fundamental differentiation between 'introjection' (the case of 'normal' mourning, whereby the lost object is internalized, idealized, etc.) and 'incorporation' (the case of 'abnormal', refused or impossible mourning). For Abraham and Torok, 'incorporation' involves the idea that the lost object is, as if magically, 'swallowed' up whole. 'Swallowed' needs to be understood as highly paradoxical here. As they note in their essay 'Introjection/Incorporation': 'It is to avoid "swallowing" the loss that one imagines swallowing, or having swallowed, what is lost, in the form of an object.'[3] In the case of the Wolf Man, both his sister and his father are incorporated. This gives rise to a highly singular crypt, as Derrida observes in 'Fors': 'The Wolf Man's crypt does not shelter his own lost and incorporated object, as a melancholic's crypt would, but the illegitimate object of another, of his sister, of his sister seduced by his father' (p. xxxvi). Once the crypt has been formed, everything in the Wolf Man's 'life' will be

concerned with its concealment. 'The Self' becomes, as Derrida
puts it, 'a cemetery guard' (p. xxxv).

What is a crypt? In 'Fors' it is described as '(1) a certain
organization of places [*lieux*] designed to *lead astray* and (2) a
topographical arrangement made to keep (conserve-hidden) the
living dead' (p. xxxvi). Thirdly, it involves 'the notion of a cipher,
a code' (p. xxxvi). Abraham and Torok's analysis is concerned
with 'words that hide'; they call these words '*cryptonyms* ...
because of their allusion to a foreign and arcane meaning' (p. 18).
It is a matter of attending to 'allosemes', that is to say to 'the
lexical contiguity of the various meanings of the same word' (p.
19). Cryptonymy consists in 'replacing a word by the synonym
of its alloseme' (p. 19). Abraham and Torok identify the Wolf
Man's crypt in the form of the word '*tieret*' (the Russian verb 'to
rub'). This is the 'magic word'. But insofar as '*tieret*' is a cipher,
a code or a word, it must, they argue, 'be called a *silent word*'; or
rather, it is a '*word-thing*', 'a word that operates only from the
Unconscious' (p. 46). Does this mean, Derrida asks, that 'the
crypt's cipher' is 'formed out of verbal, even nominal material?'
And he continues: 'The answer to this question cannot be a
simple yes or no, and its very formulation must be displaced by
the object and protocol of the book itself' (p. xxxvii). The notion
of '*tieret*' as a kind of 'thing' has nothing to do with 'the thing-in-
itself philosophers speak of'; rather it is 'a mark or a cipher', a
'trace with no present in its wake' (p. xliv). Indeed, the notion of
'the Thing' should be 'thought out *starting from* the Crypt'; the
Thing is a '"crypt effect"' (p. xiii). 'Perception itself,' Derrida
notes, 'falls under the law of the cipher ... Nothing ... can be
perceptible or verbalizable from the first, through and through.'
And it is only according to this law that we can 'even understand
the mere possibility that a crypt could take place' (p. xxxix).

Already it is clear here that the notion of the crypt has ex-
ceeded any traditional space of psychoanalytic discourse. The
correspondences between Abraham and Torok's work on the
'crypt' and Derrida's own formulation of western metaphysics
in terms of the logic of 'différance', 'the trace' and so on, are
striking. Abraham's question, articulated in 'The Shell and the
Kernel', is also Derrida's: 'how to include in a discourse – in any
one whatsoever – that very thing which in essence, by dint of

being the precondition of discourse, escapes it?'[4] The notion of the crypt is, in Derrida's account, explicitly articulated in terms of the structure of language (and indeed, the structure of 'presence') in general. 'What is a crypt?' Derrida remarks that this question 'can no longer, it seems to me, be posed' (p. xiii). The question cannot be posed, it seems, at least in part because of the meta-physico-ontological presuppositions governing the use of the third person singular present indicative 'is'; and because the notion of the crypt concerns the anasemic and pre-originary. It is because of what Derrida describes as 'the *cryptic* structure of the ultimate "referent"', that '*another* kind of writing' (p. xxvi) is necessary. Again, the correspondence with Abraham and Torok is marked. It is a question of a kind of writing, or translation, which would be appropriate to 'anasemia' – to what Derrida glosses as 'the return toward concepts which are not only originary but pre-originary, which are, in other words, on this side of meaning'.[5] A kind of writing that would be faithful to the recognition that 'A certain foreign body is here working over our household words' (p. xxv).

The Wolf Man's Magic Word is, then, the attempt at such a writing. This text, as Derrida observes, 'no longer conforms to any law and order – certainly not to philosophical order, which thus finds itself moved, to the point of no return, by a psychoanalytical lever – but neither does it abide by the common order of psychoanalysis' (p. xiii). Rather it is 'an immense polyphonic poem' (p. xliii) or 'a novel, a poem, a myth, a drama, the whole thing in a plural translation, productive and simultaneous' (p. xxv). In attempting to track down the crypt of the Wolf Man, the text becomes a cryptic writing of its own. As Derrida remarks:

> *It is a singular tale, certainly, the tale of the drama of the Wolf Man, but also the pulsing, rhythmic, step-by-step tale of the act of deciphering, decrypting, itself dramatic, the tale of a tale, of its progress, its obstacles, its interruptions, its discoveries all along a labyrinth; of its entrance hall, its corridors, its angles. (p. xxiii)*

Abraham and Torok, and no doubt Derrida in turn, are caught up in this process of decrypting: 'the act of decrypting would be impossible, the very temptation would be prohibited, if the analyst's own desire was reluctant to engage itself . . . and if he did not also work doubly, in his own name, on his own name. But here, in this case, by what name should the analyst be called?' (p. xlvii). It seems that there is no adequate or appropriate answer to this question. Derrida notes that 'The Thing (*tieret*) would perhaps be the Wolf Man's name if there were any such thing here as a name or a proper name' (p. xlv); he also, provocatively, draws attention to the distinct similarity between '*tieret*' and the name of one of these analysts, *Torok* (p. xlvii). But there is no proper name, properly speaking. Either for psychoanalyst, or for philosopher, or for the Wolf Man/S. P./'*tieret*'.

Who are we? Derrida's concern is with everything which necessarily prevents us from believing that 'the *I* signs when it authenticates the seal of an "I sign," that a proper-name phenomenon stops at what goes back to the father, to the name given by the legal father' (p. xlvi). One may not know one's own name; one's own putatively 'proper name' may not be what one thinks it is. And, in any case, no proper name, however secret or however cryptic, is ever absolutely pure, or purely proper. As Derrida remarks elsewhere, in a discussion in *The Ear of the Other*, such a name 'could not possibly occur in a pure state because of the differential structure of any mark. [It] could be what it is only in a relation of differentiation and thus also of contamination, in a network or common system' (*EO*, p. 107).

Still, there remains what 'Fors' calls 'a *desire for idiom* or an *idiom of desire*' (p. xlvi). It manifests itself undecidably, for example, in the 'TR'-effect (*tieret, Turok, Torok, Trud*) which 'Fors' explores (see p. xlvii). It is this desire, or rather this double structure of desire, which marks the text of Abraham and Torok. And it is partly on account of the necessary recognition of such a desire that we can understand Roland Barthes's injunction which I cited earlier: '*Let the commentary be itself a text*'. It cannot, it is claimed, be otherwise. Abraham and Torok clearly acknowledge such a notion when they write, at the very start of their study: 'As for us, we have to admit that the subject controlled us more than we controlled it' (p. lxxi). Far from offering itself simply as 'a critical tool', *The Wolf Man's Magic Word* appears to be a tool,

if one can still use that word, of the other, of alterity and otherness in general. One might venture to call it an allography – a
writing on behalf of another – but only if this 'other' is acknowl-
edged as being non-human, unrepresentable and irremediably
cryptic. Whether it is a matter of the relationship between the
psychoanalyst and his/her subject or between a literary critic and
a literary text, the following also applies: the analyst or critic is
being read, being determined by the text. I am not referring here
to concepts of transference or counter-transference, but rather to
a notion of 'telepathy' as I formulated it at the end of the last
chapter. Texts are for reading, but they are also reading-machines,
reading-effects. We are still concerned with the hypothesis of an
addressee who does not exist *before* the text. It is a matter of a
determination which occurs, thanks to the text. A series of questions are perhaps intertwined here. In what senses might it be
useful to speak of literary texts as allographic? What might we
hear such texts dictating, in answer to the question 'Who are
we?'? The notion of the crypt undoubtedly disturbs the grounds,
literary text not only as cryptic, but as actually *transmitting* a
crypt? Can there be a cryptonymy of literature?

Before I turn to *Wuthering Heights* in an attempt to explore such
questions, three further terms should be introduced. These are
what Torok calls 'telepathy', what Freud calls the 'death instinct'
or 'death drive', and finally the notion of the 'ghost' or 'phantom'. Just as Derrida's Foreword, 'Fors', expands and extends the
notion of the crypt, so too does Maria Torok's 'Afterword',
written nearly ten years after *The Wolf Man's Magic Word* itself
(see *WM*, p. 84). Here the crypt is related more overtly in terms
of what Torok calls 'telepathy'. In the Afterword, for example,
she argues that what Freud regarded as 'a simple instance of
thought transference (telepathy)' is in fact 'a *metapsychological
phantom*': Freud, she proposes, is 'haunted by the effects of a
crypt lodged in someone else (his patient) [the Wolf Man]'
(p. 99). Thus, she suggests, 'Freud himself carries a crypt . . . that
is quite similar in its structure to the Wolf Man's.' This 'crypt' is
glossed as 'a painful reality beyond himself (i.e., an occult telepathy)' (p. 103). In Torok's account, it is because he is 'Haunted
by the Wolf Man's crypt' that 'Freud gives a card to occultism'
(p. 99).

In order to elucidate this notion of a haunting or a 'meta-psychological phantom', we may here note a correlation made, in Abraham and Torok's work, between a crypt and a ghost. Derrida, in fact, describes it briefly, in *The Ear of the Other*: 'the theory of the "ghost" is not exactly the theory of the "crypt" ... the ghost is more precisely the effect of another's crypt in my unconscious' (*EO*, p. 59). In 'Notes on the Phantom: A Complement to Freud's Metapsychology', Nicolas Abraham observes that 'the work of the phantom coincides in every respect with Freud's description of the death instinct'.[6] Torok takes this further and suggests that 'Freud's fable of Thanatos becomes justifiable only in relation to an internal and unknown area in Freud himself': thus, 'the introduction of a "death instinct" into psychoanalytic theory makes sense only as a "foreign body"' (*WM*, p. 91). As a crypt. In this respect the 'death instinct' has a status in psychoanalytic theory identical to that of telepathy. The 'foreign body' known as 'telepathy' is, Torok declares, 'a crypt that threw psychoanalysts, Freud included, into confusion in the 1920s' (p. 86). Telepathy is a crypt. And no doubt – given the extremely strange, scarcely imaginable relaying or network of 'communications' necessary for its construction within the Self, in the core of the Ego – it would be legitimate to describe the crypt, and especially the haunted crypt or 'ghost', as telepathic.

And then, what of telepathy as a crypt in literary criticism? What of telepathy, ghosts and crypts in *Wuthering Heights*?

II

Wuthering Heights: I might begin by attempting to provide a brief summary of this text. To provide, literally: *pro*, 'before', and *videre*, 'to see': to see beforehand, to see ahead, to foresee or foretell. I might, then, in this manner of foretelling, recount how a Mr Lockwood comes to rent a house called Thrushcross Grange, how he visits a house a few miles away called Wuthering Heights, and how his housekeeper at the Grange, Nelly or Ellen Dean, provides him, in turn, with the recent history of those places: Mr and Mrs Linton live at the Grange with their children,

Edgar and Isabella. Mr and Mrs Earnshaw live at Wuthering Heights, with their children, Hindley and Catherine, and later take in an orphan boy called Heathcliff. Mr and Mrs Earnshaw die within about four years of each other, and Hindley Earnshaw meanwhile marries a lady called Frances. Catherine and Heathcliff visit the Grange and the Lintons visit the Heights. Hindley and Frances Earnshaw have a child, Hareton; Frances dies a few months later. This evidently intensifies Hindley's inclination towards alcoholism. Edgar proposes to Catherine, Heathcliff overhears her telling Nelly about it and runs off. Catherine looks for him in vain, catches a fever, is taken to the Grange to convalesce. Mr and Mrs Linton succumb to the fever and die. Edgar and Catherine get married. After about three years Heathcliff returns, apparently transformed into a 'gentleman'. Isabella becomes infatuated with him. Heathcliff, still in love with Catherine, visits and manipulates Isabella for his own ends. Edgar can tolerate no more: Heathcliff is removed from the premises. Heathcliff and Isabella run away and get married. Catherine becomes delirious from refusing to eat. Shortly after the Heathcliffs' return to the Heights, Catherine gives birth to a daughter, another Catherine, and then dies. Isabella runs away and gives birth, a few months later, to a son, Linton Heathcliff. Hindley Earnshaw dies. Heathcliff takes over the Heights.

Then we move on twelve years. Isabella dies and her son Linton is taken first to the Grange, then to the Heights. The young Catherine has seen a little of Hareton but now forms a friendship, or penfriendship, with Linton, a sickly, weak child. Edgar becomes ill. Nelly and Catherine are kidnapped and forcibly confined when they go to visit Linton at the Heights. Linton and Catherine get married. Catherine escapes to the Grange where her father, Edgar, is dying. After his funeral Catherine is brought back by Heathcliff to Wuthering Heights. Linton dies. I might explain that this takes us up to the time of Lockwood's arrival and Nelly's recounting this history, and that this is then succeeded by an account of how, over the next year or so, Heathcliff dies and Catherine and Hareton, who had been becoming increasingly friendly with one another, finally are to be married.

I said I might give such an account of the text, a brief and patently inadequate resumé of its narrative; and there would perhaps be good reasons for doing so. A chief reason might be the apparently commonsensical one, that the narrative of *Wuthering Heights* is extremely complex, bewilderingly rapid and intense. It is in certain respects extraordinarily forgettable, like a dream or a joke. But even then I would not really have said anything about the complexity of the structure of narrators as such; and in many ways, after all, it is the intricacy, the labyrinthine strangeness of this structure which constitutes the very force of this narrative.

As Joseph would say, 'Noa!' (*WH*, p. 166). The inadequacy and inappropriateness of such an approach would be intolerable. It would be to provide or foresee in the blindest fashion, and without the slightest regard or fidelity to the question of how one can or properly ought to open a reading of this text. Without, also, the slightest regard or fidelity to the notion, cited earlier, that a certain foreign body is here working over our household words.

Suppose we attempt to begin at the beginning, with the title-page of the text? 'Wuthering Heights' and 'Emily Brontë': are these not by now, nationally and internationally, 'household words'? But what does this mean?

Wuthering Heights was written by 'Ellis Bell' and first published in 1847. The phonological phenomenon known as assimilation might happily account for the fact that, in casual or everyday pronunciation, the 'b' can become imperceptible, indistinguishable from a 'p'. In this way the word or sound of 'spell' presents itself. This is completely arbitrary and unrelated to anything whatsoever, isn't it? There is nothing magical or supernatural here. Emily Brontë, we can assume, knew how to spell her name: 'Ellis Bell' spells a pseudonym, although deliberately no doubt it retains the initials 'E. B.' Judging from the author's name, *Wuthering Heights* was written by an androgyne or, at least, by someone whose sexual identity is undecidable, neuter. In the 'Biographical Notice of Ellis and Acton Bell' which precedes the text of the second edition of *Wuthering Heights*, in 1850, Charlotte Brontë notes this 'ambiguous choice' of names (*WH*, p. 4).

'Ellis Bell' is neither ' "feminine" ' nor 'positively masculine' (p. 4). What kind of ring does it have to it? It goes round and round, the first three letters, 'ell', being also the last, which become the first again, and so on, round and round, in a ring, enclosing itself, as if sealing itself, as if sealing something perhaps.

Yes, it seems undeniable: it seals or conceals the allegedly 'real' and 'true' name of the author.

The principal purpose of the 'Biographical Notice of Ellis and Acton Bell', indeed, is to reveal this name (and the 'real' and 'true' name as well of 'Acton Bell'). Thus Charlotte Brontë writes of 'Emily' and 'Anne' and concludes her account – which is also a thanatography, a double-thanatography, a narrative of the deaths of both her sisters – with a strangely sepulchral image. Adapting the word 'necropolis', the ancient Greek word for 'a cemetery', one might describe it as a necropolitical metaphor. She writes: 'This notice has been written, because I felt it a sacred duty to wipe the dust off their gravestones, and leave their dear names free from soil' (p. 8). Charlotte's duty is 'sacred' because its objects are sacred. The revelation of the name is sacred. The name is sacred. There is a strange metaphor also at work in the final word, 'soil': literally 'earth', but metaphorically 'stain', 'tarnish', 'disrepute'. As a metaphor, in fact, it is singularly inappropriate, for if the names of Emily and Anne Brontë were not revealed, if they remained concealed and unknown, how could they at the same time be soiled? But Charlotte herself, in her very next words, offers a solution to this question. At the very end of the 'Biographical Notice', alongside the date, 'September 19, 1850', she signs her name: 'Currer Bell'. So now we know. Her 'sacred' duty has been to reveal the 'sacred' name of 'Emily Bell'. Is this a revelation – that *Wuthering Heights* was, really and truly, written by a woman called Emily Bell? The name is still hidden: revealed and concealed, sacred and soiled, proper and improper, true and fictive at the same time.

Who wrote *Wuthering Heights*?

A cryptonymic account of *Wuthering Heights* might well proceed with an analysis of the title-page of the text: the possible relations between the name of the text and the name of the author, or an exploration of the way in which the name of Emily

Brontë is (and is not) concealed behind or within the name 'Ellis Bell', and then the way in which names function, often silently and uncannily, within the text. There would certainly be grounds for such an analysis. It might be objected that a proper name is a proper name, and that to treat a proper name as a common name, or to endow a proper name with features or characteristics of common names or nouns, would be illegitimate or else mere wordplay; but it is quite clear that the text itself indicates a perfectly serious preoccupation with just such modes of illegitimacy, impropriety or expropriation. Nor, it must be stressed, should this be regarded as necessarily a matter of 'authorial' or 'conscious' control. As Derrida has remarked in this relation: 'this is not something one can decide: one doesn't disseminate or play with one's name. The very structure of the proper name sets this process in motion' (*EO*, p. 76).

We have already noted some of the odd qualities of the name 'Ellis Bell' and its peculiarly proper/nor-proper relation to 'Emily Brontë'.[7] And this without needing to dwell on the resonant force of an 'ell' sound not only in Brontë's own forename, but also in the name of one of the chief characters and narrators, Ellen Dean. It might appear that the name 'Brontë' itself offers singularly little scope for homonymy or for being visibly or aurally translated or metamorphosed into other names, proper or common. The two words in the dictionary which come closest to her name, perhaps, are 'brunt' and, of all things, 'brontosaurus'. 'Brunt' is a word of obscure origin, nicely defined as 'the shock of an onset or contest: the force of a blow: the chief stress or crisis of anything'. I take this definition from *Chambers Dictionary*. (You may remember that it is 'the Messrs. Chambers, of Edinburgh' who, Charlotte tells us in the 'Biographical Notice', help the three sisters on their way into the world of publication . . .) The word is familiar enough in the phrase 'the brunt of the storm'. Coincidentally, perhaps, this can be linked to the brontosaurus. I am not suggesting that the name 'Emily Brontë' denotes a dinosaur, even if we are concerned here, ineluctably, with certain appearances or productions of the monstrous. 'Saurus' is from the Greek for 'lizard'; the Greek word 'βροντη', however, signifies 'thunder'. Such etymological peregrinations might seem no more than a quaint digression, except that Brontë herself does it, very near the start of the text: 'Wuthering Heights is the name of Mr. Heathcliff's dwelling. "Wuthering" being a significant provincial adjective, descriptive of the atmospheric tumult to which its station is exposed in stormy weather' (p. 14). The proper name, the name of the house (and of the text), is based on a 'provincial adjective', a common word connoting an 'atmospheric tumult' and 'stormy' conditions. In this way, we might observe how the title, and how the text itself, has begun to translate and encrypt – perhaps the 'name' (whatever that might be) of its 'author'.

On the basis of the text's explicit making-proper of an adjective, 'wuthering', a cryptonymic analysis, or cryptanalysis, might legitimately be led into and out of other proper names in the text. For example, 'Earnshaw' which, like an 'urn' itself, carries the bright promise of acquiring or deserving, as well as the funereal certitude of death; 'Lockwood' which, in a bizarrely overt manner, seems to indicate encryptment itself; or 'Heathcliff', a name with distinctly vertiginous associations which would in turn translate back into the 'heights' of the title of the text. 'Heathcliff' is a particularly provocative, 'non-proper' name. At one point Catherine advises Nelly to inform the infatuated Isabella: 'Tell her what Heathcliff is – an unreclaimed creature, without refinement, without cultivation; an arid wilderness of furze and whinstone' (p. 89). To come closer to decomposing the name 'Heathcliff' into a common noun or common nouns would, no doubt, strain credulity, verging (as it does even here perhaps) on the farcical. It is like Heathcliff's 'own' reference, at one point, to a 'nab [or promontory] of heath' (p. 174). Still the desire inscribed in Heathcliff's name could be described as the desire for the appropriation of all that his name so commonly embraces: Penistone Crags, for example, and the ubiquitous moors themselves. But perhaps nothing is showing when Lockwood visits the graves – the last two paragraphs of the text – and Catherine's name (though not mentioned) is 'half buried in heath', while Heathcliff's is 'still bare' (p. 266).

Thus far at least, one would be able to emphasize the extent to which a cryptonymic account admirably works against so many of the realist or naturalist assumptions which inform and govern the vast majority of critical readings of this text. A reading of 'Heathcliff', for example, in terms of name-effects and translation-effects, of the non-proper and improper, or the decomposition of the proper, would certainly demonstrate greater fidelity to the way in which the text itself (rather than its critics) characterizes 'Heathcliff' – as something rather than someone, or as a being that is inhuman, non-human or unnamable. Heathcliff is 'not a human being' (p. 128), says Isabella. He is not, thinks Nelly Dean, 'a creature of my own species' (p. 134). ' "He's not a human being," (p. 143) Isabella re-asserts later. He is less than 'half a man' (p. 149). He is 'preter-human' (p. 147), 'a monster' (p. 128), and so on.

Even at an allegedly commonsensical thematic level, it is clear that *Wuthering Heights* is deeply concerned with the notion of the translatability or the metamorphic qualities of proper names. This manifests itself quite clearly in the way in which the text more or less begins with a reference to the inscription '1500' and 'Hareton Earnshaw' above 'the principal door' (p. 14) of the house, and ends, in effect, with the reinstitution of this name – more than three hundred years later. It manifests itself also in the shifts of name, from 'Catherine Earnshaw' to 'Catherine Linton', and from 'Catherine Linton' to 'Catherine Heathcliff' to 'Catherine Earnshaw'. And it shows itself, in a distinctly eerie way, in the name – which J. Hillis Miller has described as an oxymoron – 'Linton Heathcliff'.[8] A cryptonymic account would undoubtedly need to attempt a rigorous examination of these aspects of the text.

We might here recall the fact that there is, in *Wuthering Heights*, a 'character' called 'Heathcliff Earnshaw'. When Mr Earnshaw returns from Liverpool with 'a dirty, ragged, black-haired child' speaking 'some gibberish that nobody could understand', Nelly Dean is 'frightened' by 'it'. Because Hindley and Catherine, the young children, 'refused to have it in bed with them, or even in their room', Nelly 'put it on the landing of the stairs, hoping it might be gone on the morrow'. Her 'cowardice and inhumanity' are discovered and she is 'sent out of the house'. Lockwood continues his transcription of Nelly Dean's narrative:

> *This was Heathcliff's first introduction to the family. On coming back a few days afterwards, for I did not consider my banishment perpetual, I found they had christened him 'Heathcliff'; it was the*

name of a son who died in childhood, and it has served him ever since, both for Christian and surname. (p. 39)

Death, then, is inscribed in the name of 'Heathcliff' as well, and perhaps more explicitly and more affectively than in the names of 'Earnshaw' and 'Lockwood'.

The linking of the name of 'Heathcliff' with death and commemoration is in fact at least double, since it is projected not only on the basis of the past (and present) but is also realized in a strange and singular future. When one thinks of a telepathic dream in *Wuthering Heights*, one probably thinks first of Lockwood's (in Chapter 3). But there is at least one other. It is Nelly Dean's and it comes very near the end of the text. It concerns, in an eerie foresight, the commemorative uniqueness of the name of 'Heathcliff':

> *'But where did he come from, the little dark thing, harboured by a good man to his bane?' muttered superstition, as I dozed into unconsciousness. And I began, half dreaming, to weary myself with imaging some fit parentage for him; and repeating my waking meditations, I tracked his existence over again, with grim variations; at last, picturing his death and funeral; of which, all I can remember is, being exceedingly vexed at having the task of dictating an inscription for his monument, and consulting the sexton about it; and, as he had no surname, and we could not tell his age, we were obliged to content ourselves with the single word, 'Heathcliff.' That came true; we were. If you enter the kirkyard, you'll read on his headstone only that, and the date of his death.*
>
> *Dawn restored me to common sense. (p. 260)*

It is in the name of 'Heathcliff' and its various translations, allosemes and transformations, it is in the highly enigmatic question of what is commemorated or concealed in the name of 'Heathcliff', that a cryptonymic account would perhaps be most crucially centred. On scarcely a moment's reflection, the possibilities seem to throng: for instance, heath-bare-naked, unveiled; heath-barren-refuse, bran (what might be happening then, with the game with the ball marked 'H.'? – 'the H. might be for Heathcliff, his name; but the bran came out of H.' [p. 199]),

Branwell; Brontë-brunt-brand (*OED* gives 'Bront' as an obsolete form of 'brunt', 'brand'), Brontë-brunt-height(s), storm, wuthering; cliff-crag-Penistone; cliff-nab-seize, lock, Lockwood; cliff-nab-keeper of a door-lock; heath/bell-hare-bell-Hareton, Isabella, Ellis Bell, knell, Nelly; Earn-urn-death ... But before embarking on a more detailed investigation of this field, a fundamental difficulty must be confronted. Despite its proclaimed status as 'an immense polyphonic poem', this difficulty scarcely arises in the case of Abraham and Torok's *Cryptonymy*. It is the methodological question of the distinction between what we might usefully, if tentatively, categorize as a psychobiographical cryptanalysis and a characterological cryptanalysis.

A psychobiographical cryptanalysis would perhaps, to use Nelly Dean's word, 'track' the existence of Heathcliff back to the commemorative reference to the 'son who died in childhood' – a reference which might then be linked to the deaths of Emily's sister Maria and brother Branwell (with its tantalizing 'Br-' and 'ell'-features) – and reconstruct the text on the basis of vicarious biographical identifications, that is to say along lines only slightly disarticulated from the conventional mode of the most redundant 'literary' psychoanalysis. A more strictly characterological approach would proceed from a recognition of how pervasively and how acutely the text represents characters in terms of 'unconscious' or 'semi-conscious' as well as 'conscious' states: it would read the text as if the text itself were offering a dramatization of the work of 'ghosts' or 'crypts' in the lives (and deaths) of certain fictional characters.[9] From this perspective, the question of the authorship of the text, of 'authorial intent' or (unconscious) desire, would be of negligible or only secondary importance. Let us pursue this notion of a characterological approach a little further.

As long ago as 1935, Lord David Cecil noted that

> *Emily Brontë does away with the most universally accepted of all antitheses – the antithesis between life and death ... But she does more than believe in the immortality of the soul in the orthodox Christian sense. She believes in the immortality of the soul* in this world ... *the disembodied soul continues to be active in this life.*[10]

The question as to whether one is dealing with Emily Brontë's 'own' 'belief' or with what the text of *Wuthering Heights* appears to 'believe' or to encourage us to 'believe' is one that must be left rigorously in suspense. It massively complicates, at any rate, any account of 'crypt', 'ghost' or 'soul' in *Wuthering Heights*. 'Soul' because it seems in certain respects that this word in Brontë's text can be closely linked or even identified with the notion of the 'crypt'.

There is so much in *Wuthering Heights*, and especially in the relationship between Catherine and Heathcliff, that can be regarded as telepathic in the supposedly 'ordinary', 'spiritualist' sense. It is easy, however, to underestimate Catherine's famous declaration 'I *am* Heathcliff' (p. 74) or one of her dying admonitions to Heathcliff: '. . . and should a word of mine distress you hereafter, think I feel the same distress underground' (p. 133). Notions of romantic identification have all too easily effaced the radical strangeness of the ways in which they relate to and 'inhabit' one another. For Catherine and Heathcliff do not merely testify to each other a love that is deeper than the grave: each carries the other in the form of an earlier self, regardless of their present selves and regardless of whether they are alive or dead in that present. Thus Catherine, at the end of her life, can exclaim: 'That is not *my* Heathcliff. I shall love mine yet; and take him with me – he's in my soul' (p. 134). This is not Heathcliff but *another* 'Heathcliff', an earlier self. And shortly afterwards Heathcliff says 'wildly': 'Do I want to live? What kind of living will it be when you – oh, God! would *you* like to live with your soul in the grave?' (p. 135). The soul here is separate and separable; it is like a foreign body, in oneself or in another.

Part of the historical importance of Wordsworth's 'Tintern Abbey' and *Intimations* 'Ode' is that they effectively transform the conception of English elegy: they offer themselves directly as elegies concerned with the loss or 'death' of one's own self, either in childhood or as a young adult. One of the ways of understanding Brontë's text would be to see it as an extraordinary elaboration of the theory of mourning only implicit, if nevertheless finding its first articulation, in the poetry of Wordsworth. In Brontë we are faced with the uncanny representation of mourning for one's own *or* other loved contemporaries' lost selves. Following Abraham's stress on the capacity for a crypt or 'phantom-effect' to be passed down the generations, a more characterological approach might focus not only on how Catherine and Heathcliff

inhabit one another, in death and life, but also on what is transferred in the following generation, to the second Catherine and
to Linton Heathcliff.[11] It would perhaps focus too on the role
played by Nelly Dean herself: what kind of crypt-effects does she
bear within herself and what does she pass on, even in spite of
herself, to succeeding generations?

There is so much mourning, there are so many deaths, in
Wuthering Heights that it becomes difficult to maintain a cohe-
rent sense of it. Perhaps one becomes anaesthetized. This might
appear to be Doctor Kenneth's experience, as he encounters
Nelly Dean shortly after the dealth of Catherine:

> '*Well, Nelly,*' *said he, riding into the yard one morning, too early
> not to alarm me with an instant presentiment of bad news.* '*It's
> yours and my turn to go into mourning at present. Who's given us
> the slip now, do you think?*'
> '*Who?*' *I asked in a flurry.*
> '*Why, guess!*' *he returned, dismounting, and slinging his bridle
> on a hook by the door.* '*And nip up the corner of your apron; I'm
> certain you'll need it.*'
> '*Not Mr. Heathcliff, surely?*' *I exclaimed.* (p. 152)

Nelly's guess is wrong of course: it is Hindley Earnshaw.

Because it comes in the midst of a series of so many other,
arguably more significant, deaths, it may be easy to overlook or
forget a peculiar aspect of the death of Hindley Earnshaw.
Nelly's apprehension of it – both her anticipation and her percep-
tual grasp of it – raises a very bizarre question. Is it possible for
there to be an encrypting of a loved one *while* that loved one is
still alive? It is Abraham's hypothesis that a phantom or ghost
(for example, that of Hamlet's father in Shakespeare's tragedy) 'is
meant to objectify, even if under the guise of individual or collective hallucinations, the gap that the concealment of some part
of a loved one's life produced in us'. Thus '*The phantom which
returns to haunt bears witness to the existence of the dead buried
within the other.*'[12] Some months before the death of Hindley
Earnshaw, and before the death of Catherine, Nelly has an hallucination. She is walking one 'bright, frosty afternoon' by a high-
way stone:

... I cannot say why, but all at once, a gush of child's sensations flowed into my heart. Hindley and I held it a favourite spot twenty years before.

I gazed long at the weather-worn block; and, stooping down, perceived a hole near the bottom still full of snail-shells and pebbles, which we were fond of storing there with more perishable things; and, as fresh as reality, it appeared that I beheld my early playmate seated on the withered turf, his dark, square head bent forward, and his little hand scooping out the earth with a piece of slate.

'Poor Hindley!' I exclaimed, involuntarily.

I started – my bodily eye was cheated into a momentary belief that the child lifted its face and stared straight into mine! It vanished in a twinkling; but, immediately, I felt an irresistible yearning to be at the Heights. Superstition urged me to comply with this impulse. Supposing he should be dead! I thought – or should die soon! – supposing it were a sign of death! (p. 94)

Retrospectively, one can say that this is what Freud might have wanted to class as a 'telepathic' experience: Hindley Earnshaw does die, only a few months later. But it is more – and other – than this as well. The hallucinatory presence of Hindley Earnshaw as a child: what is this ghost or ghost-effect that appears here, 'as fresh as reality'? Does Abraham's fascinating hypothesis work here? In which case, the 'ghost' of Hindley Earnshaw – even though it appears while Hindley Earnshaw is still alive – would bear witness to something, or someone, buried alive in his (and/or Nelly's) 'unconscious'. In which case – since we are confronted with a crypt-effect the origin of which is strictly beyond or before the narrative of *Wuthering Heights* – we have, a powerful allegory or representation of the crypt-as-a-trace-with-no-present-in-its-wake. This would clearly apply to the representations of Catherine-as-ghost and Heathcliff-as-ghost as well. And it would also make for a far less benign reading of the 'end' of *Wuthering Heights* than is customarily accorded to the 'return' to a 'new' Earnshaw generation.

Where has this led us? I suggested that a cryptonymic account of *Wuthering Heights* would necessitate, at some level, a methodological distinction between a psychobiographical and a more purely characterological approach. The first of these seems the least adequate, if indeed it is possible at all. A psychobiographical approach would mean treating the text of *Wuthering Heights* as if it were the equivalent, for Freud or for Abraham and Torok, of the analytical material furnished by the Wolf Man 'himself'. A characterological approach, on the other hand, would seem to end up by situating *Wuthering Heights* as equivalent to Abraham and Torok's text itself: *Wuthering Heights* would be a kind of fictional cryptonymic case-study, a weird Victorian prototype of *The Wolf Man's Magic Word*. It should by now be becoming clear that neither of these approaches is satisfactory. Jumping ahead a little, perhaps, I would argue that Wuthering Heights provides – it foresees, foretells – the necessary possibility of both and neither at the same time. And in this context it might be seen as merely an exemplary text as regards the question of a cryptonymy of literary texts in general.

But let us step back.

III

What gives us pause? Something, no doubt, related to the intensity and relentlessness with which the text involves itself, and us, with representations or experiences of encryptment.

An example: Chapter 3, where we are given 'Lockwood's dream'. Or rather, his dreams, since there are at least two. Where do they begin?[13]

Lockwood is 'sick exceedingly, and dizzy and faint' (p. 25), and has to spend the night at Wuthering Heights. Zillah – the name is from the Hebrew for 'shade' – the housekeeper shows him to a room: 'I fastened my door and glanced round for the bed' (p. 25). Already he has doubly encrypted himself: locked within a room within a house that is already effectively locked. It is labyrinthine, like a catacomb or crypt. As Heathcliff tells him later, 'Keep out of the yard ... you can only ramble about the steps and passages' (pp. 32–3). Thus inside the inside Lockwood sees the bed: 'a large oak case, with squares cut out near the top, resembling coach windows' (p. 25). He gets into this 'singular sort' of crypt: 'I slid back the panelled sides, got in with my light, pulled them together again, and felt secure against the vigilance of

Heathcliff, and everyone else' (p. 25). Now lodged within the inside of the inside of the inside, Lockwood has been apparently encrypted within the reification of his name: he has secured himself within the 'oak case', locked in wood. What is happening here? Names. Enough to send you to sleep.

Inside there is a ledge; the oak case encloses a window. The ledge is covered with the graffitied names of Catherine Earnshaw, Catherine Heathcliff, Catherine Linton. Lockwood is dropping off; but then 'a glare of white letters started from the dark, as vivid as spectres – the air swarmed with Catherines' (p. 25). He had been trying to nod off; as he later tells Heathcliff, 'spelling over the name' was 'calculated to set me asleep, like counting, or . . .' (p. 32). 'Spelling over': the text clearly allows for a homonymy in this word 'spelling'. No doubt there is reference here to the magical belief that the power of naming can materially affect the person so named.[14] As Lockwood will recount: 'reading it often over produced an impression which personified itself when I had no longer my imagination under control' (p. 32). Chiasmus of the reification and personification of proper names. Where does this lead or leave us?

Reading. Lockwood reads a book, for the 'oak case' which is the encrypting reification of his name also contains a library – and in a book, inside the inside of the inside of the inside of Wuthering Heights, there are the 'faded hieroglyphics' (p. 26) of Catherine's diary. A diary, then, within a diary, since the whole of *Wuthering Heights* is itself a diary, that of Lockwood. The act or rather (since it is never a single act or event) the activity of reading in *Wuthering Heights* is not merely something represented within the 'scene' of the text. Like Catherine and Hareton's reading together, Lockwood's reading is neither a mere representation of a supposedly real activity, nor is it merely a metaphor or metonymy for our own activity of reading the text of *Wuthering Heights*. What is it? It is neither inside nor outside the 'scene' of the text; it is both inside and outside at the same time. It's enough to send you to sleep. Ceaselessly, from one text to another – losing one's direction, losing one's head, losing one's place: 'I began to nod drowsily over the dim page; my eye wandered from manuscript to print. I saw a red ornamented title – "Seventy Times Seven, and the First of the Seventy-First. A

Pious Discourse delivered by the Reverend Jabes Branderham"'
(p. 28). The numbers, like proper names, 'calculated to set me
asleep, like counting, or . . .' 'Branderham': another instance of
what one might want to see as the BR-effect ('Brontë', 'Branwell'), and, with its 'brand', specifically evoking the notion of
imprinting a mark, naming or reifying the activity of marking or
signing a name. Later, Lockwood will even assume that this is, by
way of the mother, in an oblique or occulted manner, a family
name. As he exclaims to Heathcliff, 'I'm not going to endure the
persecutions of your hospitable ancestors again. Was not the
Reverend Jabes Branderham akin to you on the mother's side?'
(p. 31).

Where are we and who? In what place, or lost place? 'I began
to dream, almost before I ceased to be sensible of my locality' (p.
28). Then comes the dream of the book, the dream of what has
now already been 'calculated' or 'counted', as if this process of
calculation or counting has already been applied to a proper name
or proper names as well: a sermon 'Divided into *four hundred
and ninety* parts' (Brontë's italics, pp. 28–9). What is happening
here? Among other things, we discover, 'odd transgressions that
I never imagined previously' (p. 29).

Is one awake or asleep? And can one wake up in the middle of
a dream and be wakeful, make oneself wakeful, and yet continue
to sleep? This point in the text dramatizes or performs what is
characteristic of the novel as a whole. Derrida, in his work on
Freud and telepathy, speaks of 'writing' and/or 'making one read
under hypnosis' (*T*, p. 21). He is referring not only to Freud's
texts, but also to his own.[15] Like certain of Freud's and Derrida's
texts, but perhaps more entrancingly so, *Wuthering Heights* could
be described as a hypnagogics. It broaches the space of what has
been defined as 'the transitional state of consciousness experienced while falling asleep . . . [or] during the process of waking
up'.[16] But it does so by keeping you wide-awake. You're falling
asleep, you're waking up . . .

How would you know the difference?

Doing one thing while saying another. The text can appear to
keep you absolutely awake, while sending you to sleep. It can
appear to turn you – the anonymous reader – into a vigilant

observer of Lockwood's encryptment at Wuthering Heights, a meticulous and rational reader of his crazy nightmare, his blindly supernatural experience, while actually, at the same time, by the same movement, drawing you in, distracting your attention from your own inclusion. Writing 'as' Freud, in 'Telepathy', Derrida says how he 'always drew attention to the procedures of diverting attention, just like "mediums" do' (*T*, p. 27). Is this not a fundamental gesture generated by the structure of multiple narrators 'in' *Wuthering Heights* as well? Where is Ellis Bell, or Emily Brontë? That must appear to be a digression.

'As fresh as reality,' says Nelly Dean, of her telepathic hallucination. Derrida has Freud say: 'Reality, when I talk about it, it is as if to send [people] to sleep, you will understand nothing of my rhetoric otherwise' (*T*, p. 25). Let's transfer this to 'reality' or rather to the concept of 'realism', in *Wuthering Heights* or in so-called novels in general: realism, it's as if to send them to sleep. That's what realism in fiction is. Wake up. Can one wake up, be wakeful, and continue to sleep? The dream continues. 'Oh, how weary I grew. How I writhed, and yawned, and nodded, and revived! How I pinched and pricked myself, and rubbed my eyes, and stood up, and sat down again' (p. 29), says Lockwood.

But this is not the dream that really matters, if it is a dream at all. Perhaps it is a way of diverting attention.

The inaudibly audible brunt of the dream, 'the tremendous tumult', Branderham's 'shower of loud taps on the boards of the pulpit' transpires, as Lockwood appears to awaken, to be a 'branch' ('branch' with its animistic if not monstrous *root* in the Latin 'branca', the paw of a beast): 'Merely the branch of a fir tree that touched my lattice, as the blast wailed by, and rattled its dry cones against the panes!' (p. 29). Then he dreams again, and it is the central telepathic or supernatural event in the text. He dreams reality: 'I was lying in the oak closet, and I heard distinctly the gusty wind, and the driving of the snow; I heard, also, the fir-bough repeat its teasing sound' (p. 30). The sound is so 'teasing' that he breaks the window, 'stretching an arm out to seize the importunate branch: instead of which, my fingers closed on the fingers of a little, ice-cold hand!' And then, recounts Lockwood, 'The intense horror of nightmare came over me.' It is

nightmare within nightmare. And the voice of 'Catherine Linton',
who has lost her place, lost her way, cries 'Let me in – let me in!'
(p. 30).

Let me in, or let me out? The heart of the innermost inside has
already become the outside (outside the window), just as this
outside is becoming another inside. Like an ancient Egyptian
tomb which conceals (and preserves) the (living) dead, Lockwood
tries to cover it up with writing, texts, books: 'The fingers re-
laxed, I snatched mine through the hole, hurriedly piled the
books up in a pyramid against it' (p. 30). Then the pyramid
begins to move, 'as if thrust forward' from within, outside; and
Lockwood yells himself 'awake'.

The supernatural or concretely 'telepathic' nature of this
'dream' will be confirmed a few minutes afterwards when Heathcliff, believing Lockwood is out of hearing, 'wrenched open the
lattice, bursting, as he pulled at it, into an uncontrollable passion
of tears. "Come in! come in!" he sobbed' (p. 33). All burst.
Lockwood calmly tells us that this represented 'a piece of superstition on the part of my landlord, which belied, oddly, his
apparent sense' (p. 33). How are we supposed to read this? On
the verge, or in the wake, of what kind of dream? It closes the
supernatural off, at the same time as letting it in. It is a gesture
repeated, and elaborated, throughout the text. And without
letting us be assured any more that the inside and the outside,
inclusion and exclusion, can ever be distinguished – without letting us know where such a process could be claimed to begin.

IV

What is a door? *Chambers* defines it as 'the usual entrance into a
house, room, or passage: a frame for closing up the entrance'.
These two definitions, brief and apparently commonsensical as
they are, already indicate a peculiarity: a door is both the entrance and what closes up the entrance. To enter through a door
is to cross the threshold. A threshold is 'the place or point of
entering'. In its so-called figurative sense, the word also designates 'the limit of consciousness'. *Chambers* suggests its etymological derivation, from the Old English *therscan*, 'to thrash, thresh,

in its older sense of trample, tread'. The threshold is where you tread, it is what is trampled or trodden in order to enter a door. We could note, then, that the etymology of 'threshold', perhaps in a merely fortuitous or coincidental fashion, presupposes movement, a physical movement of trampling or treading. It is a movement, however, if one can say this, which by definition does not assume movement *across*, to the inside or to the outside. The 'threshold' appears to be, by this logic, merely movement: it is not rigid and static, but a place – if it is, strictly speaking, a place – of mere movement, without direction.

Doors, windows, gates, walls and frames. *Wuthering Heights* is full of them, as several critics have stressed.[17] Let us, for a moment, confine ourselves to doors. *Wuthering Heights* seems to offer itself, in fact, as an exemplary text for the elaboration of a theory of doors in literature. As we may be led to surmise from a cursory decomposition or anthonomasia of Lockwood's name, the text is pervaded by references to locked doors: for instance, when Heathcliff is locked in at Thrushcross Grange or when Linton and the second Catherine are effectively imprisoned at Wuthering Heights; when Isabella tries to escape from the Heights but Heathcliff 'ordered me in, and shut and re-fastened the door' (p. 117), or when, most horribly perhaps, Linton is transported to the Heights and Nelly rather blithely records that 'as I closed the door, I heard a cry, and a frantic repetition of the words – "Don't leave me! I'll not stay here! I'll not stay here!" Then the latch was raised and fell … and so my brief guardianship ended' (p. 171).

Such references evoke the feelings of confinement, claustrophobia or encryptment which the text as a whole tends to produce. But doors are not characterized in this way alone. They can, even when locked, be broken or bypassed. Thus Heathcliff, apparently ensnared by Edgar Linton and his servants, 'seized the poker, smashed the lock from the inner door, and made his escape as they tramped in' (p. 100). And a little later he will assure Nelly that, no matter what, he will 'find an opportunity of entering' (p. 128) Thrushcross Grange. Sometimes there are doors where one would least expect them, and where consequently they assume a certain phantasmagoric quality – for instance, there is Joseph 'shuffling down a wooden ladder that vanished in the roof, through a trap' (p. 33) or, in the grounds at the Grange, when Nelly and the second Catherine without apparent warning 'neared a door that opened on the road' (p. 187). At other times, again, doors are simply 'wide open' (p. 130) or just yield to one's hand (cf. p. 242). Finally, and most weirdly perhaps, one can encounter a situation in which it is possible 'to unlock, and re-lock the door, without shutting it' (p. 226).

Where is the key? Let's throw in this hypothesis, in passing: if there is an interpretative key to *Wuthering Heights*, it has been 'swallowed' by being thrown into the fire – even into 'the hottest part of the fire' (p. 99) – but the fire is irremediably fictive.

What is a door? Being shut or locked in, shut or locked out, doors that are open or only imagined to be closed, inner doors and outer doors, doors appearing in strange places – all of this signals a complex meditation. With entrancing effects: what we might call the entrancement of the threshold of a hypnopoetics. The text's preoccupation with doors is certainly linked to the question of the threshold. We might think of 'Mr Heathcliff, who lingered by the door, dividing his attention between the objects inside and those that lay without, pretending, that is, to observe the latter, and really noting the former alone' (pp. 175–6). This position at the threshold, complicating or confusing the inside and the outside, is also one which characterizes Heathcliff very near the end of the text, when he 'stood at the open door; he was pale, and he trembled . . .' (p. 257).

Being at the threshold: such a phrase might appear to allow for the play on the literal and the figurative. After all, it is later that same day that Heathcliff tells Nelly, 'Last night, I was on the threshold of hell. To-day, I am within sight of my heaven. I have my eyes on it – hardly three feet to sever me!' (p. 259). But suppose the question of the threshold precedes or in some uncanny way prefigures the literal and the figurative: then the capacity to distinguish between the two is conditional on having already crossed the threshold, on having made in effect an ethico-theoretical decision to exclude or pass over an interpretation of the question of the threshold.

We need not pay much attention, perhaps, to Lockwood when he responds to Catherine's humiliation of young Hareton: 'I rose, and, from a gentlemanly idea of relieving his embarrassment, took up my station in the door-way, surveying the external prospect, as I stood' (p. 239). Yet this adoption of a 'station in the door-way' immediately follows a specific reference to the notion of the threshold in terms of the capacity for reading and understanding. Lockwood has just attempted to side with Hareton, who is being 'laughed at': 'But, Mrs Heathcliff,' says Lockwood, 'we have each had a commencement, and each stumbled and tottered on the threshold, and had our teachers scorned, instead of aiding us, we should stumble and totter yet' (p. 238). To try to read and understand is, first of all, to 'stumble and totter' on the threshold. Do we ever cross it? Does the text allow us to cross the threshold, however softly, however imperceptibly, for instance like a thrush, or like a ghost?

As if to confirm his own capacity for reading and for understanding, Lockwood takes up his 'station in the door-way'. 'Station': the word suggests fixity or immobility, the opposite of the mobility, the trampling or treading, the stumbling or the tottering elsewhere associable with the 'threshold'. But let us follow the passage of this allegorical vignette a little further. Off goes Hareton, returning with 'half-a-dozen volumes in his hands'. What happens to them? What happens, as if literally and allegorically, to the capacity to read? Hareton 'gathered the books and hurled them on the fire' (p. 239). Lockwood, of course, and as if to divert our attention by using the verb in an ostensibly figurative sense, stubbornly insists on still knowing how to read:

> He afterwards gathered the books and hurled them on the fire. I read in his countenance what anguish it was to offer that sacrifice to spleen. I fancied that as they consumed, he recalled the pleasure they had already imparted, and the triumph and ever increasing pleasure he had anticipated from them; and, I fancied, I guessed ... (p. 239)

I fancied, says Lockwood, I read his mind, I had no difficulty reading: reading as imagining, guessing, hallucinating, fancying, telepathy. Thus the telepathic, foretelling, fortune-telling, mad network of narrators and narrating that constitutes the text, weaving and crisscrossing it: telepathy effect.

But what is the frame on which such telepathic embroidery achieves itself?

On the way to trying to answer that question, a final moment in this vignette. It is, as Lockwood describes it, when Hareton 'advanced hastily to the entrance, where I made way for him to pass. But, ere he had crossed the door-stones, Mr Heathcliff, coming up the causeway, encountered him and [laid] hold of his shoulder. (p. 239). There is Hareton, stumbling at the threshold. So obvious, you could see it coming. There you go.

'Ere he had crossed the door-stones': this is one example of where the text fastens on the notion of reaching or of crossing the threshold. There are others. For instance: 'the moment she [the first Catherine] crossed the threshold' (p. 45); 'she [the second Catherine] was almost at the doorstones already' (p. 174); 'We [Nelly and the second Catherine] reached the threshold; Catherine walked in; and I stood waiting' (p. 214). Or, to take one of the earliest instances last, there is Lockwood, at the beginning, on his first visit to Wuthering Heights: 'Before passing the threshold, I paused' (p. 14).

Should he go in? Should we go in? The structure of the narration will not have given any option. Already, before this, Heathcliff has 'uttered with closed teeth' the simple command: '"walk in!"' (p. 13). What is it – to walk? For at the very end of the text: 'the country folks, if you asked them, would swear on their Bible that [Heathcliff] *walks*' (p. 265). Could the text itself walk? Does it move? It is more comforting and rational to think of a text as a physical object, spatial but fixed; essentially static and immobile, like so many dead letters, and yet . . .

What makes Lockwood obey Heathcliff's injunction? The reason he gives is very strange: 'The "walk in," was uttered with closed teeth and expressed the sentiment, "Go to the Deuce!". Even the gate over which he leant manifested no sympathizing movement to the words, and I think that circumstance determined me to accept the invitation' (p. 13). He agrees because 'the gate over which he leant manifested no sympathizing movement to the words'. He goes on to provide a clarification of this reasoning – 'I felt interested in a man who seemed more exaggeratedly reserved than myself' (p. 13) – but the strangeness of the anthropomorphizing description of the gate remains. As if a gate could, of its own accord, manifest a 'sympathizing movement'. In fact, however, this is only an early example of a homonymic

motif which besets the text, like so many weird hurdles or move-
ables.

Reading, and property, in motion.

v

Just as the text unhinges, in effect, the logic of the 'door'– starting
from the paradox of being both 'entrance' and 'exclusion', and
compelling an undecidable encounter of 'threshold' and movement – so it plays at the 'gate'. Gates are described anthropomor-
phically elsewhere in *Wuthering Heights*. For example, there is
the occasion when Lockwood revisits the Heights, shortly before
the burning of the books: 'The front door stood open, but the
jealous gate was fastened' (p. 236). Despite the anthropomorphism, the gate here seems to be merely the equivalent of another
door. But there is also the other word, 'gait', a homophone or
homophonic alloseme meaning 'way'. Immediately following her
telepathic hallucination by 'the weather-worn block', or rather as
a bizarre continuation of it, Nelly Dean has come into sight of
Wuthering Heights only to discover that 'The apparition had
outstripped me; it stood looking through the gate' (p. 94).
Framed by the gate, however, is not Hindley, but Hareton: the
trace or apparition of the crypt transmitted. Like father like son.
Who is the father? 'Devil daddy' (p. 95). Hindley Earnshaw or
Heathcliff? And what does the father teach the son? Nelly tempts
Hareton, who is still behind the gate, with an orange: 'He jumped
at the fruit; I raised it higher. "What does he teach you?" I asked.
"Naught," said he, "but to keep out of his gait"' (p. 95). And
Hareton uses this word again, later on, when Catherine is attempting to befriend him. In its context, the effect of this homophone
is complemented by a double sense of the word 'side'– 'sideways',
meaning 'towards one side', but also 'side' as a verb meaning (as
one might have guessed) to 'move': '"I shall have naught to do
wi' you, and your mucky pride, and your damned, mocking
tricks!" he answered. "I'll go to hell, body and soul, before I look
sideways after you again! Side out of t' gait, now; this minute!"'
(p. 247).

Homonymic confusion of movement and supposedly fixed en-

trances. This motif finds a culmination in one of the most poised
and tantalizing sentences in the text. We are very near the end
now. You know what is happening, it is just as predicted, just as
you remember. Catherine and Hareton are to get married and
move to the Grange. But who, asks Lockwood, will live at
Wuthering Heights then? Nelly answers:

> *'Why, Joseph will take care of the house, and, perhaps, a lad to
> keep him company. They will live in the kitchen, and the rest will
> be shut up.' 'For the use of such ghosts as choose to inhabit it,' I
> observed. 'No, Mr. Lockwood,' said Nelly, shaking her head. 'I
> believe the dead are at peace, but it is not right to speak of them
> with levity.'*

A pause – in which one might be invited to think about levitation,
or in any case about the seductions of this flat denial of the
existence of ghosts, from a woman, Nelly, who has seen at least
one herself – and then the sentence, which is also a paragraph:

> *At that moment the garden gate swung to; the ramblers were
> returning.* (p. 265)

'At that moment': at what moment? This is the time of *Wuthering Heights*. Everything in the spacing, the punctuation and the
ordering of this sentence seems – like the animistic or anthropomorphic language of the novel's final sentence – to leave the
question of the supernatural closed, but open. Before we have
crossed the threshold of its semi-colon, the sentence eerily presents us with a gate that has a life of its own: 'At that moment the
garden gate swung to'.

'Gate' and 'gait'. The coincidence in relation to 'doors' in the
text might not appear to be worth mentioning. It might have been
considered a chance-effect; perhaps it is – whatever 'chance'
means here. But there is another motif, another concatenation,
another allosemic homonymy which disseminates itself in the
text, disseminating the text itself. It is the word 'frame'. It occurs
all over the place, rendering every and any place impossible to
frame. Chiefly, perhaps, it refers to the idea of a body, and
especially – as we might happily have foreseen – of a body at the

limit of its 'life', a limit or liminal state that moreover can itself vibrate, literally *or otherwise*. It vibrates; like an automaton, it moves. There is Linton, repeatedly described in terms of his 'white complexion and slim frame' (p. 168), his 'nerveless frame' (p. 212). It is a strange frame, trembling as if woven like a cobweb: 'He's such a cobweb, a pinch would annihilate him' (p. 227), says Heathcliff. There is the first Catherine, near death, in the weird scene in which Nelly covers the mirror into which Catherine is 'gazing earnestly' (p. 105), deliriously. Then 'a succession of shudders convulsed her frame, and she *would* keep straining her gaze towards the glass' (p. 106). So Nelly goes 'to the door' to call for Edgar to come, but she is 'summoned back by a piercing shriek. The shawl had dropped from the frame.' Why the repetition of 'frame' here? Simply coincidental? Arbitrary? An example of Brontë's 'flawed' writing? Chance? ' "Wake up! That is the glass, the mirror . . ." ' (p. 106). ' "There's nobody here!" '

And then again, there is Heathcliff's 'frame', which, when he comes to fetch the second Catherine back from Thrushcross Grange, is described as being 'a stone or two heavier, perhaps' (p. 227), since Nelly had last seen him. But this frame undergoes, reaches or exceeds a certain bizarre transformation at the limit or 'end' of his 'life'. The description trembles, stumbles: Heathcliff's face exhibits an 'unnatural – it was unnatural – appearance of joy'; but 'his frame' is 'shivering, not as one shivers with chill or weakness, but as a tight-stretched cord vibrates – a strong thrilling, rather than trembling' (p. 258). Thrilling, beyond a touch; or a touch beyond.

Beyond the frame. It is as if one had lost touch, or as if one were losing one's mind. For that is another sense of 'frame' – the frame of one's mind, or rather the frames. Multiplicity is presupposed. Yet it helps to believe that one's mind is always in one frame or another – even if, as the saying goes, one is not in the right frame of mind. Thus we encounter, for instance, Earnshaw returning to the Heights 'rabid drunk, ready to pull the old place about our ears (his *ordinary* frame of mind in that condition)' (p. 66, emphasis added). Yet it seems that there is also a frame of mind which can share the frame of another at the same time. Frames multiply. The mind is a frame which frames. But who, or what, frames this frame? And from the 'inside' or the 'outside'? Nelly, for example, can imagine herself in the 'frame' of Heathcliff, and tell him ' "Were I in your place, I would frame high notions of my birth" ' (pp. 54–5). Framing high notions of his birth is, you may remember, exactly what she has just been doing. Later, when the corpse of Catherine lies before her, Nelly's 'frame' of mind is composed partly of the deathly silence of another. She even becomes a sort of uncanny ventriloquist's dummy, however muted: 'I partook of the infinite calm in which she lay. My mind was never in a holier frame than while I gazed on that untroubled image of Divine rest. I instinctively echoed the words she had uttered, a few hours before. "Incomparably beyond . . ." ' (p. 137).

'Incomparably beyond': this quotation, or rather this prosopopeia, this wording from beyond life, serves as a reminder of another play, another deadly serious play, with the word 'frame'. This prosopopeia is a quotation, within a quotation, within a quotation: from Catherine to Nelly to Lockwood . . . There are numerous more extreme instances in the text. But are they 'in' the text? In accordance with what frame of reference, or frame of 'frame'? *Wuthering Heights* appears to multiply frames of narration at the same time as taking them away. It is as if there can be strict, visible demarcations and simultaneously an absolute erasure of such demarcations. For example, the presence of quotation marks. '1801 – I have just returned from a visit' (p. 13). This is the 'opening' of Lockwood's diary, but without any opening quotation marks. The effect becomes far stranger when Nelly's narrative begins, also unattended by quotation marks: 'Before I came to live here, she commenced, waiting no further invitation to her story' (p. 38). A similar formal gesture can be noted in the way in which separate chapters are framed. There seems, for instance, little reason for the end of Chapter VIII and start of Chapter IX coming where they do, except perhaps, with the latter, weirdly to mime the entering of a door, the blank and typographical threshold of another chapter: 'He [Hindley] entered, vociferating oaths dreadful to hear; and caught me in the act of stowing his son away in the kitchen cupboard' (p. 67).

Is there a true frame, or a true collection of frames, according to which we can read *Wuthering Heights*, judge it, feel or construct a detachment from it? It is striking that another use of the word 'frame' is consistently identifiable with the untrue, with falsehood and fiction. Thus we can find Nelly Dean, ostensibly for Heathcliff's benefit, 'framing a bit of a lie' (p. 100); or, later, telling the second Catherine 'I'd rather be three months ill, than hear you frame a deliberate lie' (p. 197). Or again, very near the end of the text when, wishing to see Heathcliff, she 'framed an excuse to go in' (p. 257).

Does the frame, any frame, stay still? As with the uncanny mobilization of 'door', 'threshold', 'gate' or 'gait', the paronomasia or rather the dissemination of 'frame' invites a negative response. That is the final sense of the word 'frame' for now – the sense, once more, of going, of movement. It occurs at least twice in the text. Nelly, early on, with a premonition that old Mr Earnshaw has died, orders Catherine and Heathcliff to 'frame upstairs, and make little din' (p. 44). And later, in her letter to Nelly, Isabella describes how, trying to establish a conversation with Hareton, he threatens her, telling her to 'frame off' (p. 116).

Wuthering Heights: what is the title, and where, if it can no longer be thought of as something fixed and stationary, if it somehow in itself 'wuthers', makes a sound without a sound, or a movement without movement? A movement perhaps imperceptible, in a distanceless distance: a kind of telekinesis. The title of a text and the name of a house. And from that confusion onwards, from the undecidable treading of that threshold, we would be taken in – like foreign objects.

VI

Something is raised, in the name of 'Wuthering Heights'. As the text frequently suggests, one can raise a tale (for example, p. 221), one can raise a goblin (p. 90), one can raise a ghost or phantom (for example, p. 265), one can raise a latch. Movement in each case – and perhaps starting with the movement of translation within, across and between them.

The latch is raised; it catches. So fast, so slow, the movement that is no movement: you don't know whether or not you're seeing things. Or 'reading things'. It is too late.

'Time stagnates here' (p. 32) – at Wuthering Heights, in
Wuthering Heights – and yet *at the same time* everything goes
haring on. From the vertiginous evocations of the title onwards,
from the first words – '1801 – I have just returned'; not 'I have
recently returned', but *just*, just this very moment. The suspense
of a moment that can seem to last a year: 'just' '1801', for
example. In this extraordinary immediacy – in which, also, time
stagnates – the text maintains itself, and us. Double or multiple
present in which we do not know when we are, and therefore
what is happening now, just now, or who . . .

It is the speed of life *and* death, and neither. It is the speed and
disseminatory strangeness of the word 'cant', applied to Nelly
Dean (pp. 52, 221) and, perhaps less often observed, to Nelly
Dean's mother ('canty', p. 186). It is the speed of the narrative
(Isabella's) within a narrative (Nelly's) within a narrative (Lockwood's) in which Isabella is made to recount the very imperative
of speed, what we might term the wuthering heights of speed
itself:

> In my flight through the kitchen I bid Joseph speed to his master; I
> knocked over Hareton, who was hanging a litter of puppies from a
> chair-back in the doorway; and, blest as a soul escaped from
> purgatory, I bounded, leaped, and flew down the steep road; then,
> quitting its windings, shot direct across the moor, rolling over
> banks, and wading through marshes; precipitating . . . (p. 150)

And I leave the sentence there.

There is a concept or phenomenon to which texts of parapsychology refer, known as 'cryptaesthesia'. Coined by Charles
Richet, it is defined in *OED* as 'A supernormal faculty of perception, whether clairvoyant or telepathic.' Etymologically it per-
tains to the perception (*aesthesis*) of what is hidden (*crypto-*).[18] In
his own very different texts, Jacques Derrida has demonstrated
how, in various ways, our household words are worked over by
certain kinds of crypt-effect, by otherness. He has sought to use
words 'under erasure': to employ, for example, the word 'is', but
offering it to be understood as if it were crossed out. For reasons
already given, this would have to be the status of that word in the
question 'What *is* a crypt?' Elsewhere, and in a corresponding

fashion, Derrida has introduced the notion of 'paleonymy' – where a word that is 'old' and familiar can, for strategic purposes, be retained, but as in some sense a 'new' word. The 'old' word is contaminated, deformed, worked over by a certain 'newness' and strangeness.[19]

I should like to conclude by suggesting a paleonymic use of the word 'cryptaesthesia' as a means of describing *Wuthering Heights* and, indeed, other literary texts. Perhaps this word must retain some vestiges of its more 'familiar' parapsychological sense: whether it does, or to what extent, I leave undecided for the present. It can be aligned with 'telepathy' and 'telekinesis': it too would involve a certain reinscription, a paleonymic translation. 'Cryptaesthesia' here carries a stronger sense of reference to the notion of the crypt and to aesthetics, at the same time as alluding to the telepathic capacity of the text to see us coming, read *us*, determining us and our strange inclusion, cryptaesthetically working over our 'own' language, working over us, *ourselves*. I am suggesting, then, the case for a cryptaesthetics of literature.

In relation to Abraham and Torok's *Cryptonymy*, I have attempted to indicate that *Wuthering Heights* not only seems to encrypt, but encrypts, among other things, the very language that one might use to describe a crypt. The frame of reference itself is encrypted. We are left on another threshold, silent, at the very moment of tottering. This is the telepathic dimension.[20] In a placeless place and at a kind of speed without motion, it stirs, wuthers or vibrates, in a singular telekinesis. Self, soul, ghost, crypt: these terms are deranged, no longer ordered by the topoi of 'life', 'death' or 'immortality'. The text is concerned with ghosts of the living, selves as already phantoms or phantom-effects, crypts without origins and without limits. Proper names and common names, the name of the title and of the author, 'door', 'threshold', 'gate'/'gait' and 'frame': I have sought also to show some of the strange effects produced by, within and through such 'household words'. The notion of a hypnagogics or hypnopoetics, a radical disturbance of sleeping and waking, reading and dreaming, is dynamically linked to all of these character-izations.

The analysis appears to oblige us, then, to consider the text in terms of what I would call its cryptaesthetic resistance. Such resistance, it should be clear, is not something dependent on, or derivable from, the 'intentions', the critical or rhetorical 'self-consciousness', or the 'unconscious' of an author. Rather, the text itself is a crypt – of itself, always in otherness. It is ineluctably allographic and allocryptic. Finally, the notion of cryptaesthetic resistance might offer a new and different way of accounting for what has been so often celebrated as the 'power' of *Wuthering Heights*. Indeed this proposal could be generalized: the 'stronger' or more 'powerful' a literary text, the greater its cryptaesthetic resistance. I would even venture that such a hypothesis could be adopted with respect to texts by certain other writers, certain critics, philosophers or psychoanalysts for example.

'At that moment, the garden gate swung to....'.

The impossible, moving 'outside' of 'literature': its *gaite*.

We are deposited at the door, on the threshold, with a door. But what is a threshold, what is a door, in literature?

To close – two brief quotations from another text which seems to pose the question, another text which must also promise to be both complex and extraordinary, in terms of a cryptaesthetics. This is Samuel Beckett's *The Unnamable* (1958) which, as it draws to its unnamable end, or beginning, states:

> ... *perhaps it's the door, perhaps I'm at the door, that would surprise me, perhaps it's I, perhaps somewhere or other it was I, I can depart, all this time I've journeyed without knowing it, it's I now at the door, what door, what's a door doing here, it's the last words, the true last* ...

And then

> *perhaps they have said me already, perhaps they have carried me to the threshold of my story, before the door that opens on my own story, that would surprise me, if it opens, it will be I, it will be the silence, where I am, I don't know, I'll never know, in the silence you don't know* ...[21]

4

A Note on The House with the Green Shutters

What is a note, footnote or endnote? 'In the silence you don't know' – Beckett's words – refer to being in a place or atmosphere of silence and not knowing, not knowing perhaps anything at all. And at the same time they refer to a particular kind of silence, unknown, unprecedented – a silence that is quite other, absolutely unfamiliar. In 'the silence you don't know'.

What is a novel? Though in some respects now rather dated and in others arguably incoherent, Philippe Sollers's essay 'The Novel and the Experience of Limits', originally given at a *Tel Quel* seminar in December 1965, remains a provocative and important contribution to the theory of the novel. Clearly corroborating the then-emerging work of Barthes and Derrida, Sollers affirms:

> *Thus we see that the essential question today is no longer that of the* writer *and of the* work *(and even less that of the 'work of art'), but that of* writing *and of* reading. *Consequently, we need to define a new space where these two phenomena could be seen as reciprocal and simultaneous, a curved space, a medium of exchanges and reversibility where we would finally be on the same side as our language. ('The Novel and the Experience of Limits',* in Writing and the Experience of Limits, ed. David Hayman, trans. Philip Barnard with David Hayman [New York: Columbia University Press, 1983], 195)

(We might bracket off Sollers's rather dubious final clause here, with its assumption of a language that could truly be ours, our own. And perhaps graft on instead Derrida's more precise proposition, in 'Border Lines' (in *Deconstruction and Criticism* [New York: Seabury Press, 1979]), that 'One never writes [or reads] either in one's own language or in a foreign language' [p. 101].) But what would be the 'new space' towards which Sollers is gesturing? How might we describe this 'curved space' or kind of arch? What, then, would a novel be?

Let us take a step backwards, or sideways, one way or another, or not, to the question of the footnote.

A gastropod at the edge of the world.

I would like to dedicate the present note to the memory of F. R. Leavis. More specifically I wish to dedicate it to a reading of a footnote of F. R. Leavis. One footnote might join the other, communicating with the other at a distance, across discourses and decades, at first perhaps in a sort of two-step, but elaborating a different rhythm or treading space, another threshold.

Leavis's note occurs at the end of his essay 'The Great Tradition' (in *The Great Tradition: George Eliot, Henry James, Joseph*

Conrad [London: Chatto and Windus, 1948], 1–27). We scarcely
need remind ourselves what the phrase 'the great tradition' refers
to. Jane Austen, George Eliot, Henry James, Joseph Conrad and
D. H. Lawrence: 'the great tradition of the English novel is *there*'
(p. 27), Leavis tells us. I foresee a digression, trailing off at this
point, regarding the notion of 'tradition': *traditio* and translation,
the 'English' American of Henry James and 'English' Polish, or
French, of Conrad; tradition as telepathic, as in Terry Eagleton's
ironic and suggestive characterization of T. S. Eliot's conception
of 'Tradition':

> *The existing classics within the cramped space of the Tradition*
> *politely reshuffle their positions to make room for a newcomer, and*
> *look different in the light of it; but since this newcomer must*
> *somehow have been in principle included in the Tradition all along*
> *to have gained admission at all, its entry serves to confirm that*
> *Tradition's central values. The Tradition, in other words, can never*
> *be caught napping: it has somehow mysteriously foreseen the major*
> *works still unwritten* . . . (Literary Theory: An Introduction *[Ox-*
> *ford: Basil Blackwell, 1983], 39)*

But for the moment, Leavis's footnote, which is ostensibly concerned with the Brontës, with the marginal in more than one
sense. The note concludes:

> *I have said nothing about* Wuthering Heights *because that aston-*
> *ishing work seems to me a kind of sport. It may, all the same, very*
> *well have had some influence of an essentially undetectable kind:*
> *[Emily Brontë] broke completely, and in the most challenging way,*
> *both with the Scott tradition that imposed on the novelist a roman-*
> *tic resolution of his* [sic] *themes, and with the tradition coming*
> *down from the eighteenth century that demanded a plane-mirror*
> *reflection of the surface of 'real' life. Out of her a minor tradition*
> *comes, to which belongs, most notably,* The House with the Green
> 'Shutters'. *(p. 27)*

At the margin, at the edge, at the end and after the end of 'the
great tradition', the marginal, the 'minor tradition': and so, as we
hope to show, among other things, supplementary and essential,
derivative and fundamental. *The House with the Green Shutters*:

those are the last words, the words literally at the end, of 'The Great Tradition'. Hail and farewell.

Though brief, the note is so well known, it seems, that it is not necessary for Dorothy Porter, the Penguin editor of *The House with the Green Shutters* (Harmondsworth: Penguin, 1985) to specify Leavis's name when she observes that George Douglas Brown's text has been 'not infrequently treated as a sport, compared typically to *Wuthering Heights*' (*HGS*, p. 12). What do *Wuthering Heights* and *The House with the Green Shutters* have to do with one another? How might we speak of them, together? What, as a 'minor tradition', might they imply or communicate about the 'great tradition' of the 'English' 'novel'?

The House with the Green Shutters was first published in 1901 and is classed as a Penguin Classic, though it is without doubt less widely read than Brontë's text. It is set mostly in a small 'fictive' town called Barbie, in Scotland. Barbie is generally regarded as being modelled on Brown's birthplace, Ochiltree, in Ayrshire. Some of the later chapters shift to Edinburgh. But, above all, the text is centred on the House with the Green Shutters itself, the grandest and most 'commanding' (p. 50) house in Barbie, the home of John Gourlay, his wife, his daughter Janet and his son, John Gourlay the younger. Gourlay is a fierce and unpopular man, at the outset the most powerful and successful trader in the town. He encounters a rival, however, in the form of James Wilson, who establishes an 'Emporium', 'LICENS'D TO SELL TEA & TOBACCO', 'in the midst of Barbie' (p. 95). Wilson also has a son, also of the same name, though generally referred to as 'Jimmy'. The rivals send their sons to the 'distant and expensive' High School of Skeighan, Gourlay specifically in order 'to be upsides with Wilson' (p. 128). And later both sons are sent to the university in Edinburgh. Partly as a consequence of such expenses, but situated in a larger and more complex process of tragic inevitability, Gourlay's business crumbles. Meanwhile young Gourlay in Edinburgh turns to drink and is eventually expelled from the university. Petrified of going home to confront his father, he nevertheless knows he must. The confrontation is terrible: Gourlay is murdered by his own son, who a few days afterwards poisons himself. But 'There's twa thirds of the poison left' (p. 241) and Mrs Gourlay, who is anyway (it transpires) dying of cancer, and her consumptive daughter Janet, discreetly but horrifically, finish it off.

Of Brontë's and Brown's texts one can enumerate as rapidly as possible certain similarities or correspondences. Both have titles which are also the names of houses; both are chiefly set in an isolated community; both make use of dialect, as well, which increases the kind of powerful geographical, linguistic and ideological marginality they simultaneously exhibit and exploit. Both are concerned with some form of family tragedy, in both cases partly incited by a male desire for property or appropriation and by the destructive effects of alcohol. Both are the single 'great novels' by which their authors' names have become famous. With their provoking 'BR-' in common, both authors, moreover, died young: Emily Brontë was thirty, George Douglas Brown thirty-three.

Wuthering Heights and *The House with the Green Shutters* correspond, I would like to say – by letters, by the letter, as letters. For the correspondence or correspondences are also of less obvious and more uncanny kinds. Few readers or critics, I suspect, would wish to dispute that both texts are, in various ways, uncanny. Each broadly demonstrates the efficacy of Freud's general definitions of the 'uncanny' ('The "Uncanny"', in *PFL*, 14: 335–76), whether in so-called life or literature: the familiar becoming unfamiliar, the homely becoming unhomely, or (where Freud follows Schelling) when that which *'ought to have remained ... secret and hidden ... has come to light'* (p. 345). In both Brontë's and Brown's texts one encounters important instances of what is perhaps the most general form of the uncanny, namely repetition: repetition of a feeling, situation, event, character, and so on. One can also readily find examples of some of the arguably discrete and less general forms: coincidence, animism, anthropomorphism, automatism, the fear of being buried alive (or related images or experiences of claustrophobia). To elaborate an account of *Wuthering Heights* and *The House with the Green Shutters* in these terms would be one way of attempting to pursue the question of the strangeness of these texts and of their correspondences. And of their rapport with Telepathy.

But for the present I wish to focus on another cluster of correspondences: sound and silence, ghosts, foresight and fortune-

telling, anger and hatred, images (if one can call them that) of
eyes, images (if one can call them that) of reading, the epistolary
and postal systems, hypnagogics and 'realism', a certain notion of
movement, rhythm or step, thresholds and doors. I must limit
myself to detailed consideration of only a few of these, in *The
House with the Green Shutters*. Correspondences with *Wuthering
Heights* will, perhaps, be able to carry on as if behind the scenes,
silently.

'In the silence you don't know.' Dorothy Porter remarks that
'Brown is a great poet of silence and stillness' (p. 20). Strange,
paradoxical mixing of 'poetry' and 'silence'. The question of the
threshold is at work in, and before, the text of *The House with
the Green Shutters* as well. The opening paragraph indicates it
well enough – the significance of door and doorstep – together
with strange meetings of sound and silence, and movement without movement. There is also the image of the 'arch' or 'curved
space' here, to which we will return:

> The frowsy chamber-maid of the 'Red Lion' had just finished
> washing the front door steps. She rose from her stooping posture,
> and, being of slovenly habit, flung the water from her pail, straight
> out, without moving from where she stood. The smooth round arch
> of the falling water glistened for a moment in mid-air. John Gour-
> lay, standing in front of his new house at the head of the brae,
> could hear the swash of it when it fell. The morning was of perfect
> stillness. (p. 39)

So much hinges on doors. They seem to mark the passages and
passageways by which the text leads itself on, offers a reading of
itself, and leads to, or communicates with, Wuthering Heights.
What is a door? And what is behind it? Just as one might predict, doors (and gates) in *The House with the Green Shutters* are
recurrently associated with silence and anticipation. But they are
also associated with a foresight of dread and horror.

In this way, entering in silence, one can interrupt the act of
reading, commenting without commenting, demanding the foretelling of a good story:

> Gourlay went swiftly to the kitchen from the inner yard. He had
> stood so long in silence on the step, and his coming was so noiseless,

that he surprised a long thin trollop of a woman, with a long thin scraggy neck, seated by the slatternly table, and busy with a frowsy paper-covered volume, over which her head was bent in intent perusal.

'At your novelles?' said he. 'Aye, woman; will it be a good story?'

She rose in a nervous flutter when she saw him ... (p. 51)

Anthropomorphism links the house with its owner – 'A litle dour and blunt in the outlines like Gourlay himself, it drew and satisfied your eye as he did' (p. 50). 'Your' eye, remarks the narrator: whose eye is that? Are you there? As we later learn, 'Heavy Scotsmen are fond of telling folk that they are where they are. "You're there!" said Templandmuir' (p. 107). Gourlay is there, at least, anthropomorphized in the form of his house, but most of all identified in relation to its doors. For instance, his son is hiding upstairs in the garret, a reader, once again, being disturbed from an activity of reading:

Once he heard the birr of his father's voice in the lobby and his mother speaking in shrill protest, and then – oh, horror! – his father came up the stair. Would he come into the garret? John, lying on his left side, felt his quickened heart thud against the boards, and he could not take his big frighted eyes from the bottom of the door.
(p. 82)

And later, after being expelled from university, 'He was afraid to go home to meet his father. He shrank, in visioning fear, before the dour face, loaded with scorn, that would swing round to meet him as he entered through the door' (p. 200). Actually the positions will be reversed. Young John finally takes the train, sees his father in Barbie, in the street, without being seen himself, and he realizes 'with relief' that 'He would not have to face his father the moment he went in. . . . He crept on through the gloaming to the House with the Green Shutters' (p. 201). That is the final sentence of Chapter XXIII, the movement of creeping on towards the threshold. The chapters literally close, and open, with thresholds and doors. The next chapter (XXIV) closes with the father finally trudging home. Its last sentence is a closure and an entrance, or else a kind of door that puts any distinction between them into suspense: 'So Gourlay trudged home through the darkness, beaten at last, mad with shame and anger and foreboding. The first thing he saw on entering the kitchen was his son – sitting muffled in his coat by the great fender' (p. 211).

What is the silence of the white space between this last full-stop and the onset of the succeeding chapter?

The first sentence of Chapter XXV perhaps epitomizes, epigraphs or epitaphs it: 'Janet and her mother saw a quiver run through Gourlay, as he stood and glowered from the threshold. He seemed of monstrous bulk and significance, filling the doorway in his silence' (p. 212).

All eyes are fixed around the issue of doors – on what is inside or what is outside, on what could be called the tight threshold of being. It is tempting to say that people are snails. The motif of gastropods leaves its trails in the text: so many of these Scots can exhibit a 'creeshy [or slimy] benevolence' (p. 155). So many of them are 'A "slug for the drink"' (p. 155). When young John is drunk, at one point, he is described as being 'as phull of drink as a whelk-shell's phull of whelk' (p. 179). Or – invoking Shakespeare's 'whining schoolboy, with his satchel / And shining morning face, creeping like snail / Unwillingly to school' (*As You Like It*, II, vii, 145–7) – there is young John before he finally steals 'through the Green Gate with his bag slithering at his hip': 'On school mornings the boy shrank from going out with a shrinking that was almost physical' (p. 75). Writing itself can be, echoing Tennyson's *In Memoriam*, 'nothing but a froth of words – lucky if it glistens without, like a blobber of iridescent foam' (p. 162).

Near the end now, young Gourlay buys a bottle of whisky, and walks back like a somnambulist, through a community of surreal gastropods, back to the House with the Green Shutters to die:

> *He stared before him like a man walking in his sleep, and never once looked to either side. At word of his coming the doors were filled with mutches and bald heads, keeking by the jambs to get a look. Many were indecent in their haste, not waiting till he passed ere they peeped – which was their usual way. Some even stood away out in front of their doors to glower at him advancing,*

turning slowly with him as he passed, and glowering behind him as he went. They saw they might do so with impunity; that he did not see them, but walked like a man in a dream. He passed up the street and through the Square, beneath a hundred eyes, the sun shining softly round him. Every eye followed till he disappeared through his own door. (p. 240)

Like snails: having heads that are capable of being inside and outside, but always at, their doors; having stalked eyes or stalked ears, being antennae or listening-posts. At an earlier, more triumphant moment, young John has returned to Barbie having won the Raeburn essay prize at Edinburgh. Gourlay and his son meet the parson, Mr Struthers, a man more popularly and maliciously known as 'Puffy Importance' (p. 172):

Though the elder Gourlay disconsidered the Church, and thought little of Mr Struthers, he swelled with pride to think that the minister should stop his offspring in the Main Street of Barbie, to congratulate him on his prospects. They were close to the Emporium; and with the tail of his eye he could see Wilson peeping from his door, and listening to every word. This would be a hair in Wilson's neck! (p. 174)

Just before this we are offered another eavesdropping, whereby the philosophy of Hegel seems to become something else for the gastropods – for the slugs of Barbie, but also for the text itself as a gastropod which soaks up, absorbs the work of Hegel. Struthers, pontificating, has pronounced 'auld Tam', the professor at Edinburgh, to be 'a little too fond of Hegel'; and 'Mrs Eccles, listening from the Black Bull door, wondered if Hegel was a drink' (p. 174).

To listen in or to eavesdrop is – by a current English colloquialism – 'to trunk'. *The House with the Green Shutters*, like so many other literary texts, is full of trunking. Everyone in the small community of Barbie trunks in on everyone else. This is the purpose of what Brown calls 'the bodie': 'The genus "bodie" is divided into two species: the "harmless bodies" and the "nesty bodies". The bodies of Barbie mostly belonged to the second variety' (p. 59). The 'chief occupation' of a bodie 'is the discussion of his neighbour's affairs' (p. 59); and the pursuit of this occupation is crucially dependent on trunking, on networks of gossip or trunk lines. This constitutes what I would like to call one of the telepathic structures of the text. Ultimately, as we will see, this is linked to notions of the epistolary and the postal services. Everything in the text is criss-crossed, woven up with 'speculation' (p. 59), with foreseeing, foretelling and fortune-telling. Brown in fact defines the typical Scotsman primarily in terms of a 'forecasting leap of the mind' (p. 98), and observes how 'his forecasting mind is always detecting "possibeelities"' (p. 99). Although the 'bodies', along with several other characters, are consistently preoccupied with malevolent little prophecies and visions of the future, it is chiefly James Wilson who embodies this function. He 'was a dreamer' and 'His close musing eye, peering at the dusky-brown nodge of his pony's hip through the gloom, saw not that, but visions of chances, opportunities, occasions' (p. 99). In this brief description, as elsewhere in the text, a certain hypnopoetics is at work, a form of hypnosis which elides any reality of the present.

'Speculation' or 'forecasting', however, is not a theme of the text: it is intimately bound up with the structure and possibility of its narrative. The narrator of *The House with the Green Shutters*, for example, explicitly identifies with this aspect of Wilson: Wilson's 'delight in his visions was exactly the same as the author's delight in the figments of his brain. They were the same good company along the twilight roads. The author, happy with his thronging thoughts (when they are kind enough to throng) is no happier than Wilson was on nights like these' (p. 100). The narrator's 'forecasting mind', we might say, is stamped in the telepathic, fortune-telling labyrinth of the narration itself. Like Shakespeare or Hardy, Brown relentlessly exploits the kind of prophetic or telepathic gestures by which tragic inevitability is organized. The narrator is, by definition, a clairvoyant: 'It was strange that a thing so impalpable as gossip should influence so strong a man as John Gourlay to his ruin. But it did' (p. 105).

Like the 'bodies', the narrator appears to have the uncanny facility of a medium or fortune-teller who not only predicts or prophesies, but also somehow enacts the prediction or prophecy. Brown writes:

> *The bodies of Barbie became not only the chorus to Gourlay's tragedy, buzzing it abroad and discussing his downfall; they became also, merely by their maddening tattle, a villain of the piece and an active cause of the catastrophe. Their gossip seemed to materialize into a single entity, a something propelling, that spurred Gourlay on to the schemes that ruined him. (p. 105)*

Strange, telepathic 'entity': what would it look like? Might it not bear witness, again, to the 'foreign body' that, for Maria Torok, equally identifies 'telepathy' and 'the death drive' in the work of Freud?

How should we read these references to 'the chorus' and 'tragedy'? To speak of the narrator's 'ironic tone', here and elsewhere in *The House with the Green Shutters*, would seem inadequate. Who and where is the narrator? And, by the same token, who and where is the reader? The narrator is sometimes, it appears, a member of the Barbie community itself: 'Ours is a nippy [mean or brutal] locality' (p. 92), he says at one point. At other times, he is evidently outside – a narrator of dispassionate detachment and clinical objectivity. Like Brown's description of what a novelist 'should' be, he is 'an aloof individual . . . stating all sides and taking none' (cited by Porter, p. 17). As Dorothy Porter notes, this 'uncertainty', disturbance or incoherence in the presence and role of the narrator has tended to be regarded by critics as a significant flaw in the text. Porter attempts to shift critical focus on this problem by suggesting that we see 'the narrator's uncertainty to be characterized as functional rather than helpless' (p. 18). The fact that the narrator seems to vary between being 'within' the community and 'dissociated' from it complements the idea that 'Community is both necessary and oppressive or impossible' (p. 18). Porter's suggestion needs to be radicalized. She seems to think that the 'stance' or 'uncertainty' of the narrator can be perceived and understood without 're-reading' (p. 18), and without at any point or in any way raising the question of the 'stance' or 'uncertainty' of the reader. But the reader is implicated at every level. In part it is a matter of the strangeness and disruptive power of the use of the second person 'you'. 'You' happens or it happens to 'you' abruptly, without warning: 'And there, hey presto! the transformation was achieved, and Wilson's Emporium stood before you' (p. 95). The introduction or inclusion of 'you' is as rapid and insidious as a jibe from Wilson's wife: 'her jibe was in you and out again, before you knew you were wounded' (p. 97). Taking the words of Browning in 'Childe Roland' as literally as possible, 'you're inside the den!' And the peculiarly incorporated relation of the narrator to the reader will reach a further uneasy 'communality' when the former observes, towards the end of the text, 'When we think of what Gourlay did that day, we must remember ...' (p. 197).

We are caught up, it seems, in the web or trails of the text. 'You' may be, for example, yourself 'a nippy man' (p. 98), the kind of person who is likely to 'shout carelessly' (p. 98) in the street. Or you may quite involuntarily find yourself, in the role of reader, as one of the 'bodies'. The web of trunking and 'keeking', of interpreting, speculating and forecasting, and of being some kind of 'sneck-drawer' (p. 112), no doubt encourages an imbrication of 'reader' and 'bodie'. Reading is, literally, sneckdrawing ('A sneck is a door latch': p. 263). How otherwise, for example, determine the feeling of unreality which is created when Johnny Coe, one of the 'ablest' of the bodies, relates the story of the 'great flood' that happened on the day young Gourlay was born, relates, in other words, a piece of news that is twelve years old (pp. 72–3)? The bodies know the story well enough; only they will pretend not to, in order to accommodate 'you', a new 'bodie' of sorts: 'That was at the boy's birth, Mr Coe?' asks Tam Brodie at the end. 'Ou, aye, just the laddie' (p. 73).

Or perhaps you are not there at all. Perhaps you are merely silence, a horrible absence, just a white blank.

The challenge seems to be absolute. As interlude or 'fillip' (p. 73) at this juncture, perhaps we might briefly take a glass of Hegel? In his essay 'Hypogram and Inscription', Paul de Man discusses the moment in the *Phenomenology* when we are confronted 'with the actual piece of paper on which Hegel, at that very moment and in this very place, has been writing'. De Man observes that, 'because he wrote it down, the existence of a here and a now of Hegel's text is undeniable as well as totally blank. It reduces, for example, the entire text of the *Phenomenology* to the endlessly repeated stutter: *this* piece of paper, *this* piece of paper, and so on' (*The Resistance to Theory* [Manchester: Manchester University Press, 1986], 42).

The House with the Green Shutters is a tragedy set in the time of the coming of telemedia. A little over half way through the text, that time is briefly described:

> *The grand old days – only a few years back, but seeming half a century away, so much had happened in between – the grand days ... had disappeared for ever. Now all was bustle, hurry, and confusion, the getting and sending of telegrams, quick despatches by railway, the watching of markets at a distance, rapid combinations that bewildered Gourlay's duller mind. (p. 135)*

Television has not been invented, but the text shows a fascination with images or pictures which are self-contained, apparently with a life of their own. Or rather, a death of their own – the work of 'morbid fancy' (p. 160) or of 'morbid perception' (p. 163). Not only are there the many instances where the narrative presents powerful, beautiful visuals, but this fascination is embodied in young John. It is a fascination with what the text calls 'automatic visualization' (p. 194). Repeatedly, and provocatively, it is linked to questions of reading and writing. Thus, for young Gourlay, 'reading was a painful process, and he could never remember the plot. What he liked best ... was a vivid physical picture' (p. 80). Reading, one doesn't see the words, one sees visions, a form of television.

Books are telepathic – they can read your mind, see you coming from a distance, tell you what you are thinking, tell you what you have been perceiving all along without realizing: young Gourlay's 'mind was full of perceptions of which he was unconscious, till he found one of them recorded in a book, and that was the book for him' (p. 81). Language is the 'medium', the fortune-teller inevitably out there, or deep within, at some inconceivable distance or proximity, waiting. Writing, or preparing to write, one doesn't see the words, one sees visions, tele-pictures coming independently of intention or conscious desire: '... his morbid fancy set to work of its own accord. He saw a lonely little town far off upon the verge of Lapland night, leagues and leagues across a darkling plain, dark itself and little and lonely in the gloomy splendour of a Northern sky' (p. 160). This is how John sets about writing his Raeburn essay, 'An Arctic Night'.

Finally, and most challengingly, there is the night when John cannot sleep, when the 'stupefaction of alcohol' has worn off and 'automatic visualization' – or a kind of demonic hypnopoetics – takes over: 'He was anxious to sleep, but drowsy dullness kept away. His mind began to visualize of its own accord, independent of his will; and, one after another, a crowd of pictures rose vivid in the darkness of his brain. He saw them as plainly as you see this page' (p. 193). With its identificatory though equivocal 'as', this simile is of the strongest kind. It constitutes perhaps the most critical point in the text. The rest of Brown's sentence in fact modifies the description, implying a distinction between 'plainness' and 'clearness', as well as a darker, more disturbing distinction between the natural and the unnatural, the vital or life-affirming and the morbid: 'He saw them as plainly as you see this page – but with a different clearness – for they seemed unnatural, belonging to a morbid world' (p. 193). 'This page' of written or printed words is natural, vital, life-affirming. The provocation, or the challenge, remains.

You see this page? You see it 'plainly'. What do you see? Does the text reduce to an 'endlessly repeated stutter: *this* piece of paper, *this* piece of paper ...'? Or is there another kind of automatism, another kind of entrancement or hypnotism at work? Perhaps one needs, in the words of young Gourlay, to 'hover a blink' (p. 185), to suspend one's movement for a moment, for the blinking of an eye.

There are, the text suggests, moments of vision, hypnotic moments in which one experiences a truth, a shadow of the truth perhaps which links telepathy and death. John is about to return to Edinburgh, but as the gig awaits him his sight is arrested by the 'couthie laurel by the Red Lion door':

> *Gourlay stared at the bright evergreen, and forgot for a moment where he was. His lips parted, and – as they saw in the light from the door – his look grew dreamy and far-away.... The spell lasted but a moment, but one of those moments searching a man's nature to its depths, yet flitting like a lonely shadow on the autumn wheat.*
> (p. 185)

The House with the Green Shutters is obsessed with seeing and with eyes. This obsession culminates in 'the red e'en' (p. 233), the disembodied eyes of the ghost of the murdered father that comes to 'glare at' (p. 231) the son, to haunt him 'always' (p. 234) and drive him to his death. Given the fact that the father is specifically described as a man willing and able to send his son 'slinking away *animo castrato*' (p. 212) – 'mentally and spiritually unmanned', as Dorothy Porter puts it (p. 256, n. 72) – it would be tempting to follow Freud, in his essay 'The "Uncanny"', where he argues that 'fears about the eye are derived from the fear of castration' (p. 352). But to do this would be, on the one hand, to evade the problematic but fundamental role of hypnotism and a certain hypnopoetics in psychoanalysis itself and, on the other hand, to pass over a more obvious, though no less complex, aspect of Brown's text. 'Aspect' may be an appropriately visual metaphor: I am thinking of anger, fury, rage and hatred.

There has been comparatively little study of anger and hatred in literature. It is these emotions which perhaps most strongly link the elder John Gourlay in Brown's text and Heathcliff in *Wuthering Heights*. A fuller and more systematic study might attempt to analyse anger, rage and hatred in these texts specifically in terms of notions of mourning. But I must limit myself here to only one or two provisional remarks. The first is that *The House with the Green Shutters* seems to suggest that there is a strong, 'uncanny' relationship between anger, rage or hatred, and telepathy. There are, as the narrator humorously confides, 'men whom you hear thinking' (p. 122); and 'the Scots peasant' in particular is attributed, however equivocally, with a 'character-reading eye' (p. 129). But such capacities are powerfully heightened when the context is one of rage or hatred. As the narrator observes:

> *Our insight is often deepest into those we hate, because annoyance fixes our thought on them to probe. We cannot keep our minds off them – 'Why do they do it?' we snarl, and wondering why, we find out their character. Gourlay was not an observant man, but every man is in any man somewhere, and hate to-night driving his mind into Wilson, helped him to read him like an open book. (p. 112)*

The proposition that 'every man is in any man somewhere' is scarcely one of pious humanism. It indicates rather the sort of relation which is experienced shortly after the town-meeting about 'the new railway' (p. 109), when Gourlay and Templand-muir leave together: 'They trudged together in a burning silence. Though nothing was said between them, each was in wrathful contact with the other's mind' (p. 114). Significantly, perhaps, it is not only Gourlay who demonstrates this kind of violent com-munication and 'character-reading'. Later on, for example, and as an eerily distorted foretelling of the scene in which he provokes his expulsion from the university, Gourlay's son in a rage thinks about Armstrong, the young man who had that evening teased him with the question 'would you face up to a professor?' (p. 192) Young Gourlay 'lay in brooding anger, and his mind was fluent in wrathful harangues in some imaginary encounter of the future.... He flowed in eloquent scorn of Armstrong and his ways.... He seemed gifted with uncanny insight into Arm-strong's character' (p. 193). In this way Brown's text indicates a further link between telepathy and the death drive – feelings of hate being, in Freud's work, closely identified with the latter. (See, for example, *Beyond the Pleasure Principle*, in *PFL*, 11: 327, and 'The Ego and the Id', in *PFL*, 11: 383. And one or two other observations might be made, parenthetically, at this point. As well as feelings of 'hate', Freud associates the death drive with 'the destructive instinct, the instinct for mastery, or the will to power' ['The Economic Problem of Masochism', in *PFL*, 11: 418]. This 'instinct for mastery' or 'will to power' would not only suggest another death-driven aspect of the older Gourlay, but open the thought of a further, disturbing question: to what extent is reading itself, and that of literary critics in particular, in the service of the death drive? Especially if, or to the extent that, we accept Robert Young's proposal that 'each reader reads with a secret wish and fantasy that his or her approach will at last see the literary object as it really is, finally get to it, seize it and carry it off – that his or her reading will be so complete, so final, so irrefutable, as to render all future readers powerless and dispos-sessed' ['The Politics of "The Politics of Literary Theory"', in the *Oxford Literary Review*, vol. 10 (1988), 139].)

What effects are generated by anger, hate, rage on the reader of literature? If love, kindness and placidity tend to elicit a reader's identifications, can fury and hatred form a demonic counterpart,

A Note 79

absenting but by that very rejection haunting or hypnotizing her/him?

Anger, fury, rage and hatred in *The House with the Green Shutters*: John Gourlay is their living monument. And in producing this monumentalization, the text is, paradoxically perhaps, both weakened and strengthened by a reliance on hyperbole and melodramatization. Realism, remember, it's as if to send you to sleep ... Gourlay, repeatedly, is 'infernal angry' (p. 82) and 'hellish angry' (p. 104); he is, as his name might seem to promise, 'gurly' (p. 103) – 'surly, rough, ill-tempered' (p. 260) as Porter glosses it; he is capable of 'huge disgust' (p. 52) and 'brutal dourness' (p. 65). He shows a 'vicious rage' (p. 216) and 'monstrous wrath' (p. 214); he is 'a cauldron of wrath' (p. 115), and thereby identified with the 'pretty hell-broth brewing in the little town' (p. 105).

Many of the other characters are described in terms of their eyes, and the ways in which they look. On a single page, for example, we are asked to visualize 'a heavy civic eye', 'a bargain-making eye' and 'little side-glancing eyes' (p. 60) among the bodies. But it is the eyes of John Gourlay that dominate both the people of Barbie and the text itself. Gourlay has 'awful eyes' (p. 115). He has 'a wide-open glower' that people cannot bear. The Deacon, for instance, 'simply cannot thole the look' (p. 68), and this is shown in a single-sentence paragraph quite early on: 'He glowered at the Deacon now till the Deacon blinked' (p. 69). Gourlay is a man who 'would kill ye wi' a glower' (p. 58). He has a look that can clear streets: 'And then he strode – with a look on his face that made the folk fall away' (p. 104).

But however 'vicious' (p. 217) or demonic, the rage and hatred in his eyes has uncanny 'steadiness' (p. 68) and immobility – 'like a stone head at gaze in the desert' (p. 138). He may show a face that is 'frightfully distorted' (p. 126) or 'black with the passionate blood' (p. 205) of anger, but what is haunting or hypnotic about his eyes and his rage is their strange stillness. His rage is 'steady' but 'seething' (p. 53) at the same time. His eyes are 'steady' yet 'flaming' (p. 205); and as the narrator asserts, 'There is something inhuman in a rage so still' (p. 205). It involves a kind of movement without movement – like an entrancement of motion, or like the hypnotic, hallucinative effect of sound without sound ('a dumb gowl' – or bellowing – 'of rage' [p. 206] for example), or like a glower inconceivable without a blink. Young John has skived off school and is sitting in the waiting room at the railway station, reading a novel. Again reading is interrupted, this time by the combined arrival of the baker and a terrible storm: 'The fronting heavens were a black purple.... Quick lightning stabbed the world in vicious and repeated hate' (pp. 130–1). The rain comes down in 'a white rush of slanting spears'. And then 'The heavens were rent with a crash and the earth seemed on fire' (p. 131). Young Gourlay, terrified, exclaims, 'The heavens are opening and shutting like a man's eye' (p. 131). Like shutters, or like the 'rapid blinking of the eyes' (p. 126) which appears to be the counterpart to Gourlay's 'wrath' and 'storm of anger' (p. 126). And when, suddenly, in the storm that 'roared above the town' (p. 130) of Skeighan, 'a blaze of lightning flamed wide, and a fork shot down its centre', young Gourlay, with his uncanny capacity for 'automatic visualization', says: 'That ... was like a red crack in a white-hot furnace door' (p. 131).

A white door.
To be seen 'as plainly as you see this page'.

The shutter-effect: between 'reading' and 'seeing'.
Hiding from his father, John is up in the garret, in the House with Green Shutters, reading a novel. Who is narrating? Who is reading? There is a piece of paper, like a modern 'mystic writing pad' with all its iron-filings gathered inarticulately at one place. It is a 'hollow curve', like a little arch, to be 'plainly' seen, and from which one must turn away in order to read:

> ... *A piece of glossy white paper had been flung in the untidy grate, and in the hollow curve of it a thin silt of black dust had gathered – the light showed it plainly. All these things the boy marked and was subtly aware of their unpleasantness. He was forced to read to escape the sense of them. But it was words, words, words that he read; the substance mattered not at all. His head leaned heavy on his left hand and his mouth hung open, as his eye travelled dreamily along the lines. He succeeded in hypnotizing his brain at last, by the mere process of staring at the page.* (p. 82)

It is 'endless stutter' or 'silt'. How else describe the movement of the narrative of *The House with the Green Shutters*? By way of telepathy, trunk-lines, television, telephone, a shuttling or criss-crossing backwards and forwards and sideways, from past to future, from reading to seeing, and back again, without a present. It shutters. It 'snooves' (p. 85). It 'creeps' like a gastropod; it swaggers and hirples. But finally it is movement without move-ment, it is the white door again, or its threshold. John Gourlay and his son are dead. 'Fate' now has a 'demoniac power' which sweeps Mrs Gourlay on, as she reads from I Corinthians, 13: *'For we know in part, and we prophesy in part. But when that which is perfect is come, then that which is in part shall be done away'* (p. 244). Telepathy is coming: the dissolution of knowledge and prophecy. Mrs Gourlay's voice has been transformed: 'it was a voice from beyond the world'. And to finish reading is to turn to death: Mrs Gourlay's daughter 'had clung to this reading as the one thing left to her before death' (p. 244). Then it is the door and the threshold: the two women 'looked at each other, in a curious palsy of the will. The first step to the parlour door would commit them to the deed; to take it was to take the poison' (p. 244). Then '"Come!" said her mother; "Come!" and drew her by the wrist. They went into the parlour' (p. 245).

Can we take that step? Do we follow them yet? Something stuck . . .

There is the postman, a trunking 'bandy-legged little man, with a bristle of grizzled hair about his twisted mouth' (p. 245). He has a 'quick thudding step', and his desire to know the contents of the letters he delivers at the House with the Green Shutters is equated with his desire to come as close as possible to penetrating the house itself: 'In Gourlay's day he had never got by the gateway of the yard, much as he had wanted to come farther. . . . Now that Gourlay was gone, however, Postie clattered through the yard every morning, right up to the back door' (p. 245). So, today, 'The post clattered in to Mrs Gourlay's back-door' (p. 246). This is to be, it seems, the final sneck-drawing: 'He knock-ed, but there was no answer. "The sluts!" said he, with a humph of disgust; "they're still on their backs, it seems"' (p. 246). So this final messenger, beyond the call of duty, 'turned the handle,

when to his surprise the door opened, and let him enter'. An eerie
activity of reading then: 'The leaves of a Bible fluttered in the
fresh wind from the door' (p. 246). But otherwise, not a sound;
no response to his call in that 'strange stillness' (p. 247).

What happens to the mail? Or again – since in Scots the word
'post' designates the postman as well – what happens to the
post? 'He opened the door of the parlour. "*Oh, my God!*" he
screamed, leaping back, and with his bulky bag got stuck in the
kitchen door, in his desperate hurry to be gone' (p. 247).

The postie manages to get back to the 'bunch of unshaven
bodies' who have gathered by the Square. The postie is afflicted
with 'a sudden picture in his brain', a picture which the text does
not or cannot unveil, no doubt the picture from the threshold.
And the post can only stammer: 'They have – they have – they
have a' killed themselves.' Then the final paragraph, the response
of the bodies to this 'stammered' information:

> *Their loins were loosened beneath them. The scrape of their feet on
> the road, as they turned to stare, sounded monstrous in the silence.
> No man dared to speak. They gazed with blanched faces at the
> House with the Green Shutters, sitting dark there and terrible,
> beneath the radiant arch of the dawn.* (p. 247)

The white door. For if a footnote could make a sound, it would
be that 'scrape', that turning to see, towards the threshold.

But 'in the silence you don't know'. And perhaps instead, in
the face of The House with the Green Shutters, we are blank,
without even 'blanched faces' to show, unable to communicate,
even from this unspeakable distance, with any of the many 'white
faces' (for example, pp. 80, 161, 193, 194, 201) of the text. Then
the door would be a wall, just another wall, and we turn to trying
to see, trying to conceive instead, a relation between *The House
with the Green Shutters* and *Wuthering Heights* which has nothing to do with us, from which we are entirely absent. There is
one strong simile, if 'simile' were still an appropriate word for it,
which occurs at least twice in Brown's text (pp. 77, 177) and once
in Brontë's: it is to be as white as a wall. I cite only the example
from *Wuthering Heights*. It is when the door, wall, face, or
panelling of Lockwood's oak case is being opened, and Heathcliff

is looking on, as if the dead were at last awakening: '... I turned and opened the panels – I shall not soon forget the effect my action produced. Heathcliff stood near the entrance, in his shirt and trousers, with a candle dripping over his fingers, and his face as white as the wall behind him ...' (*WH*, p. 31). No longer 'the novel'. No longer any intertextuality. Rather, there would be intratextuality: a space, like an arch, without us, linking and enclosing *The House with the Green Shutters* and *Wuthering Heights*, encrypting them together, in a telepathic Siamese transference, as white as a wall.

5

On Second Sight: George Eliot

I

At last comes the revelation, seeing into the mind of the other. It is the lifting of the veil: 'The terrible moment of complete illumination had come to me, and I saw that the darkness had hidden no landscape from me, but only a blank prosaic wall....'.[1]

II

Eliot goes back. Before the beginning. But there is no 'true beginning', only 'the make-believe of a beginning': 'Was she beautiful or not beautiful? and what was the secret of form or expression which gave the dynamic quality to her glance? Was the good or the evil genius dominant in those beams?'[2] The 'beginning' of *Daniel Deronda*. And it happens, these questions 'happen', in the essentially hazardous context of chance itself: 'She who raised these questions in Daniel Deronda's mind was occupied in gambling: not in the open air under a southern sky, tossing coppers on a ruined wall, with rags about her limbs; but in one of those splendid resorts which the enlightenment of ages has prepared for the same species of pleasure at a heavy cost of gilt mouldings, dark-toned colour and chubby nudities ...' (p. 35). *Daniel Deronda* and the chances of a beginning. The 'great tradition' of the English 'novel' is thrown; with *Daniel Deronda*, writing on George Eliot seems scarcely to have begun.[3]

III

The Lifted Veil is an explicitly supernatural novella, concerned with telepathy. It is narrated by a young man called Latimer, who is one day suddenly gifted with the ability to read people's minds. One thing that makes the tone of *The Lifted Veil* undecidable is the element of satire. To those inclined to think of telepathy as an abstract metaphysical fantasy, as a possibly delicious power over others or as a merely social amusement, the text offers a corrective. The narrator describes his new, absolutely telepathic understanding of close friends and relations:

> *the rational talk, the graceful attentions, the wittily-turned phrases, and the kindly deeds, which used to make the web of their characters, were seen as if thrust asunder by a microscopic vision, that showed all the intermediate frivolities, all the suppressed egoism, all the struggling chaos of puerilities, meanness, vague capricious memories, and indolent make-shift thoughts, from which human words and deeds emerge like leaflets covering a fermenting heap. (pp. 19–20)[4]*

The only person whose mind Latimer cannot read is Bertha Grant, the woman engaged to his brother Alfred. Latimer knows that he himself will marry her instead; and soon enough there is the appropriate 'accident': Alfred is 'pitched from his horse, and killed on the spot by a concussion of the brain' (p. 41). It is a few months after their marriage, on the evening – as 'chance' would have it – of his father's death, that Latimer is first able to see behind 'the veil which had shrouded Bertha's soul' (p. 47) – and then sees, initially, the 'blank prosaic wall'. The marriage goes along miserably. Bertha has a maid called Mrs Archer. She is 'peculiarly sensitive about this woman' (p. 60), and the account of their relationship has obvious intimations of sexuality. Archer suffers a 'sudden illness' (p. 59), however, and is dying. This gives Dr Meunier, an old friend of Latimer who happens to be visiting, an opportunity 'to try the effect of transfusing blood into her arteries after the heart has ceased to beat for some minutes' (p. 60). And indeed the woman is brought back to life. The correspondence with Poe's 'M. Valdemar' is obvious.[5] Both texts sound what Roland Barthes has called 'the cry from the heart of that positivist age', namely: 'if only one could believe scientifically in immortality!'[6] Mrs Archer comes back to life with a 'gasping eager voice' to accuse Bertha of a plan to poison Latimer. After this, he and Bertha live apart. Set in a 'Devonshire nest' (p. 66), the text closes with a flash of its opening, with the lifting of the veil, with the always foreseen death of the narrator, 'when the scene of my dying struggle has opened upon me ...' (p. 67).

The Lifted Veil is 'an aberration' (*LV*, p. 69), Beryl Gray observes, and 'the critical (and editorial) tendency has been tactfully to overlook its existence' (p. 70). In fact – and in some measure Gray's edition may be itself a manifestation of this – *The Lifted Veil* has in recent years become rather a popular Eliot text among critics.[7] One general critical conception seems nevertheless to have remained valid: *The Lifted Veil* is at odds with the realism and prevailing rationalism of her *oeuvre*. It is unlike anything else George Eliot wrote. In seeking to reverse and modify this view, we will to some extent be attempting no more than Eliot wished when she proposed: 'it will be well to put the story in harness with some other productions of mine, and not send it forth in its dismal loneliness'.[8] *The Lifted Veil* is intensely, if weirdly, representative of George Eliot's work. The other texts are, in certain crucial respects, unintelligible without it.

Eliot was fascinated by the 'spiritualist' issues emerging in Britain, and abroad, in the 1850s; and, as Gray notes, she engaged enthusiastically 'with the interrelated and highly topical subjects of phrenology, mesmerism (or animal magnetism), and clairvoyance' (*LV*, p. 77). It is not that these interests are treated only in that strange novella, *The Lifted Veil*. Even as dry and dignified an authority as *OED*, for example, cites Eliot's *Silas Marner* (1861) for the use of the noun 'clairvoyant(e)' as 'One who possesses, or is alleged to possess, the faculty of clairvoyance' (sense 2): '"Did he wear ear-rings?" Mr Crackenthorp wished to know, having some acquaintance with foreign customs. "Well – stay – let me see," said Mr Snell, like a docile clairvoyante, who would really not make a mistake if she could help it.'[9] Perhaps, as Gray suggests, Eliot's interest in such 'spiritualist' questions became less practically oriented after George Henry Lewes 'entered and anchored her life' (*LV*, p. 77); but conceptually and rhetorically this interest pervades and even dominates her work. One could begin with *Silas Marner* itself, stressing its preoccupation with the force of superstition, its fantastical coincidences, its overt interest in states of trance and in 'the conditions of ghostly phenomena' (p. 105). Or one could begin with *The Mill on the*

Floss, the composition of which was interrupted so that Eliot could write *The Lifted Veil*.[10] Thus, already, the opening of the intratextual: *The Lifted Veil* in *The Mill on the Floss*, and vice versa, a self-encrypting network without true exit or entrance. Intratextuality and all the metaphors, motifs, concepts, representations of webs and weaving in Eliot ... But we will try not to get caught that way, instead seeking to move as quickly as possible towards *Daniel Deronda*.

IV

Works in silence. If this is writing, in what senses is it not silent? How can one, however madly, hear writing? What would it mean for words to touch? Could one conceive a non-humanist 'spirit' of fiction? Can a text look at you? Surely that would be pure imagination, hallucination? Beyond sense ...

V

George Eliot – or Marian Evans – speaks to us in her own voice: this could be taken as one of the norms of 'English' literary criticism. If it is something which readers have found sometimes tedious or irritating, it has also been a basis for her position as cultural spokesperson and moral legislator over the past century or so. It is no doubt too early to calculate the inevitable transmutations of that position under the effects of feminist criticism, such as Gillian Beer's fine monograph, or, on another level, of a study such as Simon Dentith's, with its lucid demonstration that Eliot is considerably less socially and politically 'egalitarian' than she might seem.[11] It would appear less difficult to predict a continuing critical adherence to the comforts and reassurances of a fundamental phonocentrism in George Eliot's texts. Whether in the descriptions of the voices of characters, or in the projected actualization of the speaking voice of the author/narrator, there is a consistent set of assumptions at work linking voice with spontaneity, self-expression and self-presence, the integrity and truth of a speaking self. Maurice Blanchot's notion of 'the narrative voice' – as a voiceless voice, disembodied, in a placeless place, beyond or outside 'ego' or 'I' – does not seem immediately pertinent to an understanding of these texts.[12] If anything, Eliot's might seem a prime example of what Blanchot distinguishes as the 'narratorial voice' – a voice of calm and reason, carrying with it an easy conviction of its self-identity.

In fact, it would be quite possible to show how narratorial perspective breaks down; the actualization of a speaking voice bursts apart. It could be done by examining a relatively small number of instances, for example in *Middlemarch*.[13] The reader of *Middlemarch* is in a double-bind, and 'George Eliot' knows all about it. On the one hand, the reader does not know what is going to happen, the text is a process of revelation. Thus 'Eliot' can address the reader: 'I am sorry to add ...' (*M*, p. 224); 'pardon these details ...' (p. 265); 'But I must first say ...' (p. 384). On the other hand, 'Eliot' uses the royal 'we', and the reader is directly amalgamated: 'Enough. We are concerned with ...' (p. 564); or, on the final page, 'we insignificant people' (p. 896). If this makes us wonder who or where we are, the question is clearly just as dizzying in relation to 'our' author or narrator. The weird, if inevitable, androgyny or mixing of genders incumbent upon a female author who speaks or writes as an explicitly masculine 'diligent narrator' (*M*, p. 375) and who likewise confers an explicitly masculine identity on 'her' reader illustrates, though perhaps in itself insuperable, only one level of the difficulty.

Another undoubtedly concerns the notion of the 'omniscient narrator'. The narrator of *Middlemarch* is everywhere and everyone, moving in and out of characters' minds with the ease and precision of a needle, reading their thoughts, summarizing, transcribing or concealing them, as 'occasion' might seem to require. Quotation marks because 'occasion' here is a thoroughly telepathic construction. Sometimes the omniscience is presented hesitantly, the element of doubt ('I think') constituting a tease, a figure of seduction. Of Dorothea and Celia, for instance, we are told: 'I think they both cried a little in a furtive manner, while Dorothea ran down-stairs to greet her uncle' (p. 309). Or of Will Ladislaw's meeting Dorothea once more: 'I think his own feelings at that moment were perfect, for we mortals have our divine moments, when love is satisfied in the completeness of the beloved object' (p. 398). Here 'we' are again, this time attributed with divinity, even though we are mere 'mortals' like the narrator or (it goes without saying) like Will and Dorothea. And in passing 'we' might wonder, given the equalization of 'mortals' here, what prevents an interpretation of this 'love' as being between the narrator and the character. What would this make 'the author'?

Romance of telepathy and non-telepathy of romance. Thus on a single page 'we' can be provided with an account of Lydgate's thoughts and another of Rosamond's: it is, from more than one point of view, part of a 'foreseen development', the opening of 'a preconceived romance'. But what doubles the stakes of this romance, and of the possible seductiveness of the fortune-telling, is the extraordinary explicitness of the narrator's knowledge: 'Poor Lydgate! or shall I say, Poor Rosamond! Each lived in a world of which the other knew nothing' (p. 195). This is knowledge as a kind of clairvoyeurism. The narrator of *Middlemarch* can even be discovered breaking an entry on the mind of the reader – at one moment in the form of a potential survey of 'my reader's imagination' (p. 375), at another in the form of a patently mad assertion: 'pardon these details for once – you would have learned to love them if you had known Caleb Garth' (p. 265). Who or what – we may reasonably ask – is this male-female-author-metafictional character-narrator phantasmagoric collage of narratorial positions? It is this monstrosity, this narrator-madness, which both supports and simultaneously silences 'George Eliot' speaking 'in her own voice'.

Simply forgotten. We have suggested an essential relation between 'telepathy' and 'the novel'; its most obvious manifestation is the omniscient narrator. No 'psychological realism' without telepathy: it is enough to send you to sleep. A double-question imposes: Why do we accept the very institution of an omniscient narrator? And what is happening – 'unconsciously' or otherwise – when we do? To accept the telepathic transfer ... A conventional answer might be that it is the 'magic' of literature, it is a matter of identification, we identify with a particular conception of the author and with particular characters, nothing could be plainer or more natural. The logic of all of this is massively facilitated by an underlying adherence to the notion of a unified self, and perhaps the most fundamental problem with any attempt to shake up the

texts (or readings) of Eliot is that they themselves seem to adhere
to such a notion so solidly.

That Eliot stresses the notion of unified self has been a key to
'her' 'success' as an author – educationally, culturally, ideological-
ly. *Middlemarch*, for example, highlights the value and importance of the idea that 'A human being in this aged nation of ours is
a very wonderful whole' (p. 444). Even if, like Lydgate, one
experiences a certain internal division, or a sense of having 'two
selves', there is always 'the wide plain where our persistent self
pauses and awaits us' (p. 182). With such a notion of self in place,
movements of projection and identification would seem to be able
to carry on without difficulty. And what makes Eliot's texts even
richer and more winning is their clear and critical awareness of
such ruses and constructions of narcissism. It is this critical
awareness that gives the reader some power of foresight, organizing responses to particular relationships. For instance, near
the start of the relationship between Dorothea and Casaubon:
'Dorothea by this time had looked deep into the ungauged res-
ervoir of Mr Casaubon's mind, seeing reflected there in vague
labyrinthine extension every quality she herself brought' (p. 46).
Or the relations between Fred Vincy and old Peter Featherstone:
'Fred fancied that he saw to the bottom of his uncle Featherstone's soul, though in reality half what he saw there was no
more than the reflex of his own inclinations' (p. 147). 'Half what
he saw there': for if Eliot's texts are polemically directed against
the naked ugliness of egotism, they are equally directed against
that of solipsism. Hence the insistent concern, announced on the
first page but running through *Middlemarch* for example, with
'the rapturous consciousness of life beyond self' (p. 25).

This will be the focus: the networks according to which, in
George Eliot's texts, one self is able to communicate with, ap-
preciate or understand another; along with the demonstration
that *Daniel Deronda* manifests a decisive shift in the conception
of the unity of the self. Everything depends on the concept of
sympathy.[14] One may have 'a small hungry shivering self', like
Mr Casaubon, but this is not much use unless it is capable of
'transformation into sympathy' (*M*, pp. 313–14). From *Middlemarch* to *Daniel Deronda*, and beyond, sympathy will occupy a
space of continuing conceptual elaboration. What happens?

VI

'To telegraph secrets' (*DD*, p. 465): without beginning, and without knowing how it might be doing so, this is one of the desires of *Daniel Deronda*. It is no longer possible to think of this text as a 'novel'. It gambles, and gambols, in another 'space' of 'literature'.[15] Works in silence. For example, Gillian Beer has noted: 'The silence in which so much of *Daniel Deronda* takes place is a terrifying seal over the crowded and various discourses of the text. Here, the process of reading is assimilated very tightly to the silent movement of thought within us'.[16] But what is silence? Nothing stable or familiar. No silence without hallucination. Eliot explores its limits. Her texts repeatedly evoke and question the perception of silence, and of something other, within or beyond it. Even in what may be her most celebrated speculation, in *Middlemarch*: 'If we had a keen vision and feeling of all ordinary human life, it would be like hearing the grass grow and the squirrel's heart beat, and we should die of that roar which lies on the other side of silence' (*M*, p. 226). In *The Lifted Veil*, this is the 'roar' of telepathy. Latimer describes the German courier 'whose stream of thought rushed upon me like a ringing in the ears not to be got rid of. . . . It was like a preternaturally heightened sense of hearing, making audible to one a roar of sound where others find perfect stillness' (*LV*, p. 26).[17]

In *Daniel Deronda* 'the other side of silence' is rendered more complex and more strange. For instance in a brief description of Hans and Mirah: 'Thus the two went side by side in a companionship that yet seemed an agitated communication, like that of two chords whose quick vibrations lie outside our hearing' (p. 798). It is impossible to judge the tone of this sentence, given our ironic awareness of fundamental differences between these two characters. For between them, as between Lydgate and Rosamond in *Middlemarch*, there seems to be not so much a 'telepathic' correspondence as merely a 'total missing of each other's mental track' (*M*, p. 632).

'Agitated communication': nothing in *Daniel Deronda* stays still. The superficial adherence to a fixed, stable concept of the self in *Middlemarch* dissolves. *Daniel Deronda* is concerned with 'the transmutation of self' (*DD*, p. 523), with awakenings of 'a new consciousness' (p. 355), with 'self' as 'many-sided' (p. 647), with 'unconsciousness' (p. 717), with such notions as that of a mind 'breaking into several, one jarring the other into impulsive action' (p. 700). 'Self' is represented in terms of multiplicity, indeterminacy, conflicting forces and agitations. What is 'agitated communication'? With the point of disintegration of the self goes the event, the present, thought: '"events come upon us like evil enchantments: and thoughts, feelings, apparitions in the darkness are events – are they not?"' (p. 693). In *Daniel Deronda*, no sense is left undisturbed, everything unsettled. Whether it is the activities of the so-called five senses or the principle of reason itself: even 'The driest argument has its hallucinations' (p. 572).

In *Middlemarch* we are told that there are certain 'states of mind' in which even 'the most incredulous person has a private leaning towards miracle' (p. 650). This is the very air of *Daniel Deronda*. It is a come-on even to the least credulous reader. It simultaneously explores and encourages precisely such 'states of mind'. It is pervaded by ghosts and 'spirits', by forecasting, foresight and 'second-sight', by strange intuitions, fantastical coincidences, instances of apparent telepathy or omniscience. There is not only the haunting and superb Gwendolen whose force of presence is such

> that if she came into the room on a rainy day when everybody else was flaccid and the use of things in general was not apparent to them, there seemed to be a sudden, sufficient reason for keeping up the forms of life; and even the waiters at hotels showed the more alacrity in doing away with crumbs and creases and dregs with struggling flies in them. (p. 71)

Gwendolen is a 'young witch' (p. 127) no doubt, and evidently with 'devil' (p. 487) or 'demon ancestry' (p. 99), perhaps including the orphan Bertha Grant. Gwendolen can look 'like one who had visited the spirit-world' (p. 832), her feelings as 'dim and alarming as a crowd of ghosts' (p. 662). 'Fantasies' move 'within her like ghosts' (p. 669). But there is also Grandcourt's first 'wife', Mrs Glasher, emphatically a 'sorceress' (p. 616) and 'Medusa-apparition' (p. 668); and there is Daniel Deronda's mother, who appears to have 'ties with some world which is independent of ours' (p. 688).

Throughout the text, there seems to be a play on such words as 'spirit', 'spirits', 'spiritual'. Their more or less relentless recurrence highlights the polysemic strangeness. Gwendolen, above all, is a young woman of 'spirit' (p. 663); 'she has a high spirit' (p. 111). She can 'carry her troubles with spirit' (p. 483), or she can be 'possessed by a spirit of general disappointment' (p. 320). She has, we are told, 'no permanent consciousness' of 'spiritual restraints', though she is liable to 'fits of spiritual dread' (p. 94). These last two references are especially thespian, since they occur at the end of the chapter in which we are presented with the theatricals at Offendene – when 'the movable panel ... flew open', terrifying Gwendolen into looking, *pace* Shakespeare's Hermione, 'like a statue into which a soul of Fear had entered' (p. 91). This is followed by the 'quick fire of undertoned question and answer' (p. 92) in which Eliot appears to satirize the putative crankiness of spiritualism:

> *'Was the door locked? It is very mysterious. It must be the spirits.'*
> *'But there is no medium present.'*
> *'How do you know that? We must conclude that there is when such things happen.'* (p. 92)

But then the word 'spirits' comes back again, scarcely perceptible. New paragraph: 'However, Gwendolen soon reappeared, showing her usual spirits, and evidently determined to ignore as far as she could the striking change she had made in the part of Hermione' (p. 92). 'Spirit', 'spirits', 'spiritual': these words float and glide. It is as if their 'ordinary sense' is visited; or as if that 'ordinary sense' is flickering, constantly subject to the instability of the light. Difficult to see. The unique, solitary encounter with – what? The 'tremor' of 'spiritual dread' could come to Gwendolen 'on suddenly feeling herself alone, when, for example, she was walking without companionship and there came some rapid change in the light' (p. 94). Elsewhere, 'spirits' are unequivocally from the 'other world', as we have seen. Thus, at the close of

Chapter 63 for example, the sensuously rhetorical question, 'What spirit was there among the boughs?' (p. 823), a question in at least one other sense relaying the 'spirit' of Wordsworth's 'Nutting'.[18]

Eliot seems to be exploring what Oppenheim has so suggestively pointed to as the contemporary synonymity of the 'spiritual' and 'psychological'.[19] Denying the networks of spiritualism, telepathy or clairvoyance, while nevertheless using them; displacing the crankiness, employing the 'same' words; letting the 'old' words acquire or accumulate a floating strangeness, producing a paleonymy of spiritualist vocabulary, generating within the surface of *Daniel Deronda* another kind of writing, signalling the agitation of other kinds of 'communication'. Disintegrating the subject. Three paragraphs after Gwendolen's reappearance 'showing her usual spirits', George Eliot starts another: 'There had really been a medium concerned in the starting open of the panel: one who had quitted the room in haste and crept to bed in much alarm of conscience. It was the small Isabel' (p. 93). There is always a medium, one or the other, one next to or on top of the other. Most of all, there is writing itself – what is described at one point as 'the medium of a little black and white' (p. 250). This puts us in touch with everything, including for example the brilliantly Mr-Snake-like Lush, who is the figure of the 'medium' in more than two senses. Thus Grandcourt wishes to communicate with his wife: 'To Grandcourt it did not even occur that he should, would, or could write to Gwendolen the information in question; and the only medium of communication he could use was Lush, who, to his mind, was as much of an implement as pen and paper' (p. 657). 'Lush' mediates between the two ostensibly non-'spiritualist' senses of 'medium', figuring (at the threshold of sense) a medium that is quite other.

The text inhabits the space of what might have seemed 'an impossible contradiction' – 'to be superstitious and rationalising at the same time' (p. 48). Denying while using and, with use, irrevocable displacement. Whether favourable or unfavourable, whether true or false, whether realized or unrealized, the text is teeming with 'fortune-telling', 'presentiments', 'speculation', 'clairvoyantes', 'phantoms of the future', 'vague foreboding', 'foreshadowing', 'divination', 'forecasting imagination' and 'fore-sight'.[20]

This is something worth looking at twice. For instance, in relation to the notion of 'second-sight', which the Scotsmen W. and R. Chambers describe as 'a gift of prophetic vision attributed to certain persons, esp. Highlanders'. 'Second-sight' would be another term subjected to a strange dissolve. At first sight it might seem worthy of straightforward denial or rejection. Thus, for example, we read the final sentence of chapter 37: 'Deronda's was not one of those quiveringly-poised natures that lend themselves to second-sight' (p. 527). With this denial, then, forget anything earlier that might have intimated that Deronda possesses special or uncanny powers? But the first sentence of the following chapter allows us a second sight: ' "Second-sight" is a flag over disputed ground' (p. 527). Eliot's text, with its paleonymic and disseminatory effects, ensures that 'second-sight' is a disputed flag, an uncanny, flickering sign. Chapter 38 goes on, with almost indecent speed, to assert that 'it is a matter of knowledge that there are persons whose yearnings, conceptions – nay, travelled conclusions – continually take the form of images which have a foreshadowing power' (p. 527). It is a matter of knowledge at least partly because we have encountered it earlier in the text: for instance, ' "Don't let Gwendolen ride after the hounds, Rex," said Anna, whose fears gifted her with second-sight' (p. 98).[21] Or – as a second example – there is Lush again, regarding Grand-court 'as something like a man who was *fey* – led on by an ominous fatality.... Having protested against the marriage [between Grandcourt and Gwendolen], Lush had a second-sight for its evil consequences' (p. 362).

The word *'fey'* is given a nice gloss by Barbara Hardy: 'Used nowadays to mean "odd" or "clairvoyant" but used by George Eliot in the earlier Scottish sense of "pursued by fate" or "doomed" ' (*DD*, pp. 892–3). But Grandcourt is 'fey' in at least both senses. More than once he seems possessed of strange, even omniscient power. Although for the most part he looks 'as neutral as an alligator' (p. 195) and speaks in a 'superficial drawl' (p. 654), he is a man with 'a ghostly army at his back' (p. 503). He can manifest 'a silence ... formidable with omniscience' (p. 674) and show a frightening 'power of suspicious divination' (p. 670). He can be 'diabolical' (p. 654). And in this way at least, he is a kind of double for the musician Klesmer – whose name itself invokes Mesmer. He is another sort of 'monster' (p. 300). As Mrs Meyrick suggests, ' "He has magic spectacles and sees everything through them, depend upon it" ' (p. 544).

VII

As for 'second-sight', that is also what the text has. It becomes a metaphor for reading. Which does not mean that we know what it is. Any more than we know what 'coincidence' means. Coincidences are the bridges in the city of fiction. Imagine a Dickens text without coincidences. But the city is strange. Like Wittgenstein's metaphor for language, it is 'an ancient city: a maze of little streets and squares'; there are 'suburbs', and we don't know if or where they finish.[22] Coincidences will happen. As George Eliot suggests, quoting Aristotle quoting Agathon: ' "It is a part of probability that many improbable things will happen" ' (*DD*, p. 567). And one might want to agree with Amy Meyrick and simply say, 'Such things are going on every day' (p. 718). But a level-headed awareness of the improbable probabilities of coincidence and a cavalier disregard for such niceties seem to be on a collision course. *Daniel Deronda* takes the notion of coincidence to a bizarre kind of limit. A question, perhaps, of reading the 'spirit' of coincidence.

There are those little coincidences, in the face of which no eyebrows need ascend. There is the way Rex and Anna Gascoigne and Gwendolen link up with the Meyricks (pp. 515, 707) – though Hans at least considers this worth three exclamation marks!!! (p. 707). There is the way in which, as Deronda tells his mother, ' "for months events have been preparing me to be glad that I am a Jew" ' (p. 698). There is the coincidence – which can in turn be linked to *The Lifted Veil* – of the synagogue at Frankfort.[23] This is when Joseph Kalonymos – with his beautiful name – sees Deronda and is led to discover his name and identity and the whereabouts of his mother. As if Kalonymos was omniscient or telepathic: 'It was as if everything had been whispered to him in the air' (p. 701). Perhaps we too are letters, opened in the post; telephone calls, tapped in advance. Or other media, other mediums, interrupted, being read or performed elsewhere, unnamable.

There is a breeze on the flag of 'second-sight'. Grandcourt and Gwendolen are yachting: 'So the days passed, taking them with light breezes beyond and about the Balearic Isles, and then to Sardinia, and then with gentle change persuading them northward again towards Corsica. But this floating, gently-wafted existence, with its apparently peaceful influences, was becoming as bad as a nightmare to Gwendolen' (p. 738). Bad as a nightmare, bad as the dream of 'some fiercely impulsive deed' she has been imagining – 'a dream that she would instantaneously wake from to find the effects real' (p. 737). This was 'the palsy of a new terror'; she has a vision of 'a white dead face from which she was for ever trying to flee and for ever held back' (p. 738). An agitated vision which brings back the 'upturned dead face' (p. 56) behind the panel at Offendene but which is also prophetic of the 'dead face' of Grandcourt, a face which 'will not be seen above the water again' (p. 753).

In the meantime, the wind increases: there is 'a squall'. Afterwards, Grandcourt comes to her and says: 'There's been the devil's own work in the night. The skipper says we shall have to stay at Genoa for a week while things are set right' (p. 739). The Grandcourts do not know this but Genoa is where Deronda has gone, to meet his mother for the 'first' time. The coincidence makes the idea of a prophetic or telepathic dream seem mere jetsam. To emphasize the point – or perhaps properly to smudge it – Eliot adds another: Gwendolen

> was waked the next morning by the casting of the anchor in the port of Genoa – waked from a strangely-mixed dream in which she felt herself escaping over the Mont Cenis, and wondering to find it warmer even in the moonlight on the snow, till suddenly she met Deronda, who told her to go back. In an hour or so from that dream she actually met Deronda. (p. 740)

Adds another what? Gets difficult to tell the difference between a dream and a coincidence. Glimpsing spanners in the works of Freud.

That Deronda should be in Genoa 'of all places' (p. 740), at the same hotel needless to say, is a coincidence which Grandcourt finds 'disgusting'. He cannot believe in 'a miraculous foreknowledge' on the part of Gwendolen – he cannot believe that she 'had posted a letter to [Deronda] from Marseilles or Barcelona, advising him to travel to Genoa in time for the chance of meeting her there'. Yet neither can Grandcourt believe that the whole thing is 'a mere accident' (p. 741). Like Freud at the end of his speculations on the 'death instincts' – or (which may come to the same thing) in his ruminations on 'telepathy' – when he says, 'I do not know how far I believe' but anyway 'the emotional factor of conviction' is not important.[24] Coincidences in *Daniel Deronda* are no longer either credible or incredible. Like Freud's texts, but arguably in a more 'conscious' fashion, *Daniel Deronda* seems rather to be concerned to explore a space of the acredible.[25]

To equate Sigmund Freud and Henleigh Mallinger Grandcourt may seem outrageous; but like Grandcourt, the Freud of *Beyond the Pleasure Principle* is 'fey', playing *'advocatus diaboli'* while apparently 'led on by an ominous fatality' or (in Freud's words) 'possessed by some "daemonic" power'.[26] The equation would also highlight a difference, namely the presence and power of 'woman'. Should they go out in the boat, for a 'pleasant sail', or not? ' "Let us go, then," said Gwendolen, impetuously. "Perhaps we shall be drowned" ' (p. 743). So they go – he to death, she (decidedly) 'to live' (p. 879). Watch the flag: 'Some suggestions were proffered concerning a possible change in the breeze ...' (p. 745). But off they go: 'This handsome, fair-skinned English couple manifesting the usual eccentricity of their nation, both of them proud, pale, and calm, without a smile on their faces, moving like creatures who were fulfilling a supernatural destiny' (p. 745).

VIII

Walking the plank ... To the acredibility of the Daniel-Mirah-Mordecai triad. What Deronda himself lacks in 'second-sight', Mordecai more than makes up for; he is without doubt the character in whom questions of prophecy, 'spirit' and telepathy can be most straightforwardly focused. But Mirah, his sister, has her share – for instance, when she walks home one day 'after singing at a charitable morning concert in a wealthy house' in Knightsbridge, and 'began to feel herself dogged by footsteps that kept an even pace with her own'. No doubt about it: 'She immediately thought of her father, and could no more look round than if she had felt herself tracked by a ghost'. Thus she goes on 'picturing what was about to happen as if she had the full certainty that the man behind her was her father' (p. 804). And she is right.[27]

Mirah and Mordecai are enmeshed with 'coincidence' and 'second-sight' from the start. There is the 'darting presentiment' (p. 230) which Daniel has when he first meets Mirah, and the way in which her arrival at the Meyricks' seems, at least to Mab Meyrick, 'preternatural' (p. 240). There is the 'coincidental' similarity between Mirah and Daniel regarding their estrangement from their mothers: 'Something in his own experience caused Mirah's search after her mother to lay hold with peculiar force on his imagination' (p. 245). There is the eventual 'coincidence' that Daniel's mother should transpire to be a singer; to have been, just like Mirah, 'brought up as a singer for the stage' (p. 729). Then there is the whole acredible thread of the search for Mirah's mother and brother – starting with Daniel's coming across the name 'Ezra Cohen' above a jewellery shop down 'a little side street out of the noise and obstructions of Holborn' (p. 432). Is this a remarkable 'coincidence' or not? 'There might be a hundred Ezra Cohens lettered above shop-windows, but Deronda had not seen them' (p. 433). Again 'coincidence' is subjected to strange displacement under the effects of simultaneous denial and affirmation, or rationality and superstition: 'Who is absolutely neutral?' (p. 432) asks Eliot. On the one hand the apparent denial: 'To find an Ezra Cohen when the name was running in your head was no more extraordinary than to find a Josiah Smith under like circumstances; and as to the coincidence about the daughter, it would probably turn out to be a difference' (p. 445). On the other hand, the bizarre 'coincidence' that – while deciding 'that all likelihood was against this man's being Mirah's brother' (p. 435) – Daniel defers his visit to the jeweller's by going into a second-hand bookshop (in the name of the search and in search of the name, the textual labyrinth of 'coincidence' finds itself lost here, in the manner of Borges) where he meets, unknowingly, a man who looks like 'a prophet' (p. 436) and turns out to be Mirah's brother. Or, again, as a kind of overpass, hidden alongside the original coincidence, there is the weird 'fact' that the name of 'Ezra Cohen' over the shop is not the 'real' name of Mirah's brother in any case; *and yet* it leads to him. ' "Mordecai is really my name – Ezra Mordecai Cohen" ' (p. 632).[28] Given this context it becomes impossible to know whether or how far to believe one's eyes, or Deronda's lack of 'second-sight', when Mordecai finally, inadvertently, reveals his sister's name: ' "Mirah?" Deronda repeated, wishing to assure himself that his ears had not been deceived by a forecasting imagination. "Did you say Mirah?" ' (p. 602)[29]

IX

Other bridges. *The Lifted Veil* is recognizably traditional in its linking telepathic experience with 'rapt passivity' rather than 'prosaic effort' (*LV*, p. 14). In a more original way, perhaps, it suggests a link, or a bridge, between telepathy and aposiopesis. What sets off Latimer's first 'vision' is an aposiopesis in his father's speech: ' " . . . Alfred will join us at Basle, and we shall all go together to Vienna, and back by Prague" . . . My father was called away before he had finished his sentence, and he left my mind resting on the word *Prague*, with a strange sense that a new and wondrous scene was breaking upon me' (p. 11). Then comes Latimer's vision, which takes place on an 'unending bridge' (p. 11). And later when he really does go to Prague, it is ultimately for this bridge, the bridge where telepathy will be 'realized': 'I felt a sudden overpowering impulse to go on at once to the bridge, and put an end to the suspense I had been wishing to protract' (p. 34). 'Rapt passivity', aposiopesis, telepathy: bridges.

Daniel Deronda first sees Mirah on the riverbank near Kew Bridge. He carries on rowing to Richmond Bridge and then comes back. Aposiopesis is now represented as pure sound, a piece of music: 'the approach of his favourite hour – with its deepening stillness, and darkening masses of tree and building between the double glow of the sky and the river – disposed him to linger as if they had been an unfinished strain of music' (p. 229). He decides to stop 'in the bend of the river just opposite Kew Gardens, where he had a great breadth of water before him reflecting the glory of the sky, while he himself was in shadow' (p. 229). And then the strange experience of sympathy which gives way:

> *for a long while he never turned his eyes from the view right in front of him. He was forgetting everything else in a half-speculative, half-involuntary identification of himself with the objects he was looking at, thinking how far it might be possible habitually to shift his centre till his own personality would be no less outside him than the landscape, – when the sense of something moving on the bank opposite him ... (p. 229)*

And then immediately his 'darting presentiment' in realizing it is the girl again: second sight.

Sympathy and second-sight, medium and spirit, agitated communication: all of these concern the figure of Mordecai. He is dying of consumption: his trust has turned into 'an agitated watch for the fulfilment that must be at hand'. He is waiting for 'the deliverer' who will rescue his 'spiritual travail from oblivion, and give it an abiding place in the best heritage of his people' (p. 531). He is thinking of 'the Being answering to his need as one distantly approaching or turning his back towards him, darkly painted against a golden sky' (p. 530). He is on a bridge, 'a favourite resort', borne up by eerie and unfinished music:

> *Leaning on the parapet of Blackfriars bridge, and gazing meditatively, the breadth and calm of the river, with its long vista half hazy, half luminous, the grand dim masses or tall forms of buildings which were the signs of world-commerce, the oncoming of boats and barges from the still distance into sound and colour, entered into his mood and blent themselves indistinguishably with his thinking, as a fine symphony to which we can hardly be said to listen makes a medium that bears up our spiritual wings. (pp. 530–1)*

This is the first sight of Mordecai on the bridge. It is not Wordsworth's 'Westminster Bridge'; but his poetry, in particular its representations of forms of sympathy, haunts *Daniel Deronda* perhaps more acutely than any other Eliot text.

The second sight of Mordecai on the bridge comes in Chapter 40, following an epigraph from Wordsworth's *Excursion*, B, IV, which describes the rising moon that

> *Burns, like an unconsuming fire of light,*
> *In the green trees; and, kindling on all sides*
> *Their leafy umbrage, turns the dusky veil*
> *Into a substance glorious as her own,*
> *Yea, with her own incorporated, by power*
> *Capacious and serene.*[30]

Needless to say that, at this moment, who should come rowing towards the bridge but Daniel Deronda, 'come from the golden background' (p. 550). And Mordecai's 'inward prophecy' is 'fulfilled': 'Obstacles, incongruities, all melted into the sense of completion with which his soul was flooded by this outward satisfaction of his longing' (p. 550). It is like an experiment, scientific, spiritualist, artistic or otherwise: 'His exultation was not widely different from that of the experimenter, bending over the first stirrings of change that correspond to what in the fervour of concentrated prevision his thought has foreshadowed' (p. 550). Mordecai tells Daniel: 'I expected you to come down the river. I have been waiting for you these five years' (p. 550). He defines the bridge: 'It is a meeting-place for the spiritual messengers' (p. 551). It is on this bridge that Mordecai, in true Wordsworthian fashion, has 'listened to the messages of earth and sky' (p. 551). Wordsworth's 'power / Capacious and serene' – an animistic or anthropomorphic form of sympathy – is translated into the 'sympathetic' and 'receptive' feelings between two individuals. Mordecai's 'exultation' and 'excited calm' (p. 551) meet with Deronda's 'sympathetic emotiveness' and 'his speculative tendency' (p. 553). This is another bridge: 'Receptiveness is a rare and massive power, like fortitude; and this state of mind now gave Deronda's face its utmost expression of calm benignant force – an expression which nourished Mordecai's confidence and made an open way before him. He began to speak' (p. 553).

Now Mordecai can seem to be a mind-reader, as in the brief exchange: ' "You are not sure of your own origin." "How do you know that?" said Daniel' (p. 558). He can announce aposiopesis and prophesy to Deronda: 'You have risen within me like a thought not fully spelled: my soul is shaken before the words are all there' (p. 559). Mordecai is not interested in being remembered as the author of the writings he leaves for Deronda to read: 'Call nothing mine that I have written' (p. 820), he says. He is not interested in leaving some monument or work of art – an 'imperfect image' of his 'thought', such as 'the ill-shapen work of the youthful carver who has seen a heavenly pattern'. His concern is, as he tells Daniel, 'that my vision and passion should enter into yours' (p. 821). And Daniel has agreed, declaring: 'I mean to work in your spirit' (p. 820). To read this 'spirit', and the acredible network of exchanges and relays in which it is inscribed, 'simply' in terms of Judaism and of the future history of the Jews would be to skip and miss the amazing originality of this text's 'spiritualism'.

In what ways can a text possess and communicate 'spirit'? When Deronda goes to Mainz, to meet Joseph Kalonymos, to collect the writings which his grandfather has left for him, the encounter is electrifying:

> *in the presence of one linked still in zealous friendship with the grandfather whose hope had yearned towards him when he was unborn, and who though dead was yet to speak with him in those written memorials which, says Milton, "contain a potency of life in them to be as active as that soul whose progeny they are," he seemed to himself to be touching the electric chain of his own ancestry.* (p. 787)

This description evokes all sorts of questions, for instance about Bloomian 'influence', genetic archivism, the 'unconscious' and 'telepathy'.[31] The description is governed by the rhetorical figure of prosopopoeia, the figure which Paul de Man has defined as 'the fiction of an apostrophe to an absent, deceased, or voiceless entity, which posits the possibility of the latter's reply and confers upon it the power of speech'. It is 'the fiction of the voice-from-beyond-the grave'.[32] De Man also draws attention to the etymology of the word 'prosopopoeia': *prosopon poiein*: to con-

fer, or make, a face or mask. Prosopopoeia allows for the transmission of thought or speech, of what Milton calls 'potency of
life' or 'soul'. It is the means by which Daniel's grandfather can
'speak'; it is also, in a larger sense, the means by which the text of
Daniel Deronda communicates.

Daniel Deronda is a physiognomy. It appears to make a face at
the same time as offering a study of the face. The text's almost
obsessive concern with faces is no doubt linked to what we might
call the prosopo-poetic drive – the desire to 'perpetuate', for
instance, the faces of Daniel and Mordecai when 'the two men,
with as intense a consciousness as if they had been two unde-
clared lovers, felt themselves alone in the small gas-lit book-shop
and turned face to face' (p. 552). The desire to 'perpetuate those
two faces' leads directly to the notion of perpetuating 'spirit' and
to the notion of the 'maternal'. The reader is asked to give to
Mordecai's 'yearning consumptive glance something of the slowly
dying mother's look when her one loved son visits her bedside,
and the flickering power of gladness leaps out as she says, "My
boy!" – for the sense of spiritual perpetuation in another resem-
bles that maternal transference of self' (p. 553).

Two observations may be noted here. First: 'spiritual perpetuation' is not (merely) masculine. If there is something 'spiritual'
transmitted – something 'telepathic' insofar as it appears to
exceed, elude or circumvent 'the recognized channels of sense'
(Myers), even including genetics, psychoanalysis or rhetoric –
it is both feminine and masculine, or neither. 'Telepathy' and
'androgyny' seem to be in touch with one another. *The Lifted
Veil* strongly implies a relationship: Latimer, the telepathic male
narrator, has 'a sort of half-womanish, half-ghostly beauty' (*LV*,
p. 20). And in Eliot's representation of Deronda, especially of his
sympathetic capacities, there is a marked emphasis on 'the mental
balance in [him]', on 'an affectionateness such as we are apt to call
feminine' (p. 367).[33] Second observation: as prosopopoeia, *Daniel
Deronda* not only 'posits the possibility' of a reply, not only
'confers . . . the power of speech', as de Man puts it, but seems to
recognize this possibility as constitutive. A text becomes a face
thanks to its reader. Eliot's concept of 'receptiveness' incorporates 'reception-theory'. For as she observes, 'often the grand
meanings of faces as well as of written words may lie chiefly in
the impressions of those who look on them' (p. 226).[34]

Faces haunt. When Deronda looks in the mirror he sees not only his own face, whatever that might mean: 'His own face in the glass had during many years been associated for him with thoughts of some one whom he must be like' (p. 226). When Gwendolen thinks of her mother she thinks of her 'dear face' (p. 277), 'the dear beautiful face with fresh lines of sadness in it' (p. 271) for example. And when Mirah begins to recount her 'life' to Mrs Meyrick, she begins: 'I remember my mother's face better than anything; yet I was not seven when I was taken away, and I am nineteen now' (p. 250). Mirah is also able to recognize a face before she sees it, as she describes being nearly kidnapped: 'I knew it – before the face was turned, as it fell into shadow, I knew who it was' (p. 261). At the end of her first meeting with him at Genoa, Daniel's mother, after 'perusing his features', says: 'But perhaps now I have satisfied my father's will, your face will come instead of his – your young, loving face' (p. 704).

Faces come. In *Daniel Deronda* faces come haunting but also haunt coming, from and before the beginning: 'Was she beautiful or not beautiful? and what was the secret of form or expression which gave the dynamic quality to her glance? Was the good or the evil genius dominant in those beams?' The face with which the text opens demands to be seen again in the light of later outlines. First, there is the fact that these questions are 'in Daniel Deronda's mind' (p. 35) – as if, despite the provocative absence of quotation marks, the questions remain absolutely silent, confined to the 'thoughts' of one character. Second, the text appears to start with the 'glance' of Gwendolen; but there is at least one eye before this, the 'evil eye' of Deronda himself: ' "Oh, you cast an evil eye on my play," said Gwendolen, with a turn of her head and a smile. "I began to lose as soon as you came to look on" ' (p. 375). Third, a correspondence is explicitly made between the face at the opening of the text and the first encounter with an original work of art: 'Some faces which are peculiar in their beauty are like original works of art: for the first time they are almost always met with question' (p. 459).

This is part of the originality of *Daniel Deronda*. With what kind of face does it come or haunt? If it is a physiognomy, it is undecidably 'good' or 'evil', and is unstable, unrecognizable. Perhaps its unveiling is still to come; or else has just begun: a sketching or tracing of the face which would be a kind of visual aposiopesis. One might risk an 'analogy' with what was known in Eliot's time as 'spirit photography': visual invocations of the faces of the dead, to be made out, or not, from the shadows and the blurs, the play of lights and multiple exposures.[35] *Daniel Deronda* seems to touch, and thereby change, the frame within which 'prosopopoeia' is traditionally conceived. Insofar as this rhetorical figure supposes the giving or the making of a face, it presupposes that this face is alive. It should be capable of speech. At least one face hidden in *Daniel Deronda*, however, is a dead face. A face, a picture or a work of art can foreshadow or determine the future. 'The picture of the dead face and the fleeing figure, brought out in pale definiteness by the position of the wax-lights' (p. 91), when 'the movable panel' flies open, is a face which haunts; and it clearly foreshadows, with its own 'pale definiteness', the nameless 'white dead face' (p. 738) and the 'dead face' of Grandcourt which Gwendolen will 'never get away from' (p. 753).[36]

Is a face – seen or imagined, in a pictorial or mental representation – living or dead? And is it human? More than once the text encourages the idea of seeking out 'what one may call the elementary expressions of the face' (p. 438). Another exposure. For if *Daniel Deronda* is a physiognomy, if it is attempting a kind of verbal translation of 'spirit photography', the face revealed may not only transpire to be dead: it may not appear human at all. It may be, for instance, the face of an insect. Such a face is apparently in Gwendolen's mind, if only as a negative, when she stops gambling:

> *And in five seconds Gwendolen turned from the table, but turned resolutely with her face towards Deronda and looked at him. There was a smile of irony in his eyes as their glances met; but it was at least better that he should have kept his attention fixed on her than that he should have disregarded her as one of an insect swarm who had no individual physiognomy. (pp. 39–40)*

And when Mrs Davilow, overwhelmed by a sense of Gwendolen's powers of 'divination', asks her how she imagines Mr Grandcourt, whom neither of them has yet met, the 'young witch' foresees that after their first encounter: 'I shall dream that night that I am looking at the extraordinary face of a magnified insect – and the next morning he will make me an offer of his hand' (p. 128).

Dream or hallucination? Past or future? Let us suggest in passing the need for an entomology of literature. The texts of George Eliot would furnish excellent breeding-grounds. When George Eliot refers to insects it is invariably in what we could call a telepathic atmosphere. This is true even if the purpose of entomological allusions seems to be a denial of 'telepathy'. Thus, for example, in *Daniel Deronda*, the reference to adults, such as Mr Gascoigne, 'who were running their eyes over the Guardian or the Clerical Gazette, and regarded the trivialities of the young ones with scarcely more interpretation than they gave to the actions of lively ants' (p. 97). Or, towards the end, the reference to the idea that, without 'creators and feeders' like Mordecai, life 'would dwindle and shrivel into the narrow tenacity of insects, unshaken by thoughts beyond the reaches of their antennae' (p. 749). However strong the denials may seem, there is an evident interest throughout Eliot's work in what is described in *Middlemarch* as 'the possible histories of creatures that converse compendiously with their antennae, and for aught we know may hold reformed parliaments' (*M*, p. 843). On this topic, in fact, Eliot would seem more satirically descriptive, more playfully lucid, than Freud. Freud observes: 'It is a familiar fact that we do not know how the common purpose comes about in the great insect communities: possibly it is done by means of a direct psychical transference'.[37] 'Common purpose', 'communities', 'direct psychical transference': anthropomorphism is telepathy, it is the trope of the telepathic. But there is no proper of 'telepathy': insofar as it might be thought in relation to the proper, 'telepathy' would be without *telos*. Or, simultaneously, a *tele* must henceforth prefix every field and designation of communication, media, psychology.

Daniel Deronda has a strange kind of enthusiasm or excitement, a sense of 'agitated communication' most obviously embodied in the figure of Mordecai and in his relationship with Deronda. The text foresees – not merely itself. It foresees its first reading, if one can say such a thing, but calls also for a reading at 'second sight'. It is a text fascinated by the notion that 'superstitions carry consequences which often verify their hope or their foreboding' (p. 375) – by the shared imagining of 'when an event, not disagreeable, seems to be confirming and carrying out our private constructions' (p. 794). In an uncanny way, this seems to adumbrate an account of Freud's instituting the 'science' of psychoanalysis. Part of the importance of Mordecai is clearly as a character in whom 'a wise estimate of consequences is fused in the fires of that passionate belief which determines the consequences it believes in'. Eliot – transcribing the thoughts of Daniel Deronda – continues:

> *The inspirations of the world have come in that way too: even strictly-measuring science could hardly have got on without that forecasting ardour which feels the agitations of discovery beforehand, and has a faith in its preconception that surmounts many failures of experiment. And in relation to human motives and actions, passionate belief has a fuller efficacy. Here enthusiasm may have the validity of proof, and, happening in one soul, give the type of what will one day be general. (p. 572)*

While this description can resonate, as if prochronically, with the notion of the Freudian 'science', the way it carries on is still stranger:

> *Men may dream in demonstrations, and cut out an illusory world in the shape of axioms, definitions, and propositions, with a final exclusion of fact signed Q.E.D. No formulas for thinking will save us mortals from mistake in our imperfect apprehension of the matter to be thought about. And since the unemotional intellect may carry us into a mathematical dreamland where nothing is but what is not, perhaps an emotional intellect may have absorbed into its passionate vision of possibilities some truth of what will be – the more comprehensive massive life feeding theory with new material, as the sensibility of the artist seizes combinations which science explains and justifies. (p. 572)*

Paradox: the last part of the final sentence might have been written by Freud. Psychoanalysis – old style – is the 'science' which supposedly 'explains and justifies' the otherwise strange creations of 'the artist'. Yet the strangeness of *Daniel Deronda* seems still to include the enigma of some half-sunk visage.

X

Daniel Deronda would become, then, a kind of unsynthesizable alternative to a Freud text. At the time of publication, in 1876, the word 'telepathy' did not exist: 'sympathetic clairvoyance' was perhaps the most obvious contemporary equivalent.[38] *Daniel Deronda* takes the notions of 'sympathy' and 'clairvoyance' to a limit which is exemplary – a limit for which there are no comparisons, and which has the structure of a multiple aposiopesis: musical, architectural, rhetorical, the necessarily unfinished sketch of an uncanny physiognomy, of a fateful gambol and gambling. In some ways it scarcely understands what it is doing, and urges a corresponding daredevilry in its readers.[39] So *Daniel Deronda*, like a Freud text, would be not so much a 'novel' as a hypnopoetics, a foresight-sympathy-saga-machine of a passionate vision of possibilities.[40] However, there seem to be at least two crucial distinctions between *Daniel Deronda* and the work of Freud – distinctions which may be said still to haunt contemporary psychoanalysis and psychology.

First: Freud's work, and consequently the fundamental burden of post-Freudian psychoanalysis and psychology, derives from the coherence of an epistemology of solipsism. *Ego: ergo sum.* *Daniel Deronda*, while elaborating the beginnings of what can readily be described as a decentred self, maintains a decisive stress on notions of 'sympathy'. This maintenance leads to a kind of paleonymic threshold – after *Daniel Deronda*, what is 'sympathy'? The question of 'solipsism' is, however imperceptibly, fundamentally displaced.

Second: in Freud's work, for instance in Chapter XII of *The Psychopathology of Everyday Life*, 'telepathy' and 'spiritualism', 'determinism', 'belief in chance' and 'superstition' are effectively foreign bodies.[41] In the amazing final work of George Eliot they are allowed in. With what effect?

There are forms of sense, agitation, communication, reception, sympathy – at least some of which continue to elude 'explanation and justification'. *Daniel Deronda* would not claim to know either, but there is the striking concern with the possibilities of 'a tacit language' (p. 687), of the 'acute point' at which 'emotion ... is not distinguishable from sensation' (p. 650), of 'invisible fibres'

(p. 633) with which two individuals can touch each other, of changes in mood 'as dim as the sense of approaching weather-change' (p. 715), of 'words' which can act 'like the touch of a miraculous hand' (p. 840), of the 'strange spiritual chemistry going on within us' (p. 364), of the still-remaining 'great deal of unmapped country within us' (p. 321), or of 'faces' which seem 'full of speech, as if their minds had been shelled, after the manner of horse-chestnuts, and become brightly visible' (pp. 238–9).

Psychoanalysis should not be viewed as coming, after the event, to explain phrases such as 'strange spiritual chemistry' or the 'unmapped country within us'. Eliot's text should be seen as following a quite different track. With its highly non-Freudian insistence on the 'impossible contradiction' of being 'superstitious and rationalising at the same time' (p. 48), with its apparent affirmation that even 'The driest argument has its hallucinations' (p. 572), with its liminal explorations of 'sympathy', 'coincidence' and 'second-sight', and with its restless fascination with forms of unconsciousness, semi- or quasi-consciousness, fantasy and dream, *Daniel Deronda* seems to open up the possibility of something else altogether: *telepsychology*, or a radically literary, non-subject-centred telepathology of everyday life.

6

A Walk in 'Kew Gardens'

Are ye the representatives
Of other peoples' distant lives?

(Thomas Traherne, 'Shadows in the Water')

There is nothing one can fish up in a spoon; nothing one can
call an event.

(Virginia Woolf, *The Waves*)

Virginia Woolf's 'Kew Gardens' (1919) seems to satirize telepathy
and spiritualism.[1] A married couple, Simon and Eleanor, come
by with their children; then come two men, the younger called
William, the elder an unnamed summoner of spirits. They are
succeeded by two elderly women, and finally by a young man
and a young woman called Trissie. We learn that while the old
spiritualist gentleman was speaking, William 'wore an expression
of perhaps unnatural calm' (p. 122). The old man seems at once
an object of sympathy and a spectacle of futility:

> *The elder man had a curiously uneven and shaky method of
> walking, jerking his hand forward and throwing up his head
> abruptly, rather in the manner of an impatient carriage horse tired
> of waiting outside a house; but in the man these gestures were
> irresolute and pointless. (p. 122)*

All this time he is 'talking about spirits – the spirits of the dead,
who, according to him, were even now telling him all sorts of odd
things about their experiences in Heaven' (p. 122). The word
'odd' here functions as satirical marker.

The old man's account of the practical business of communicating with the dead is frankly comical:

You have a small electric battery and a piece of rubber to insulate
the wire – isolate? – insulate? – well, we'll skip the details, no good
going into details that wouldn't be understood – and in short the
little machine stands in any convenient position by the head of the
bed, we will say, on a neat mahogany stand. All arrangements
being properly fixed by workmen under my direction, the widow
applies her ear and summons the spirit by sign as agreed. (p. 122)

That the old man may have some other, arguably ulterior motive
regarding such widows is hinted by the distraction of his attention:

'Women! Widows! Women in black –' Here he seemed to have
caught sight of a woman's dress in the distance, which in the shade
looked a purple black. He took off his hat, placed his hand upon his
heart, and hurried towards her muttering and gesticulating fever-
ishly. But William caught him by the sleeve ... (pp. 122–3)

The text is apparently ridiculing notions of spiritualism and telepathy, talking to the dead, picking up messages from them. The
old man is either 'merely eccentric or genuinely mad' (p. 123).
In any case, it seems, he can be treated as lightly as the man
who instituted the use of the words 'telepathy' and 'telesthesia',
F. W. H. Myers, to whom Woolf fleetingly refers in one of her
letters as 'the man who saw ghosts'.[2]
    But this would be falling back into a repressive and superficial
delimitation of such notions. The paleonymy and dissemination
of George Eliot's 'spiritualism' continues. 'Telesthesia' is on the
move, working all over these textual gardens. We might try to
track it through the rhetorical figure of anthropomorphism. Aesthetics at a distance, and the distances of the aesthetic. We might
try to assess these distances by focusing on the dubiously named
'stream of consciousness' technique or 'omniscient narrator' of
the text. Life during wartime: 'Kew Gardens' might also lead to
some reflections on telepathy and war.
    Trying to get in touch with Robbe-Grillet. Only in the last
words of the long first paragraph of 'Kew Gardens' is there
explicit reference to the presence of human beings: 'Then the

breeze stirred rather more briskly overhead and the colour was flashed into the air above, into the eyes of the men and women who walk in Kew Gardens in July' (p. 119). But up until then it seems to be all a matter of shapes and colours, light, textures, starting:

> From the oval-shaped flower-bed there rose perhaps a hundred stalks spreading into heart-shaped or tongue-shaped leaves half way up and unfurling at the tip red or blue or yellow petals marked with spots of colour raised upon the surface; and from the red, blue or yellow gloom of the throat emerged a straight bar, rough with gold dust and slightly clubbed at the end. (p. 119)

The uneasily distancing anonymity of this presentation is modified by the text's first examples of animism or anthropomorphism – 'heart-shaped', 'tongue-shaped', 'throat' – linking feeling and articulation, body and expression, in a kind of homonymic anthology of flower-sense. Animal, human and plant life is already cross-fertilizing.

Most of all – and Daniel Deronda, rowing down the river 'just opposite Kew Gardens', even in another time, another text, might never have spotted this – there is the gastropod: 'The light fell either upon the smooth grey back of a pebble, or the shell of a snail with its brown circular veins, or, falling into a raindrop, it expanded with such intensity of red, blue and yellow the thin walls of water that one expected them to burst and disappear' (p. 119). The syntax enclosing the transitive use of the verb 'to expand' mimes the near-bursting of the walls, and introduces the question of another wall. Not necessarily the question of Woolf 'herself' (she who nevertheless occasionally referred to herself as 'Wall'), but rather of the partition – in the sentence cited – between a snail and a human observer or narrator.[3] 'One expected them to burst and disappear': this 'one', observing or narrating, writing or reading, is ineluctably *at the level of* the gastropod. The entire text is oriented, given its perspective, from the position of a snail; the movements of this snail anchor the narrative.[4]

After Simon and Eleanor have gone by with their children, the description returns to the snail in the oval flower-bed. A paragraph is devoted to its, by comparison, miniature manoeuvres:

It appeared to have a definite goal in front of it, differing in this respect from the singular high stepping angular green insect who attempted to cross in front of it, and waited for a second with its antennae trembling as if in deliberation, and then stepped off as rapidly and strangely in the opposite direction. . . . Before he [i.e., the snail] had decided whether to circumvent the arched tent of a dead leaf or to breast it there came past the bed the feet of other human beings. (p. 121)

After William and the spiritualist, and the two elderly women have gone by, the account again reverts. This time the anthropomorphism is even more intense: 'The snail had now considered every possible method of reaching his goal without going round the dead leaf or climbing over it' (p. 124). The frailty of the leaf

determined him finally to creep beneath it, for there was a point where the leaf curved high enough from the ground to admit him. He had just inserted his head in the opening and was taking stock of the high brown roof and was getting used to the cool brown light when two other people came past outside on the turf. (p. 124)

The snail leaves its trail on any attempt to distinguish between a 'human' and 'non-human' psychology, or between 'spiritualist' and 'non-spiritualist' aspects of the text. A zoom lens, at least, remains necessarily focused on the relationship between anthropomorphism and telepathy. As I suggested in the previous essay, anthropomorphism seems to be constituted by telepathic invitation. Even to refer to the legs of a table, or the face of a clock, and thereby to confer anthropomorphic (or animistic) qualities on these non-'human' non-'living' objects, appears to involve not merely the one-way projection of 'human' characteristics, but the necessary possibility of their own active communication or *response* (linguistic or not). A conception of the telepathic structure of anthropomorphism poses a number of disturbances. Remaining for the moment within the context of the visual and aesthetic contemplation of objects, it no doubt poses a disturbance of all principles of objectivity, distance and detachment. The force and singularity of Woolf's work lies here – in its registering of this disturbance; in its undecidable scrambling, spinning and overturning of the animate and inanimate, the human and non-human; in its ghostly apprehensions of a new aesthetics of 'atmosphere'; in its kind of mad confusions and dissolutions of the experience of distance as such.[5] I venture to use the term 'telesthesia', in paleonymic fashion, to refer to these inextricably related dimensions of Woolf's text. The telesthetic density of 'Kew Gardens' derives also from an exploration of the apparent inverse of anthropomorphism, that is to say a questioning and displacement of notions of the categorically 'human' by reference to the non-human. As a perhaps trivial example, it is what Woolf does in a contemporary letter when she describes seeing Walter Lamb during a walk in Kew Gardens and comments, 'He knows he's but a slug.'[6]

In the final sentences of her essay 'The Supernatural in Fiction' (1918), Woolf writes of 'the sense of the unseen' and of the importance of having 'a quickened perception of the relations existing between men and plants, or houses and their inhabitants, or any one of those innumerable alliances which somehow or other we spin between ourselves and other objects in our passage'.[7] The description is in some respects essentially commonsensical: these curious 'alliances' involve a clear pre-existing distinction *between* 'men' and 'plants' or 'ourselves' and 'other objects'. 'Kew Gardens', however, radically undermines such assumptions. Its telesthetic force casts certain questions in a sort of delirious or lunatic light: What are 'people'? Is it really conceivable to be 'with other people, like other people' (p. 125)? What is it to 'walk' in Kew Gardens?

Perhaps, *pace* Lacan, we are butterflies for nobody, a dream or no.[8] 'Kew Gardens' drifts at various speeds, in different rhythms, describing the 'irregular and aimless movement' (p. 126) of people – whatever they might be – walking. But what is 'walking', given the text's eerie concourse of the human with the non-human? And what of the 'movements' of the text itself? There is the 'high stepping angular green insect'; there is the old man with his 'curiously uneven and shaky method of walking'; there is the thrush which hops 'like a mechanical bird' (p. 126). Above all, however, there is the second paragraph which starts: 'The figures of men and women straggled past the flower-bed with a curiously irregular movement not unlike that of the white and blue butterflies who crossed the turf in zig-zag flights from bed to bed' (pp. 119–20). The last butterflies to be described are scarcely old enough to fly: 'They were both in the prime of youth, or even in that season which precedes the prime of youth, the season before the smooth pink folds of the flower have burst their gummy case, when the wings of the butterfly, though fully grown, are motionless in the sun' (p. 124). And the final paragraph of the text evokes the momentary ruins of a monument, built by butterflies, by butterflies building: 'instead of rambling vaguely the white butterflies danced one above another, making with their white shifting flakes the outline of a shattered marble column above the tallest flowers . . .' (p. 126). Would monumentalization be possible without such butterfly-effects?

Superstition, the omnipotence of thoughts, telepathy zig-zag around 'Kew Gardens'. As if with the antennae of a singular butterfly or gastropod, the putative 'omniscient narrator' makes this possible. But the term 'omniscient narrator' is no longer tenable here: paradoxically perhaps, it is revealed as too simply anthropomorphic. (And telepathy, we might note in passing, will be among other things a name for the radical interruption and unsettling of any notion of 'stream of consciousness'.) The zig-zagging as if for nobody, then, consists not only in the old man who bends his ear to a flower 'and seemed to answer a voice speaking from it' (p. 123). It is also, for instance, the tentativeness of the young motionless butterflies: ' "Lucky it isn't Friday," he observed. "Why? [she replied] D'you believe in luck?" ' (p. 124) And it is the prophetic dragonfly which can answer Simon's marriage proposal to Lily: ' "And my love, my desire, were in the dragonfly; for some reason I thought that if it settled there, on that leaf, the broad one with the red flower in the middle of it . . . she would say 'Yes' at once" ' (p. 120).

Just as anthropomorphism cannot be conceived without a theory of telepathy, so the 'human' cannot be conceived. Woolf's classifications of the 'human' as 'non-human' – as butterflies or flowers, for example – cannot be assimilated to traditional notions of organic metaphor. While 'Kew Gardens' contains everyday instances of such organicism – describing a woman as 'rosy-cheeked' (p. 123) and so on – it compounds all the difficulties through its representations of words themselves. It draws attention to such difficulties in what is at once the most mundane and most singular example: the proper name. Simon, going on alone with his thoughts, thinks of Lily, the woman he might have married, fifteen years ago. Eleanor, his wife, is thinking of lilies – '"down by the side of a lake, painting the water-lilies, the first red water-lilies I'd ever seen"' (p. 121), twenty years ago. 'Telepa-lily': what are words?

The two elderly women talk as they walk, and the flowers, 'through the pattern of falling words' (p. 123), become hypnotic. This 'heavy woman' is like 'a sleeper waking from a heavy sleep [who] sees a brass candlestick reflecting the light in an unfamiliar way ...' (pp. 123–4). Enough to make you start to fall asleep on your feet: 'So the heavy woman came to a standstill opposite the oval-shaped flower-bed, and ceased even to pretend to listen to what the other woman was saying. She stood there letting the words fall over her, swaying the top part of her body slowly backwards and forwards, looking at the flowers' (p. 124). Then a little later there is the most 'classically' telepathic moment in the text, or on its edge, on another threshold, between the young man and woman, when their 'short insignificant words' ('"D'you believe in luck?"', '"Isn't it worth sixpence?"', '"What's 'it' ... ?"', '"you know what I mean"') are described as 'words with short wings for their heavy body of meaning, inadequate to carry them far and thus alighting awkwardly upon the very common objects that surrounded them' (p. 125). Hypnopoetic mixing of senses, words and things, word-things of flowers, falling light, colour, imperceptible textures, insects or birds, the unseen in the distance, a tele-anthology at the abyss. Of words, but perhaps without them, outside them, the text continues: 'who knows (so *they thought* [my emphasis] as they pressed the parasol into the earth) what precipices aren't concealed in them, or what slopes of ice don't shine in the sun on the other side? Who knows? Who has ever seen this before?' (p. 125) Words or feelings in the distance, or rather in the hallucinations of distance. 'Kew Gardens' propagates the uncanny materiality of words, intimating the madness of a non-animistic, non-anthropomorphic conception of them at the same time as insisting, as if in the furrow of a delirium: 'Who knows? Who has ever seen this before?'

It is gone now. It was never here. There is no present, no past. Just ghosts. As Eleanor says to her husband: '"Doesn't one always think of the past, in a garden with men and women lying under the trees? Aren't they one's past, all that remains of it, those men and women, those ghosts lying under the trees, ... one's happiness, one's reality?"' (p. 120) Ghosts of the present, present ghosts, present arms. Even the 'moments' of Walter Pater's 'Conclusion' to *The Renaissance* will have turned into ghosts. What are 'ghosts' here? In her review of Dorothy Scarborough's *The Supernatural in Modern English Fiction* in 1918, Woolf concurs that, in recent times, 'our sense of our own ghostliness has much quickened'. Woolf's concern is not with 'the ghosts of the dead' but with what she calls 'those ghosts which are living within ourselves'.[9] And in a similar way, in her essay on Henry James's ghost stories (1921), she notes:

> *Henry James's ghosts have nothing in common with the violent old ghosts – the blood-stained sea captains, the white horses, the headless ladies of dark lanes and windy commons. They have their origin within us. They are present whenever the significant overflows our powers of expressing it; whenever the ordinary appears ringed by the strange.*[10]

The early paragraphs of 'Kew Gardens' are peculiar enough, but the final paragraph seems to overflow, as if driven mad by further ringings. As 'one couple after another' pass the flowerbed and are 'enveloped in layer after layer of a green-blue vapour', finally being 'dissolved' in an hallucinatory 'green-blue' or 'yellow and green' or faintly 'red and blue' (p. 126) atmosphere, 'Kew Gardens' moves to another footing, shifting to a different limit of what is speakable.

Apophrades: this term refers to the return of the dead, the time when the dead come back to claim their homes or whatever else may be theirs. Harold Bloom regards it as a recurrent feature of 'strong' poetry, especially as a figure or trope manifested near the close of a text.[11] Woolf's 'Kew Gardens' may transpire to be, among other things, a powerful piece of war literature, or perhaps war poetry. In its own singularly ghostly fashion, the final paragraph seems to be attempting the impossibility of catching something like the strange oxymoron of 'spirit matter' to which the old man refers: '"Heaven was known to the ancients as Thessaly,

William, and now, with this war, the spirit matter is rolling between the hills like thunder"' (p. 122). War is rolling, it is all around: overhead, for example, 'in the drone of the aeroplane the voice of the summer sky murmured its fierce soul' (p. 126). Such a non-human 'voice' might be read as a peculiar embodiment of the relations between the First World War and spiritualism, between war and telepathy.[12]

Indeterminably haunted by the rhythms and sounds of Pater's 'Conclusion' – for example, its description of the passing of life ('Some spend this interval in listlessness, some in high passions, the wisest, at least among "the children of this world", in art and song') – 'Kew Gardens' closes with a weird synaesthesia of voices and light.[13] It attempts sound within silence, a non-'human' voice, voices without words, silence without silence. It affirms. The 'hard gemlike flame' of Pater's text has gone ecstatically soft.[14] The hypnotic impression of the brass candlestick multiplies. The text ends with voices

> *wavering . . . as if they were flames lolling from the thick waxen bodies of candles. Voices, yes, voices, wordless voices, breaking the silence suddenly with such depth of contentment, such passion of desire, or, in the voices of children, such freshness of surprise; breaking the silence? But there was no silence . . . voices cried aloud and the petals of myriads of flowers flashed their colours into the air. (pp. 126–7)*

Virginia Woolf referred to 'Kew Gardens' as a 'short story'.[15] If so, it is certainly a ghost story. But such generic descriptions seem misleading. As the narrator in Maurice Blanchot's 'The Madness of the Day' would say: 'A story? No. No stories, never again'.[16] Suspended, like so many of Woolf's texts, in its own kind of madness of the day, 'Kew Gardens' strikes into more demonic hallucinations of distance, generating an aerial perspective in the wild and ghostly light of which 'all these colours, men, women and children, were spotted for a second upon the horizon' before 'dissolving like drops of water in the yellow and green atmosphere, staining it faintly with red and blue' (p. 126). All of them have already gone to seek 'shade beneath the trees' (p. 126): just ghosts. And in the undecidable anthropomorphism of another last ghostly 'murmur', in a final vertiginous turn, in an amassing of revolutions which may remind us of the etymology which links the verb 'to walk' with the Old English *wealcan*, 'to roll, revolve', comes the break of another silence:

> *breaking the silence? But there was no silence; all the time the motor omnibuses were turning their wheels and changing their gear; like a vast nest of Chinese boxes all of wrought steel turning ceaselessly one within another the city murmured; on the top of which the voices cried aloud and the petals of myriads of flowers flashed their colours into the air. (p. 127)*

Without destination, 'Kew Gardens' seems to gather the ghosts of ancestral voices, including the voices of children, bringing war into the phantom nosegay of a moment's rhetoric.[17] It joins the waves, among others, the silent and invisible choir of *Daniel Deronda* – releasing like a cloud, a discursive formation, tele-psychology and telesthesia.

7

A Letter on Poetry

20–1–1989

My love,
     is it you? is it? You said it: hilarity. Was it for this? And why
are you always flying away from me? It's enough almost to make
me weep, yes now the tears have begun to roll; they are walking
down my cheeks. But then the thought of you, your thought, like
a cobweb, brushes them away. You will come back won't you?
Even now, I can feel it, you will come to me, you are coming.
     But is it hilarity or terror? I'm becoming hysterical. Is it joy or
horror? I am hysterical now, I've picked up the thought of
so-and-so's 'sweet birthplace' and I don't know what to do; can't
you see I'm dreaming? At least two things at once. First, let me
tell you, Wordsworth's dream. But then, even before that, Coleridge and his so-called Conversation Poem, 'Frost at Midnight'
(1798), the one that no one can hear, the one that comes while
'The Frost performs its secret ministry' (1), in that calm which
'disturbs/And vexes meditation with its strange/And extreme
silentness' (8–10).[1] Everything and everywhere is as 'inaudible as
dreams' (13), apart from the 'stranger' – that 'thin blue film' (13)
which 'flutters' (16) on the grate.[2] Staring at it is hypnotic. It
mixes sleep and wakefulness, thinking and dreaming, perception
and prophecy, present and future:

> But O! how oft,
> How oft, at school, with most believing mind,
> Presageful, have I gazed upon the bars,
> To watch that fluttering stranger! and as oft
> With unclosed lids, already had I dreamt
> Of my sweet birth-place, and the old church-tower,
> Whose bells, the poor man's only music, rang

From morn to evening, all the hot Fair-day,
So sweetly, that they stirred and haunted me
With a wild pleasure, falling on mine ear
Most like articulate sounds of things to come! (23–33)

Then it is the following day, still in a state of seeming trance, a dream of reading, glancing towards the door, and the eerie entrance of another 'stranger':

So gazed I, till the soothing things, I dreamt,
Lulled me to sleep, and sleep prolonged my dreams!
And so I brooded all the following morn,
Awed by the stern preceptor's face, mine eye
Fixed with mock study on my swimming book:
Save if the door half opened, and I snatched
A hasty glance, and still my heart leaped up,
For still I hoped to see the stranger's *face,*
Townsman, or aunt, or sister more beloved,
My play-mate when we both were clothed alike! (34–43)

Coleridge addresses his 'Dear Babe, that sleepest cradled by [his] side' (44), imagining 'The lovely shapes and sounds' (59) the baby may experience in the future, and he concludes with a benediction – 'Therefore all seasons shall be sweet to thee' (65) – whether it is summer or winter. The poem is doubly futuristic, for the putative addressee, the 'babe so beautiful' (48), could only become its reader in the future, after ceasing to exist, ceasing to be a 'babe'. 'Frost at Midnight' is a love letter, which ends by returning to its beginning. Like 'Kubla Khan' it seems to come full circle, adding a telepathic and prophetic dimension to the 'new' 'time' of its opening:

> *whether the eave-drops fall*
> *Heard only in the trances of the blast,*
> *Or if the secret ministry of frost*
> *Shall hang them up in silent icicles,*
> *Quietly shining to the quiet moon. (70–4)*[3]

But it's not going to last. Lemman, my love, you see it? Or do you hear? Tell me quickly, read our futures together, quickly, tell me, tell me, faster than any 'return of post'.

Only fragment. Forster will have been wrong (again).[4] And yet even a fragment, a ruin, a person in ruins, or a non-person, can transfer, may be able to produce transferences, but then perhaps 'transference' is no longer the word. What 'sort of thing' am I talking about? It shouldn't be necessary to tell you, writing to you now it is as though my pen had lips and you could read them. What is a poem? It is a making, it is a love letter. For writing a love letter, as Lacan affirms, is 'the only thing one can do with a measure of seriousness'.[5] No need to remind you, is there, of how much he emphasizes as well 'that speaking of love is in itself a *jouissance*'. He even suggests that it might be for this reason that psychoanalysis, psychoanalytic discourse, 'emerged at a certain point of scientific discourse'.[6]

That's it. I'm hysterical, you make me hysterical, poetry. Ecstasy, ec-stasis. Hysteria without determinable subjects. In the 'Adagia', in *Opus Posthumous*, Wallace Stevens offers a little impressionism, a sketch which touches on synaesthesia:

> *The poet seems to confer his identity on the reader. It is easiest to recognize this when listening to music – I mean this sort of thing: the transference.*[7]

'Sort of thing': analogy with a purely auditory form, 'music', but not (only) music; 'transference', but only 'sort of', not quite or not only; 'identity', but nothing personal, as Stevens indicates in another note, elsewhere: 'The poet confers his identity on the reader. But he cannot do this if he intrudes personally.'[8] And it might seem, fastening on an apparently sexist pronoun, that the poet is by definition masculine, but she's not, he's not, it's not, we'll come to it, if there is time, I promise, my love, I promise.

'One text reads another,' says Derrida: 'Each "text" is a machine with multiple reading heads for other texts.'[9] Medusacology. I am addressing you now, are you unable to listen? Then you are listening. A poem is a letter: it is the most powerful weapon on earth, still and always, to be invented. And to think, my darling, that you are the machine, now, to whom it is addressed. No, as Derrida notes in 'Telepathy', the addressee, he or she, does not exist before the letter. I'm feeling calmer now, calmer all the time, but then

I think of hysteria, I look at Freud and Breuer's *Studies on Hysteria* and scarcely need glance at the list of possible hysterical symptoms: amnesia (is that what I was reading?); anaesthesia; anxiety; auditory (do you hear this?) disturbances; feeling of cold; convulsions; deafness (I'm sorry); deliria; depression; diplopia, I repeat, diplopia; dizziness; dumbness; euphoria; fainting fits; fatigue; gastric pain; hallucination; headache; *idées fixes*; insomnia; migraine; disturbances of smell; disturbances of speech; stammer; stupor; tears; throat constriction (that's enough, I hear you say); tremor; twitching; disturbances of vision; disturbances of walking ... I select only a few,[10] I'm getting lost, I'm lost already

Euphoria, hallucination, tears ... It must be so-and-so's 'sweet birthplace', here, can't you hear I'm dreaming? 'Already had I dreamt ...' Hallucination ... It is the wild pleasure and frightening beauty of this poem for nobody, where (along the Kantian–Foucauldian lines suggested by David Carroll) the beauty of the text 'lies in the fact that it cannot be judged according to any existing rules, that no concept is adequate to it, no form of knowledge able to measure up to it'.[11] Tears ... I was hardly attending: anaesthesia, what is that? Breuer, discussing 'hypnoid states', gives one or two examples:

> *An investigator who is deep in a problem is ... no doubt anaesthetic to a certain degree, and he has large groups of sensations of which he forms no conscious perception; and the same is true of anyone who is using his creative imagination actively ... [I interrupt the citation: does that mean me, and you, and poetry? To continue:] But in such states energetic mental work is carried on, and the excitation of the nervous system which is liberated is used up in this work. In states of abstraction and dreaminess, on the other hand [that's not us is it, nothing we recognize?] intracerebral excitation sinks below its clear waking level. These states border on sleepiness and pass over into sleep ...* [12]

Was it for this? Things have passed out of my control. I can scarcely hear myself think. It is no longer possible. It is no longer I. It is: 'Imagine that I am walking like him, to his rhythm: between fifty and sixty years old' (*T*, p. 20). But who? Wordsworth between the time of initial composition and the time that he was drawing together revisions for a 'final' version of *The Prelude*? Or Coleridge, in all the aleatoriness of alienation, so close to death? Freud around the time that he was 'still' unde-cided, before his 'conversion' to telepathy?[13] Or Derrida around the time that he was writing his 'Telepathy', writing-as-Freud? It is as if writing, or reading, being dictated to, were carrying on under hypnosis. Carrying on, keeping on, keeping pace. Disturb-ances of walking, tears, my love, you've got to believe me, I'm trying to reach out

I'm hysterical. What am I saying? That poetry is inextricably linked to hypnosis and hysteria, that these can no longer be thought without a theory of telepathy.

21–1–89
                    something gets carried away, every time. Focusing on the historical emergence of psychoanalysis, underlining what we already knew even if it was without know-ing or without realizing, namely that the very 'origins' of psychoanalysis lie in the study of hysteria, Jacqueline Rose con-tends that 'hallucination and telepathy could be described as the vanishing points of what was to become the psychoanalytic account of hysteria'.[14] They have always been in contact with one another, even if illicitly, secretly, cryptically.

21–1–89
There you are, I wondered where you'd been. I can feel it now, lemman, I've fallen to pieces, it's death, it's me, befallen. There will always be a horizon of hallucination, at the centre. Forget 'perception without objective reality' (*Chambers*) or 'dis-eased perception' – as bad as Hobbes's definition of imagination as diseased or 'decaying sense'.[15] There is no 'pure' hallucination any more than there is 'pure perception'.[16] Wandering in the mind, *hallucinatus*: I'm trying to take steps. For instance to reformulate Bloom's theory of poetic influence, omitting or dis-placing its emphasis on what de Man called the 'naturalistic lan-guage of desire, possession, and power', its emphasis on subjec-

tivity, on 'strong' and 'weak' poets, and elaborating on Derrida's proposal that 'a text can stand in a relationship of transference (primarily in the psychoanalytical sense) to another text', elaborating an intratextuality, a kind of telepathic crypt-network, a cryptic hysteria-network, misprision as hallucination, but hallucination without any self-identical subject.[17]

I can't carry on. I'm genuinely 'seeing things'.

24–1–89

and as if I keep coming to.

On the one hand it is a question of following de Man's observation that 'the text imposes its own understanding and shapes the reader's evasions'.[18] The poem confers its identity ... The poem reads the reader: the reader is determined by the poem. On the other it is a case of the snail, the tracks going off in all directions in time and space linking poetry and magic, hypnosis, spells and incantation, poetry and the hypnagogic. I'm trying not to get them confused – tucking one under one arm and one under the other, I feel like another Descartes trying to establish the grounds for hyperbolic doubt while looking down at my hands unable to believe any longer whose or what they are, unable to resist the terror and joy, affirming madness in a dream, no longer stopping at what Dalia Judovitz refers to as the transformation of 'skeptical doubt into internal doubt, based on a subjective system of verification', fragmenting in fiction, no longer bound.[19]

It is not a matter of alternatives or of synthesizing a dittology. For example with *The Prelude* and in particular with the opening of Book V (1–139), the book of 'Books', which meditates on their material fragility, their comparative ephemerality, before going on to present the account of a dream in which an Arab in the desert is hurrying to bury a stone (geometry) and a shell (poetry) before the end of the world which is coming imminently, any moment.[20] It is what is called 'the dream of the Arab'. Sympathy and imagination, telepathy and hysteria: they all cross here while everything is falling to pieces, it's no good, I could hold on no longer, 'I breathe again – /Trances of thought and mountings of the mind/Come fast upon me' (I, 19–21), now it's happening. Yes, this is affirmation – affirmation even if 'trance' is to be linked up with the death drive, as it is by Paul Hirst and Penny Woolley when they suggest that

> *prolonged trance is a state of self-obliteration which corresponds to the 'wishes' Freud considers to be at the heart of the Death Instinct. Repeated entry into trance could be viewed as a form of 'compulsion to repeat' – a phenomenon analogous to shell-shock victims of the Great War who returned to their experiences in dreams, a phenomenon generally regarded as pathological.*[21]

Imagine this: a madness, writing, 'beyond the death drive'. In Coleridge, as well, 'trances of thought' are everywhere. Quite apart from the hypnopoetics of 'Kubla Khan', *The Ancient Mariner* or 'Christabel', or the uncanny figure, in 'Limbo', with 'his eyeless Face all Eye' (*Poems*, p. 325), there is the recurring fascination with whatever entrances, whatever is generated for example 'Whilst thro' my half-clos'd eyelids I behold/The sunbeams dance, like diamonds, on the main' ('The Eolian Harp', *Poems*, p. 53), whatever is generated by 'the dark green file of long lank weeds, /That all at once (a most fantastic sight!)/Still nod and drip beneath the dripping edge/Of the blue clay-stone' ('This Lime-Tree Bower', *Poems*, p. 119), whatever is generated by 'the stranger' and 'makes a toy of Thought' ('Frost at Midnight').

The intratextual entrancement and fragmentation of the poetry of Wordsworth and Coleridge. All along, *The Prelude* was the 'Poem to Coleridge'.[22] It is a letter, addressed to you, Coleridge: 'O friend, O poet, brother of my soul' (V, 180), as Wordsworth says. Yet the briefest survey of the multiplication of apostrophes in Wordsworth's poem would cause any notion of the single addressee ('Coleridge') to tremble – and the relentless instances of animism and anthropomorphism throughout scarcely make the destinerrance of such apostrophes more familiar or comforting:

> *Oh there is blessing in this gentle breeze,*
> *That blows from the green fields and from the clouds*
> *And from the sky; it beats against my cheek,*
> *And seems half conscious of the joy it gives.*
> *O welcome messenger! O welcome friend! (I, 1–5)*

Anaesthesia, euphoria, it is you: was it for this? Hallucination: there is 'a voice that flowed along my dreams' (I, 275–6), capable of composing thoughts, it is to the 'voice' of a river that *The Prelude* is addressed:

> *Was it for this . . .?*
> *For this didst thou,*
> *O Derwent, travelling over the green plains*
> *Near my 'sweet birthplace', didst thou, beauteous stream,*
> *Make ceaseless music through the night and day,*
> *Which with its steady cadence tempering*
> *Our human waywardness, composed my thoughts . . .*
> *(I, 271, 276–81)*

Whose '"sweet birthplace"'? Needless to say the question of this quotational encrypting does not come to rest simply with the proposition that Wordsworth is citing Coleridge.[23] *The Prelude* cites 'Frost at Midnight'. What is a 'birthplace' if it can be quoted, if it is seen to be textual in this way, if a text identifies with another in this way? And then what of our 'sweet birthplace' too, yours and mine, my love?

Everything in the late nineteenth-century formulation of the term 'telepathy' can be traced back through the concept of sympathy. Back to Hume, for example, who in his *Treatise* had asserted that 'Whatever other passions we may be actuated by; pride, ambition, avarice, curiosity, revenge or lust; the soul or animating principle of them all is sympathy'; who proposed that 'No quality of human nature is more remarkable, both in itself and in its consequences, than that propensity we have to sympathize with others, and to receive by communication their inclinations and sentiments, however different from, or even contrary to our own'; but who also regarded 'the mind' as 'a kind of theatre' and 'personal identity' as 'fictitious'.[24] Back to Adam Smith, who observed that 'We sympathize even with the dead' – and by this example alone demonstrated not only the inescapable fictiveness of sympathy but indicated the space for a notion of sympathy no longer constrained by the boundaries of life and death.[25] Back to Coleridge and Wordsworth. And thence to a question of a theory of reading as a theory of telepathy, and the question of the 'birthplace' of a subject, poet, reader.

24–1–89

So the 'dream of the Arab', my love, whose dream is that, where does that dream begin, to whom or what is it addressed?

Calmly, calm down, calmly now; does it not start in Book V, at line 71: 'He saw before him an Arabian waste . . .'? And isn't it addressed, beyond 'Coleridge', to everyone, all of us, 'man' or humanity in general? And isn't it written in a mood of calm, with a calmness which, in the 1850 text, is compared with the 'tranquillizing power' of 'the night-calm felt/Through earth and sky' (1850: V, 1–3)? But the panic has already begun:

> *Even in the steadiest mood of reason, when*
> *All sorrow for thy transitory pains*
> *Goes out, it grieves me for thy state, O man,*
> *Thou paramount creature, and thy race, while ye*
> *Shall sojourn on this planet, not for woes*
> *Which thou endur'st – that weight, albeit huge,*
> *I charm away – but for those palms atchieved*
> *Through length of time, by study and hard thought,*
> *The honours of thy high endowments; there*
> *My sadness finds its fuel. (V, 1–10)*

In this calm, this 'steadiest mood', comes the apocalyptic vision and overwhelming concern with the materiality of writing, with the dreadful impermanence of poetry itself. No need to linger on those moments in which the language of Book V explicitly involves witchcraft, the supernatural and telepathic – here where Wordsworth is able to 'charm away' the everyday 'woes' of humanity; where until now there has apparently been no troubling of the telepathic network between 'mind', nature and 'God' (or what's called 'the one great mind', or 'the One Life', and here more than ever the shapes and sounds of 'God', 'sympathy' and 'telepathy' begin to blur):

> *Hitherto*
> *In progress through this verse my mind hath looked*
> *Upon the speaking face of earth and heaven*
> *As her prime teacher, intercourse with man*
> *Established by the Sovereign Intellect,*
> *Who through that bodily image hath diffused*

> *A soul divine which we participate,*
> *A deathless spirit. (V, 10–17)*[26]

Still, we might note in passing the shadow of one hysterical element: 'the mind', the one which can magically read 'the speaking face of earth and heaven'. Two strands could be drawn together quickly. In his essay 'A "Word Scarce Said": Hysteria and Witchcraft in Wordsworth's "Experimental" Poetry of 1797–1798', Alan J. Bewell emphasizes the importance of the history of hysteria – 'its intimate connection with witchcraft' and its links with the concept of imagination – for an understanding of Wordsworth's poetry.[27] He suggests that, for Wordsworth and for Freud, hysteria – and '"hysterical women"' in particular – constitutes a powerful 'medium [*sic*] of speculative argument' (p. 360). He concludes that 'the witch/hysteric remains an ambivalent figure to Wordsworth, as threatening and as fascinating to him as his imagination' (p. 385). Apparent belief here that 'hysteria' and the 'feminine' are intrinsically connected; but let us emphasize a second strand. This is what Karen Swann underlines in her reading of hysteria in Coleridge's 'Christabel'. This poem, she says, 'mockingly and dreamily informs us that hysteria is the condition of all subjects in discourse, and that the attribution of this condition to feminine bodies is a conventional, hysterical response'.[28] Partly then, it is a matter of the Lacanian proposal that at the base of 'hysteria' is the question, 'Am I a man or a woman?'[29] Hysteria and the undecidability or loss of gender. The question at the core of Book V is a question concerning the mind, and Wordsworth's 'mind' is 'feminine'. Like the (male) 'murmurs' of 'the fairest of all rivers' and 'my nurse's song' (I, 272–3), like the 'Unmanageable thoughts' of the (male) 'lover' or 'poet' and the (female) 'meditative mind' (I, 145–52 ff.), 'femininity' is there and no poetry would be possible without it. The muse, imagination, the mother, *hysteria*: the necessity of her realization, of corresponding with her, communication at a distance without distance. Poetry will always pose the question of such a *hystera*: unfathered, undecidably gendered, it is to have a foreign womb in one's head. Poetry, it is you

27–1–89

The question of a feminine monumentalization, undecidable, double:

> Oh, why hath not the mind
> *Some element to stamp her image on*
> *In nature somewhat nearer to her own?*
> *Why, gifted with such powers to send abroad*
> *Her spirit, must it lodge in shrines so frail? (V, 44–8)*

She, 'the mind'; but 'it', 'Her spirit' . . . This seems to be asking for the moon, for some kind of mental cryonics which nothing in our tele-culture would render more conceivable.[30]

Wordsworth – whose very name is thus endangered, literally and paronomastically – is necessarily anxious, frightened. It is an anxiety about the fact that poetry – whether Shakespeare's, Milton's, Wordsworth's or another's – cannot last. It is an anxiety about the frailty of texts, about what Michel Foucault calls that 'transitory existence which admittedly is destined to be effaced, but according to a time-scale which is not ours...'.[31]

28–1–89

It is death. My dearest, can't you see it, here it comes, the space of literature, the stony shell. This anxiety, this singular and exemplary hysteria, which encloses and traverses the 'tale' of the dream of the Arab, is 'death'. It gives 'Tremblings of the heart' (V, 21) which link it up, as it were by 'sympathy', with Shakespeare – with the death of Shakespeare's thought, and Shakespeare's thought as death. As regards the great works which will not last forever,

> man,
> *As long as he shall be the child of earth,*
> *Might almost 'weep to have' what he may lose –*
> *Nor be himself extinguished, but survive*
> *Abject, depressed, forlorn, disconsolate. (V, 23–7)*

Living on. These lines cite and rehearse the deathly thought of
Shakespeare's sonnet 64:

> *Ruin hath taught me thus to ruminate,*
> *That Time will come and take my love away.*
> *   This thought is as a death, which cannot choose*
> *   But weep to have that which it fears to lose.*

Thinking death, writing in the face of death, writing (on) it:
writing will thus have an affinity with death which disturbs the
conceptuality of Freud's 'death drive'.[32] There is a triad – writing,
telepathy and death – and it's in there, enough to turn us all into
ghosts or over in our graves.

Or sleep. Poetry, Hypnos, it is you, can't you see, can't you
hear I'm dreaming, I'm in ruins, 'me' and 'Ruin', we 'ruminate'.
That's what it is: rumination or meditation as the end of the
world, calm hysteria, the contemplation and *apokalupsis* of St
John.[33]

I'm having to write so fast now, so little time, I am trying to
catch the last post, I am trying to remain calm, but perhaps this
will never reach you, none of us will ever have been here, my
dearest, I can already feel myself at a distance, I can feel myself
passing   but you follow

> *He saw before him an Arabian waste,*
> *A desart, and he fancied that himself*
> *Was sitting there in the wide wilderness*
> *Alone upon the sands. Distress of mind*
> *Was growing in him when, behold, at once*   75
> *To his great joy a man was at his side,*
> *Upon a dromedary mounted high.*
> *He seemed an arab of the Bedouin tribes;*
> *A lance he bore, and underneath one arm*
> *A stone, and in the opposite hand a shell*   80
> *Of a surpassing brightness. Much rejoiced*
> *The dreaming man that he should have a guide*
> *To lead him through the desart; and he thought,*
> *While questioning himself what this strange freight*
> *Which the newcomer carried through the waste*   85

Could mean, the arab told him that the stone –
To give it in the language of the dream –
Was Euclid's Elements. 'And this' said he,
'This other', pointing to the shell, 'this book
Is something of more worth.' 'And, at the word,   90
The stranger', said my friend continuing,
'Stretched forth the shell towards me, with command
That I should hold it to my ear. I did so
And heard that instant in an unknown tongue,
Which yet I understood, articulate sounds,   95
A loud prophetic blast of harmony,
An ode in passion uttered, which foretold
Destruction to the children of the earth
By deluge now at hand. No sooner ceased
The song, but with calm look the arab said   100
That all was true, that it was even so
As had been spoken, and that he himself
Was going then to bury those two books –
The one that held acquaintance with the stars,
And wedded man to man by purest bond   105
Of nature, undisturbed by space or time;
Th'other that was a god, yea many gods,
Had voices more than all the winds, and was
A joy, a consolation, and a hope.'
My friend continued, 'Strange as it may seem   110
I wondered not, although I plainly saw
The one to be a stone, th'other a shell,
Nor doubted once but that they both were books,
Having a perfect faith in all that passed.
A wish was now engendered in my fear   115
To cleave unto this man, and I begged leave
To share his errand with him. On he passed
Not heeding me; I followed, and took note
That he looked often backward with wild look,
Grasping his twofold treasure to his side.   120
Upon a dromedary, lance in rest,
He rode, I keeping pace with him; and now
I fancied that he was the very knight
Whose tale Cervantes tells, yet not the knight,
But was an arab of the desart too,   125
Of these was neither, and was both at once.
His countenance meanwhile grew more disturbed,

> *And looking backwards when he looked I saw*
> *A glittering light, and asked him whence it came.*
> *"It is", said he, "the waters of the deep*   130
> *Gathering upon us." Quickening then his pace*
> *He left me; I called after him aloud;*
> *He heeded not, but with his twofold charge*
> *Beneath his arm – before me full in view –*
> *I saw him riding o'er the desart sands*   135
> *With the fleet waters of the drowning world*
> *In chace of him; whereat I waked in terror,*
> *And saw the sea before me, and the book*
> *In which I had been reading at my side.'*

crypt-hysteria and the 'dream of the Arab': to refer to the fact that Freud clearly equates hysteria and dreams – for instance, when he states 'In view of the complete identity between the characteristic features of the dream-work and those of the psychical activity which issues in psychoneurotic symptoms, we feel justified in carrying over to dreams the conclusions we have been led to by hysteria', or when he equates 'hallucinations in hysteria and paranoia and ... visions in mentally normal subjects' – won't help much to clarify or understand the 'dream of the Arab'.[34]

Sigmund Freud, joy of the world, can you hear me? Deep down you knew all along. Partly it's a question of the dream as a kind of 'unconscious consciousness', and that idea is itself enough to make you a trifle hysterical, as around the moment you declare – in that short text you wrote in English, 'A Note on the Unconscious in Psychoanalysis' (1912), which was first published in the *Proceedings* of the Society for Psychical Research of all places and which contains all sorts of curious 'transfers' and 'translations' (for example, consistently in the original English text, the word 'psychical' rather than 'mental': Why? A bit of 'bad English'? A complimentary gesture towards the SPR? But what would that mean? Or does it signal something else, even more enigmatic? And again in the text of 1912, instead of 'preconscious' you use 'foreconscious': was this just to be diverting, to draw attention to a prophetic streak?) – you declare:

> *We have no right to extend the meaning of this word ['conscious']*
> *so far as to make it include a consciousness of which the owner*

himself is not aware. If philosophers find difficulty in accepting the existence of unconscious ideas, the existence of an unconscious consciousness seems to me even more objectionable.[35]

There might be a temptation to see the 'dream' in this way, in which case it would be a matter of the hypnagogic 'experience' of an individual. J. Hillis Miller seems to succumb:

the relation between dream and waking is so immediate and is made so explicit that the dream may almost be called a daydream, or at any rate a so-called 'hypnagogic' dream, that sort of dream which provides an immediate reworking by a man who has just fallen asleep of what he has been perceiving and thinking, rather than the rising up within deep sleep of buried images and memories.[36]

Partly it is this, but it is also immeasurably complicated, in at least four ways:

(i)   by the way in which the text of the 'dream itself' – if it were ever really possible to say such a thing – is embedded and encrypted in a context of other texts and dreams, books and readings: it is cryptaesthetic; it buries itself, uncannily performing what it describes.[37]

(ii) by the way readings and recitations are themselves represented in terms of their hypnagogic or hypnopompic powers, their capacity for 'deep entrancement' (V, 162), their capacity to 'bewitch' or soothe (178), to 'charm away the wakeful night' (520), or to become 'airy fancies/More bright than madness or the dreams of wine' (591–2);

(iii) by the way the figure of the Arab 'in the dream' spills over, repeatedly ('Full often') contaminating any wider context of distinctions between sleep and wakefulness: the 'arab phantom' coming out of 'the world of sleep' acquires 'A substance' (140–3), appears 'a living man' endowed with 'internal thought' (145), this last phrase eerily inviting us to conceive the possibility of an opposite, that is to say 'external thought'; and finally

(iv) by the question of the identity of 'the dreamer' and what happens to this identity through 'the dream'.

In each instance, also, a question of telepathy.

Starting with this weird treatment of the word 'thought'. Is 'thought' individual and personal, whatever that might mean? Or is it in some sense subversive of these notions? Is it essentially autonomous, as if disembodied but capable of occupying any mind at any time, unthinkable except as coming from an outside which would itself be unthinkable? Like the thought of Shakespeare, this came to me, the thought of you, so infinitely close and fragile, inside 'me', thought the other:

> *A thought is with me sometimes, and I say,*
> *'Should earth by inward throes be wrenched throughout,*
> *Or fire be sent from far to wither all*
> *Her pleasant habitations, and dry up*
> *Old Ocean in his bed, left singed and bare ...' (V, 28–32)*

This thought, which rapidly becomes plural, can be transmitted, as though in the mad 'silence' of a so-called Conversation poem: 'One day, when in the hearing of a friend/I had given utterance to thoughts like these ...' (49–50). Even in this apparently conventional formulation there is something slightly uncanny, as if 'the hearing' is not quite fitting, or as if the utterance has a sort of anaesthetic indifference to whether there is 'hearing' or not.

But then these thoughts are ghosts of a kind: the 'friend' confesses to having 'Yielded' – and soon everything will be yielding, minds yielding like the senses, passing into one another – 'Yielded', says the 'friend', 'to kindred hauntings' (55). The 1805 text of course attributes the 'dream' to this 'friend'; the 1850 text presents 'the dreamer' as Wordsworth 'himself'. One reason for concentrating on the earlier version is its greater strangeness in treating the question of the identity of the dreamer. But the mere fact that the two quite distinct versions exist shows up the telepathic frame: try placing yourself, placing your reading, somewhere between the two, reading 'neither' and 'both at once', enough to drive you mad (as though you wouldn't have to be mad already, as though being mad were not the necessary condition of the readability of this text in the first place: no longer the distinction between dream and event, sleeping and waking, that might once have kept guard, if only at the last outpost, before the desert-empire of the dream, over Freud's early recognition that 'we all are [insane] in dreams' ...[38]

Who is the dreamer? A footnote in the Norton edition is perfectly clear on this point: 'The dream of the Arab and his two "books," ascribed to a friend in 1805 and to Wordsworth himself in 1850, is in fact a brilliantly imaginative transformation of a dream experienced by the philosopher Descartes in 1619. It had presumably been related to Wordsworth by Coleridge.'[39] For a moment I can't help it, I find it hysterical, hilarious, my love: 'in fact', 'experienced', 'the philosopher'. And in the hands of this argument I just see 'Descartes' falling to pieces, collapsing like a house of cards, a rope of sand, or fragmenting in any case into irreducible and affirmative plurality, as if the hands covering his face in fear were suddenly translucent and he could see

                         But it's time to stop, there's no more time: Descartes the unconscious philosopher, his parents, his grandparents and the rest, the philosophical 'unconscious': is this what constitutes the dreamer? Or is it Shakespeare, Coleridge, the 'friend', Michel Beaupuy, Wordsworth? Or the Discharged Soldier, or Cervantes, Quixote, the quixotic phantom, the dream of the Arab 'himself' . . .[40] Imagine the sweet birthplace of this dream; and try picturing the dreamer.[41] Would it not be better to think of something more dramatic, like a theatre of undecidably external/internal thought, unstoppably fictive and literary, a multiple birthplace, a collage or network of personae intratextually linked up but irreducible to the self-identity of a subject, to a single self, to consciousness or unconsciousness, waking or dreaming, madness or reason?[42]

But here comes 'the dream'. What did you expect? There are, according to Gurney, Myers and Podmore in *Phantasms of the Living*, 'transient hallucinations of the sane', of which perhaps the most common examples are 'arrival-cases'.[43] *Phantasms of the Living* argues that 'There is definite evidence to show that mere *expectancy* may produce hallucination', especially in the case of 'the delusive impression of seeing or hearing a person whose *arrival* is expected'.[44] Such, then, would be the space of 'Frost at Midnight', with its bizarre footnoted representation of 'films' and its recounted anticipations of 'the *stranger's* face' at the door.[45] Reading as itself a process of arrival-cases. And for a fleeting moment one might see – as if at the threshold of both the Arab dream and 'Frost at Midnight' – it is a matter of the 'stranger' (V, 91). But this is the letter, Wordsworth's poem, yielding the telepathic, the uncanny transmission of the 'same thoughts':

> *once upon a summer's noon*
> *While he was sitting in a rocky cave*
> *By the seaside, perusing as it chanced,*
> *The famous history of the errant knight*
> *Recorded by Cervantes, these same thoughts*
> *Came to him, and to height unusual rose ... (V, 56–61)*

Until 'at length, /His senses yielding to the sultry air, /Sleep seized him and he passed into a dream' (68–70). *Exeunt omnes.*

29–1–89

What was it: telepathy, dream, poem, hysteria, stone, shell, book, burial, sea, desart 'now/Dead in my eyes as is a theatre/Fresh emptied of spectators' (V, 550–2)?

But in the scattered moments remaining, before what I cannot help conceiving as the 'great overthrow' (158), let me scribble a few last thoughts, perhaps the same as will have come to you by now: being in a dream, that is what Wordsworth is going to tell you, you will pass into another. Everything is passing, and yet:

> *Strange as it may seem*
> *I wondered not, although I plainly saw*
> *The one to be a stone, th' other a shell,*
> *Nor doubted once but that they both were books,*
> *Having a perfect faith in all that passed. (110–14)*

We are all insane in our dreams, reading, following them nothing need surprise us, even 'terror', we could see the writing on the wall. It is like Coleridge reporting in his notebook in 1802: 'October 3 – Night – My Dreams uncommonly illustrative of the non-existence of Surprize in sleep'.[46] Then again, remaining for a moment within the fiction of a single self-identical dreamer, is there not a sense in which dreams involve a kind of internal clairvoyance? And is this not mimed in the thought of Wordsworth's syntax, in the 'turnings intricate of verse' (V, 627)? For example in those lines:

> *Much rejoiced*
> *The dreaming man that he should have a guide*
> *To lead him through the desart; and he thought,*
> *While questioning himself what this strange freight*
> *Which the newcomer carried through the waste*
> *Could mean, the arab told him that the stone –*
> *To give it in the language of the dream –*
> *Was* Euclid's Elements ... *(81–8)*

'The arab' seems to answer thought. The word 'thought', suspended at the end of a line, might have an object ('he thought ...
that ...', 'he thought ... of ...') or not (first he rejoiced and
then, more seriously, but perhaps no less hysterically, 'he
thought'), who knows? Is it that 'he thought' *that* 'the arab told
him ...', though he may have been completely deluded, just
hearing things, there's no way of knowing? Or was it that 'he
thought' (period) and the arab – 'To give it in the language of the
dream' – 'really' did tell him...? Like that of other so-called
'labourers divine' (165), Wordsworth's syntax is a work of rap-
ture, a seizure you may only follow and, without destination, as
if a mere prelude, just as he thought, just as you thought, the end.
A certain clairvoyancing, then, even in Wordsworth's bathos.

For, no matter what we may think, the 'dream of the Arab'
insists on the prophetic power of poetry, the clairvoyant or
telepathic powers of the shell. This shell, says the Arab, 'this
book/Is something of more worth' (89–90). Then 'at the word'
(as it happens – is it by chance, but what could chance any longer
mean here? – that word is 'worth', the word's 'worth'); and, still
here in parentheses, we might suggest that it is only at the
juxtaposition of such incommensurable narrative frames, of the
putative utterance of *more than two* speakers [stranger, dreamer,
poet, and so on], it is only in this impossible linking, already
buried alive, that 'Wordsworth' might be spoken, that 'Wordsworth', the name, might 'speak into the air'):[47]

> *'And this' said he,*
> *'This other', pointing to the shell, 'this book*
> *Is something of more worth.' 'And, at the word,*
> *The stranger', said my friend continuing,*
> *'Stretched forth the shell towards me, with command*

> *That I should hold it to my ear. I did so*
> *And heard that instant in an unknown tongue,*
> *Which yet I understood, articulate sounds,*
> *A loud prophetic blast of harmony,*
> *An ode in passion uttered, which foretold*
> *Destruction to the children of the earth*
> *By deluge now at hand. (88–99)*

This 'blast of harmony' seems to be understood as if telepathically by the so-called dreamer, and by the 'stranger' who is able,
immediately and apparently without batting an eyelid ('with calm
look'), to confirm the prophecy. The arab's description of the
shell as 'a god, yea many gods' and having 'voices more than all
the winds' (107–8) is like a 'promise scarcely earthly' (488) which
in turn seems to prophesy or foreshadow the later stark affirmation: 'Visionary power/Attends upon the motions of the winds/
Embodied in the mystery of words' (619–21). And 'in' the
'dream' – the entrancing 'blast', its 'articulate sounds' (95; 'Frost
at Midnight', 33) – the shell's prophecy of apocalypse comes true
or rather comes to the crest, comes to the fleet point of coming
true:

> *before me full in view –*
> *I saw him riding o'er the desart sands*
> *With the fleet waters of the drowning world*
> *In chace of him; whereat I waked in terror,*
> *And saw the sea before me, and the book*
> *In which I had been reading at my side. (134–9)*

'Riding': 'reading'. What 'sea'? what 'book'? Suspension and dissemination. Even now, has the dream finished? Or begun?

'Even so' (101), as the 'arab'/'dreamer'/'poet'/'narrator' says,
citing the end of the Bible (Revelation 22: 20). Come quickly.
Everything is mixed up. The mixing of voices and identities, the
multiplication of addressors and addressees is, as Derrida has
noted in another context, itself apocalyptic.[48] Of the apocalyptic
'deluge' or 'glittering wall' which is approaching, Hillis Miller
states: 'This apocalyptic news is the fundamental theme of poetry.' 'Poetry,' he remarks, 'both soothes and is apocalyptic'.[49]
Calm hysteria: the 'calm look' (V, 100) with the 'wild look' (119).
But the 'dream of the Arab' is apocalyptic, as well, in its notion

of transmitting the 'same thoughts'. As Wallace Stevens writes, in 'Owl's Clover':

> *Is each man thinking his separate thoughts or, for once,*
> *Are all men thinking together as one, thinking*
> *Each other's thoughts, thinking a single thought,*
> *Disclosed in everything, transcended, poised*
> *For the syllable, poised for the touch? But that*
> *Apocalypse was not contrived for parks* ...[50]

The most alluring and mad fantasy of all, the very 'dream of reading': that which identifies telepathy and apocalypse, everyone having the same thoughts at the same time. No longer 'everyone', but rather everyone 'together as one', a single one, 'thinking a single thought'.

And then I read again, one more time, Derrida's definition of the truth: 'The truth,' he says, 'what I always have difficulty getting used to: that non-telepathy is possible. Always difficult to imagine that one can think something to oneself, deep down inside, without being surprised by the other, without the other being immediately informed' (*T*, p. 13). Suppose this is wrong. Suppose non-telepathy is not possible. This might be one of the thoughts communicated by the 'dream of the Arab': the necessity of formulating a notion of the poet, or dreamer, or reader, as ineluctably and affirmatively plural, inescapably fragmentary and fictive. This would not be to propose what Jacqueline Rose calls 'an endless dispersal of subjectivity', or 'a pure fragmentation which would be as futile as it would be psychically unmanageable for the subject'.[51] For what, after all, is 'pure' fragmentation? And how do we *know*, without tautology, what is 'psychically unmanageable'? No, it is rather to attempt to mark another space, both contextual and intratextual – to adumbrate a conception of the subject that would be strategically aligned with the notion of literature as a discursive formation. 'Telepathy': might that not serve, finally, as a term to describe the uncanny, multiple and heterogeneous composition and operation, the *work* of such a subject?

But I can't see anymore, only that it will happen any moment now, noon or midnight, you won't come, this will never have reached you, my love, it is not you, it's the stranger, always the stranger, in the trances of the blast, silent as icicles, quiet as the moon.

Some Thoughts on Antony and Cleopatra by Moonlight

To see the moon, to see it preside as final addressee, the exterior paramour of death, the cold selenic crypt. Or to see nothing, only the air and the dark, to speak into the air, blindly, into the falling darkness of the air. 'The night/Is shiny' (IV, ix, 2–3).[1] It would be telepathic – to have seen death coming, at the last possible moment, and beyond it, to have foreseen it truly; or to think it so radically, so thoroughly, so nearly that it happens, it comes. Shakespeare's *Antony and Cleopatra* lives on the dissolution of these apparent alternatives. It is possible, however strangely, to 'Think, and die' (III, xiii, 1). 'Thought' (IV, vi, 35), as Enobarbus says, can kill. Enobarbus's drive towards death collides, in the moonlight, with the moon, with the melancholy madness of the moon and with the anthropomorphic lunacy of the moon as addressee:

> *O sovereign mistress of true melancholy,*
> *The poisonous damp of night disponge upon me,*
> *That life, a very rebel to my will,*
> *May hang no longer on me. Throw my heart*
> *Against the flint and hardness of my fault,*
> *Which, being dried with grief, will break to powder,*
> *And finish all foul thoughts ...*   *(IV, ix, 12–18)*

II

Everywhere in *Antony* and *Cleopatra* there is the concatenation of the foreseeing of 'death', reading the future, prophecy, the text of telepathy. No doubt it is most crystal-clear in the case of the Soothsayer, who 'know(s) things' (I, ii, 7) and can read 'In Nature's infinite book of secrecy' (I, ii, 8); who foresees the deaths of Cleopatra, Charmian and Iras, and foresees Antony's fate against Caesar. The Soothsayer cannot give reasons; it is something on the move, in his brain: 'I see it in my motion, have it not in my tongue' (II, iii, 13). But elsewhere there are the Roman 'augurers' who 'Say they know not, they cannot tell, look grimly, /And dare not speak their knowledge' (IV, xii, 4–6). There are the Egyptians who

> take the flow o' th' Nile
> By certain scales i' th' pyramid. They know
> By th' height, the lowness, or the mean, if dearth
> Or foison follow ...   (II, vii, 15–18)

There is Cleopatra with her second or first sight: 'O, never was there queen/So mightily betrayed! Yet at the first/I saw the treasons planted' (I, iii, 24–6). She can foresee and prophesy, and like everything else in *Antony and Cleopatra* you can never tell how deadly serious it may be. Of love letters to Antony, she declares: 'Who's born that day/When I forget to send to Antony/Shall die a beggar' (I, v, 63–5). As for his suicide, she will have had 'a prophesying fear' (IV, xiv, 119) of it. Needless to say it is she who most of all is identified with witchcraft: she is the 'enchanting Queen' (I, ii, 119), the 'great fairy' (IV, viii, 12), the 'grave charm' (IV, xii, 25) or 'spell' (IV, xii, 30) whose 'magic' is Antony's 'noble ruin' (III, x, 18). Yet 'ordinary' soldiers, too, seem open to uncanny or supernatural phenomena and can even specify their precise import:

2nd Soldier: *Peace! What noise?*
1st: *List, list!*
2nd: *Hark!*
1st: *Music i' th'air.*
3rd: *Under the earth.*
4th: *It signs well, does it not?*
3rd: *No.*
1st: *Peace, I say!*
        What should this mean?

2nd:	'Tis the god Hercules, whom Antony loved,
	Now leaves him. (IV, iii, 11–16)

Then there is Enobarbus who, in the context of Antony's marriage with Octavia, seems glad that he is not 'bound to divine of this unity' (II, vi, 113) but can prophesy in any case, however negatively. And there is Caesar, whose chances are themselves beyond chance, beyond 'natural luck' (II, iii, 26). The Soothsayer says so, and even Antony has sufficient foresight to recognize it. One has to imagine a hapless 'hap', beyond 'chance':

> Be it art or hap,
> He hath spoken true. The very dice obey him,
> And in our sports my better cunning faints
> Under his chance.   (II, iii, 32–5)

In military terms his 'speed . . . / Carries beyond belief' (III, vii, 74–5), and he is the figure most explicitly and most ruthlessly concerned to 'Possess' (II, vii, 94) or control time itself. But in more ways than one, we know, Caesar will have transpired to be 'too sure an augurer' (V, ii, 330). The same goes for Pompey, for all his moony visions:

> I shall do well:
> The people love me, and the sea is mine;
> My powers are crescent, and my auguring hope
> Says it will come to th' full.   (II, i, 8–11)

Kirby Farrell has recently argued that there is a 'principle that governs Shakespeare's judgment of prophetic behavior', namely 'the deep taboo in the plays against attempts to seize the future by force'.[2] This suggestive schema has its underside. For there is no prophecy without history, and a play such as *Antony and Cleopatra* seems marked by a 'motion' in motion between the two, exceeding dialectics. There is of course the extraordinary conservatism of the 'national history' plays, Greek, Roman, English: no matter what happens the end is known, everyone knows it all in advance. History is already prophecy here, and vice versa. It is also clear, as K. M. Briggs has stressed, that, 'dramatically speaking, a prophecy is not likely to be made unless it is to come true'.[3] Yet prophecy is in no way merely thematic. Prophecy structures. And it will not be possible to specify the time of all this 'motion'. Rather it will be a matter of an overflowing and dissolving, fragmentation and vanishing, something no doubt too riskily compared to Antony and Cleopatra's 'separation', which 'abides and flies' (I, iii, 103), is 'residing' and 'fleeting' (104–5) at the same (impossible) time. It will be a matter of thinking in the dark, perhaps by moonlight. Or else of 'fleeting' (V, ii, 240) in its absence.

III

No 'living present'. The play 'starts' in mid-discussion ('Nay, but . . .'). Even the Roman admonition which then doubly frames the onset of Antony and Cleopatra, as spectacle within spectacle, theatre within theatre, the entrance and entrancement of the play and its namesakes, is twisted, with its singular transformational grammar:

> *Look, where they come.*
> *Take but good note, and you shall see in him*
> *The triple pillar of the world transformed*
> *Into a strumpet's fool. Behold and see.*
> *(I, i, 10–13)*

'Shall see . . . transformed': is this transformation past, or passing, or to come? This is the time – in motion – of the play. Foretelling and prophecy will have helped to set up the 'strong toil' of this uncanny temporality. It is the net and network of 'tragic inevitability', darkness overtaking the traveller in the past, and the continual coming of other moons. It is a kind of temporal lunacy. For Antony: 'I am so lated in the world that I / Have lost my way for ever' (III, xi, 3–4). Again and again.

What is the moon? It is Cleopatra. It is changing:

Antony: *Alack, our terrene moon*
         Is now eclipsed, and it portends alone
         The fall of Antony.
Cleopatra: *I must stay his time.*
                                   (III, xiii, 153–5)

What does 'stay' mean? Cleopatra will wait till he recovers.[4]
Antony's time and Cleopatra's time: the time of Antony and
Cleopatra. Antony's fall happens, over and over; and never happens. Keep recovering, living on: stay. The moon is motion, time
in motion. It is changeability, metamorphosis. It may, coming and
going, be the only remarkable thing left, for instance after
Antony's so-called death, after the apocalypse: 'The odds is gone, /
And there is nothing left remarkable / Beneath the visiting moon'
(IV, xv, 66–8), as Cleopatra says. But then again later – in the
dream of 'another sleep', in a telepathic vision that is 'past the size
of dreaming' (V, ii, 97) – we will hear of another moon, watchful,
staying on the move: 'His face was as the heavens, and therein
stuck / A sun and moon, which kept their course, and lighted / The
little O, the earth' (V, ii, 79–81).

IV

A telepathic vision might, with the qualifications we propose to
elaborate here, be one way of describing *Antony and Cleopatra*.
For there are all kinds of telepathic threads, not only those which
ensnare history and prophecy, which entangle the lunatic death-
drive of an Enobarbus, or weave the shirt of Nessus (IV, xii, 43) for
an Antony. There is, for example, the provocative oddity, encountered elsewhere in Shakespeare's plays, of a sort of telepathic
repetition of utterance, apparent displays of telepathy or thought-
transmission which no amount of textual scholarship or editorial
argumentation will efface. They may be 'coincidences', 'felicities',
'infelicities' or 'errors', but in any case they leave their trace; they
stain, they stay. The critical question indeed, as we will see, is how
or even whether their empire and effects can be delimited.
    For example, Cleopatra declares to Enobarbus that she will act
as if she were a man:

> *Sink Rome, and their tongues rot*
> *That speak against us! A charge we bear i' th' war,*
> *And as the president of my kingdom will*
> *Appear there for a man ...*   *(III, vii, 15–18)*

Then Antony and Canidius enter, and within ten lines Antony is comparing her with a man:

> Cleopatra: *Celerity is never more admired*
> *Than by the negligent.*
> Antony: *A good rebuke,*
> *Which might have well becomed the best of men,*
> *To taunt at slackness.*   *(III, vii, 24–7)*

Or, with the passing of further moons, there is the example of Euphronius, the tutor of Antony and Cleopatra's children, when he plays the role of ambassador; and Dolabella's comment comes to be weirdly reiterated by Euphronius himself:

> Caesar: *Let him appear that's come from Antony.*
> *Know you him?*
> Dolabella: *Caesar, 'tis his schoolmaster –*
> *An argument that he is plucked, when hither*
> *He sends so poor a pinion of his wing,*
> *Which had superfluous kings for messengers*
> *Not many moons gone by.*
> Enter *AMBASSADOR* from *ANTONY.*
> Caesar: *Approach, and speak.*
> Ambassador: *Such as I am, I come from Antony.*
> *I was of late as petty to his ends*
> *As is the morn-dew on the myrtle leaf*
> *To his grand sea.*   *(III, xii, 1–10)*

Or again, in what may be classed as another type of example, there is the uncanny rapport between Charmian's 'O excellent! I love long life better than figs' (I, ii, 30) and the fig-laden context of her own and her mistress's death. Such modulated or displaced 'repetitions' are instances of what might be described as dramaturgic telepathy.[5] They indicate possibilities for a quite different space of drama. They bear witness to the thought that the form of drama itself allows for telepathic possibilities, telepathic structures more 'advanced' than in any other 'literary' genre.

When Antony leaves Egypt, having declared that he will simultaneously 'remain' (I, iii, 105), Cleopatra's thoughts 'fly forth of Egypt' (I, v, 12) – after or before him, to or with him. Her

thoughts form a kind of moving sculpture, or a strange prosopo-
poetic machine smoothly curving from a present listener (Charmian), to a horse, to the telepathic prosopopoeia of what the
absent Antony is 'speaking now':

> *O Charmian!*
> *Where think'st thou he is now? Stands he, or sits he?*
> *Or does he walk? Or is he on his horse?*
> *O happy horse, to bear the weight of Antony!*
> *Do bravely, horse, for wot'st thou whom thou mov'st,*
> *The demi-Atlas of this earth, the arm*
> *And burgonet of men. He's speaking now,*
> *Or murmuring, 'Where's my serpent of old Nile?'*
> *For so he calls me. Now I feed myself*
> *With most delicious poison.*   (I, v, 18–27)

For so he calls her, and so he calls. He will call to her again. The
oxymoron of 'delicious poison' will become sentiently mixed up
with her definition of Antony, a few lines later, as 'that great
med'cine' (I, v, 36). And when the messenger, Alexas, arrives
with news of Antony, the account will seem to function as a
telepathic confirmation of Cleopatra's vision. Antony, we are
told, gets on his horse, as if to prepare for the speech to be
transmitted to his 'serpent of old Nile':

> *So he nodded*
> *And soberly did mount an arm-gaunt steed,*
> *Who neighed so high that what I would have spoke*
> *Was beastly dumbed by him.*   (I, v, 47–50)

In the peculiarity of this dramaturgic telepathy, Alexas's speech
and the thought of Antony's question ('Where's my serpent of
old Nile?') have been beastly dumbed.[6]

                              v

But then, before the entrance of Alexas, there is the remaining
serpentine passage of Cleopatra's speech – its turn from Antony's
speech, to an imperative addressed to his mind, to deathly invocation and prosopopoeia:

> *Think on me,*
> *That am with Phoebus' amorous pinches black,*
> *And wrinkled deep in time. Broad-fronted Caesar,*
> *When thou wast here above the ground, I was*
> *A morsel for a monarch: and great Pompey*
> *Would stand and make his eyes grow in my brow;*
> *There would he anchor his aspéct, and die*
> *With looking on his life.*   *(I, v, 27–34)*

Gnaeus, son of Pompey the Great, is brought back to life in Cleopatra's speech, only to 'die / With looking on his life'. Shakespeare's text undoubtedly plays on the contemporary, sexual sense of 'die', but this scarcely encapsulates the paronomastic force of the word. Rather, in *Antony and Cleopatra*, 'die' and 'death' disseminate, they dissolve. As does 'life'.

To be 'above the ground', to be alive, to be so intensely alive that, in Antony's words, 'There's not a minute of our lives should stretch / Without some pleasure now' (I, i, 46–7). And yet, there is no life in *Antony and Cleopatra*, no 'life' before or without the ecstatic affirmation and eroticism, or the uncanny commingling, of 'death'. It is partly this which makes the notion of telepathic love in *Antony and Cleopatra* so exorbitant, so idiomatically *beyond recall*. A horse, after all, can turn into a serpent; or what is not living can magically come to life. 'Life' and 'death' fuse undecidably, yet this aporia is figured as affirmative metamorphosis: 'Much is breeding,' as Antony says, 'Which, like the courser's hair, hath yet but life, / And not a serpent's poison' (I, ii, 180–2).

No longer the end-point or opposite of 'life', no longer teleologically governing or governed, what is 'death'? How many times does Cleopatra die, for example? As Enobarbus states, in response to Antony's proposal to return to Rome: 'Cleopatra, catching but the least noise of this, dies instantly, I have seen her die twenty times upon far poorer moment' (I, ii, 130–2). Foreshadowing her own description of Gnaeus's anchored 'aspéct', she will tell Antony: 'But sir, forgive me, / Since my becomings kill me when they do not / Eye well to you' (I, iii, 95–7). And later, after she has encouraged Antony's retreat to Alexandria, Eros will warn him: 'Most noble sir, arise, the Queen approaches: / Her head's declined, and death will seize her, but / Your

comfort makes the rescue' (III, xi, 46–8). Then, in keeping with
the tragi-comic irony of *Romeo and Juliet*, Cleopatra's mock-
death ('Mardian, go tell him I have slain myself' [IV, xiii, 7]) will
bring about the death of her lover which in turn will lead to her
own ...

Her own what? Cleopatra's 'final' 'death' requires to be seen in
the context of this heterogeneous multiplicity of 'deaths'. Her
'final' 'death' is articulated on to the 'death' of Antony. They will
seemingly have 'mingled ... entirely' (IV, xiv, 24–5). Antony
cannot live or die without Cleopatra, Cleopatra cannot live or die
without Antony: they seem to be encrypted within each other, as
if the name of each is 'buried' (IV, xiv, 34) in the other, buried in
the conjunctive 'and' of the play's title. From the beginning her
'death' is linked to his:

> Messenger: *Madam, madam –*
> Cleopatra: *Antonio's dead! If thou say so, villain,*
>   *Thou kill'st thy mistress ...*
>   *(II, v, 25–7)*

Cleopatra's death will always have been foreseen, not only thanks
to 'history' or to 'prophecy', and not only thanks to her own
foresight – for example, that she 'hath pursued conclusions infinite / Of easy ways to die' (V, ii, 351–2) or that she can declare,
in all the equivocal lightness of a rhyme: 'Now I see, I see / In
Fulvia's death, how mine received shall be' (I, iii, 64–5). Rather,
her death (and Antony's) will finally have been foreseen, if it is
possible to risk this paradox, insofar as it does not happen. Or: it
is happening all the time and it never happens. In the direction
of 'life', we are presented with a multiplicity of heterogeneous
'deaths': 'death' does not come at the end of 'life', 'death' is
happening repeatedly, continually, discandying or dissolving any
notion of 'life' that might ever have been opposed to it. In the
direction of 'death', we are presented with affirmation and erotic
triumph: 'death' is 'a lover's bed' (IV, xiv, 101) and you must 'run
into't' (IV, xiv, 100); 'death' is as uninjurious and as desirable as
'a lover's pinch' (V, ii, 291). And yet ...

VI

Playing a kind of 'fast and loose' (IV, xii, 28) with some of the threads which seem to put telepathy in touch with androgyny, with apocalypse and with aposiopesis, *Antony and Cleopatra* sees beyond foresight. There is telepathic vision. Everything goes dark. 'The long day's task is done' (IV, xiv, 35), 'the torch is out' (IV, xiv, 46), as Antony says. It is the end of the world: 'The star is fall'n'; 'And time is at his period' (IV, xiv, 106–7). The sun can fall or consume itself: 'O sun, / Burn the great sphere thou mov'st in! Darkling stand / The varying shore o' th'world!' (IV, xv, 9–11). For 'the bright day is done', as Iras puts it, 'And we are for the dark' (V, ii, 193–4). And beyond the 'visiting moon' beneath which there is 'nothing left remarkable', there is another, the final abnegation of another moon:

> *My resolution's placed, and I have nothing*
> *Of woman in me: now from head to foot*
> *I am marble-constant; now the fleeting moon*
> *No planet is of mine.* 　　*(V, ii, 238–41)*

Having lost gender or become sexually undecidable, become statuesque, a moonless still-life, what of the dark after that?

There is telepathic love, and it sees beyond death. 'The pretty worm of Nilus' (V, ii, 243) has come, and we return to the moving sculpture, the slithering apostrophes and prosopopoeias of the 'serpent of old Nile':

> *Give me my robe, put on my crown; I have*
> *Immortal longings in me. Now no more*
> *The juice of Egypt's grape shall moist this lip.*
> *Yare, yare, good Iras, quick. Methinks I hear*
> *Antony call. I see him rouse himself*
> *To praise my noble act. I hear him mock*
> *The luck of Caesar, which the gods give men*
> *To excuse their after wrath. Husband, I come.*
> *Now to that name my courage prove my title!*
> *I am fire and air; my other elements*
> *I give to baser life. So, have you done?*
> 　　　　　　　　*(V, ii, 276–86)*

The serpent whose 'biting is immortal' (246) will meet with Cleopatra's 'immortal longings'. Her speech moves from apostrophizing Iras to apostrophizing the 'dead' Antony. What begins as the supposition of hearing 'Antony call' ('Methinks') becomes steadily more assertive, until triumphantly direct: 'Methinks I hear / Antony call. I *see him*.... / I *hear him* ... / ... / Husband, I come.'

What makes this 'call' so irresistible is partly that it has been heard already. It is another instance of dramaturgic telepathy. For Antony calls Cleopatra, apostrophizes her in a soliloquy seemingly created for that uncanny purpose, when he believes she is already dead:

> *I will o'ertake thee, Cleopatra, and*
> *Weep for my pardon. So it must be, for now*
> *All length is torture. Since the torch is out,*
> *Lie down and stray no farther. Now all labour*
> *Mars what it does: yea, very force entangles*
> *Itself with strength. Seal then, and all is done.*
> *Eros! – I come my Queen – Eros! – Stay for me ...*
> (IV, xiv, 44–50)

'The torch is out', yet Cleopatra has still to live on, still to become 'fire and air': 'Husband, I come', 'I come my Queen ... Stay for me.' Their mutual apostrophes seem to lead into one another chiastically – the turning of a Möbius strip whereby it is no longer possible to know what is apostrophe or what prosopopoeia, at what point a voice 'above the ground' becomes a voice beyond the grave. For Cleopatra's affirmation of an 'after-life' (if, for what is perhaps the most affirmative death-scene in 'English Literature', this word were still appropriate or intelligible) is decisively and telepathically dependent also on Antony's:

> *I come my Queen ... Stay for me;*
> *Where souls do couch on flowers, we'll hand in hand,*
> *And with our sprightly port make the ghosts gaze.*
> *Dido and her Aeneas shall want troops,*
> *And all the haunt be ours.*   (IV, xiv, 50–4)

Death is beyond the light of a sun or moon, or even an 'eastern star' (V, ii, 304); it is 'the dark', it is 'darkness' (III, xiii, 181) itself. And yet there is light. Cleopatra can 'see'; there are flowers; 'the ghosts gaze'. There is sound: Antony can 'call', Cleopatra can 'hear'. There is touch: being 'hand in hand', the heaven of a kiss ... What is this vision of the senses, as if 'Condemning shadows quite' (V, ii, 100)?

VII

Of course the apocalypse, the never-ending night, befalls only Enobarbus, Eros, Antony, Iras, Cleopatra, Charmian. The thought of death drives them all to their deaths. There will be light after them even if, with the death of Cleopatra, Charmian can demand that 'golden Phoebus never be beheld / Of eyes again so royal!' (V, ii, 313–14). But *Antony and Cleopatra* moves, with its own kind of 'sprightly port', its own ghostly walk, step or hop, on an affirmative, telepathic edge which, unprecedentedly, suspends.[7] It is the 'medium' of being – as visible and invisible as air.

Cleopatra nurses the asp, as if she were the mother of her own death; she takes the 'delicious poison' of herself, the serpent:

As sweet as balm, as soft as air, as gentle.
O Antony! Nay, I will take thee too.
                               [Applying another asp to her arm
What should I stay –   [She dies
                                        (V, ii, 307–09)

Living, dying, the serpent, death, her own identity, or Antony's: all are indistinguishably 'as soft as air'. Apostrophizing the 'dead' ('O Antony!'), addressing 'another asp' ('Nay ...') as if she were administering rather than receiving, Cleopatra's final speech finishes with an aposiopesis: 'What should I stay –'. In other words, it does not finish. It cannot finish even if Charmian attempts to finish it: 'In this wild world?' (V, II, 310). Rather it is arrested on the word ('stay') which seems telepathically to call back to Antony's earlier ghostly call, 'Stay for me'.[8] Eclipse of

Antony's 'terrene moon': Cleopatra can or need no longer 'stay his time'. All will have dissolved, disintegrated, vanished. And yet 'stay' must stay. Everything will have been gathered up, drama-turgically telepathized in this suspense, in this 'air' of 'stay'. Aposiopesis and telepathy: suspension at the eclipse.

VIII

Perhaps it is the suspension of a kind of sleep, as Caesar unchar-acteristically intimates, gazing on Cleopatra's supposedly lifeless body, in the monument: 'she looks like sleep, / As she would catch another Antony / In her strong toil of grace' (V, ii, 342–4).[9] Then it would be another sleep, another Antony, another dream that's 'past the size of dreaming' (V, ii, 97). For it is Cleopatra's 'dream' of the 'demi-Atlas' Antony as a colossus which finally, and perhaps most of all, establishes this play's colossal quality, its exorbitance in relation to distinctions between 'life' and 'death', or 'nature' and 'fancy', its uncanny power as a kind of telepathic vision. There is never one Cleopatra, nor ever one Antony. Each is always divided, doubling and proliferating. The dream of 'another' Antony which Cleopatra describes to Dolabella is ostensibly without referent:

> Cleopatra: *Think you there was, or might be, such a man*
> *As this I dreamt of?*
> Dolabella: *Gentle madam, no.*
> Cleopatra: *You lie up to the hearing of the gods.*
> *But if there be, or ever were one such,*
> *It's past the size of dreaming: nature wants stuff*
> *To vie strange forms with fancy, yet t'imagine*
> *An Antony were nature's piece 'gainst fancy,*
> *Condemning shadows quite.*   *(V, ii, 93–100)*

The vision is impossible or impossibly contradictory. Cleopatra, in effect, tells Dolabella: You are lying, but you are telling the truth. 'But if': this marks the impossible at the same time as confirming that this passage, more than any other in the play, itself accedes to the colossal. Neither 'nature' nor 'fancy', and yet both at once, it is colossal beyond dreams. And in referring to the distance between the earth and 'the hearing of the gods', she evokes once more the colossal or sublime measure she has envisioned for herself, and for her 'Antony'.[10]

This is the passage, the words of Cleopatra's 'dream', telepathy in the colossus of mourning:

Cleopatra: *You laugh when boys or women tell their dreams;*
              Is't not your trick?
Dolabella: *I understand not, madam.*
Cleopatra: *I dreamt there was an Emperor Antony.*
              O such another sleep, that I might see
              But such another man!
Dolabella: *If it please ye –*
Cleopatra: *His face was as the heavens, and therein stuck*
              A sun and moon, which kept their course, and lighted
              The little O, the earth.
Dolabella: *Most sovereign creature –*
Cleopatra: *His legs bestrid the ocean, his reared arm*
              Crested the world; his voice was propertied
              As all the tunèd spheres, and that to friends.
              But when he meant to quail and shake the orb,
              He was as rattling thunder. For his bounty,
              There was no winter in 't; an autumn 'twas
              That grew the more by reaping. His delights
              Were dolphin-like, they showed his back above
              The element they lived in. In his livery
              Walked crowns and crownets; realms and islands were
              As plates dropped from his pocket.
Dolabella: *Cleopatra!*
                                      (V, ii, 74–92)

It is 'An Antony', precisely as Cleopatra describes; and it is not. It exists and does not exist. In this respect it has striking parallels with the colossos (or colossus) as it has been theorized by Jean Pierre Vernant, in his essay on 'The Representation of the Invisible and the Psychological Category of the Double'. Concerned with a commemorative but strange double, with something 'separate from the person who sees it', something which is neither 'nature' nor 'fancy', and which is at once existent ('a bridge') and non-existent (a 'gap'), Vernant's account would seem appropriate to the colossal Antony of Cleopatra's 'dream'-description.[11]

But there is another characteristic of the colossos to which Vernant gives special emphasis and which it may be possible to link up with what we have earlier or elsewhere suggested concerning notions of telekinesis, motion without motion, a 'sprightly port' or ghostly walk and a simultaneous capacity to 'stay'. Vernant declares: 'In the true sense of the term, colossoi are those who cannot move their legs in order to walk' (p. 313). For Vernant, it is the *'psuché'* which is 'forever in movement and forever elusive' and which the colossos is supposed to 'fix, immobilize, localize in one definite spot of the earth' (p. 313). Everything in Cleopatra's description stays still, and stays movement. The colossus of Antony does not move, yet the language in which this colossus is constructed consistently suggests otherwise: Antony's sun and moon keep their course; his arm is 'reared' and has 'crested'; he can 'quail' and 'shake', like 'rattling thunder'; his bounty is seen, visibly, still growing and still responsive to 'reaping'; it is, to borrow Pompey's word, 'crescent' (II, i, 10), still increasing; his back shows, in a dolphin-flash; things drop from him.

The uncanny motion without motion will have been inscribed, above all, in the overarching verb 'to bestride'. *OED* gives, as sense (2), 'To stand over (a place) with the legs astride; to straddle over, bestraddle'. This indication of the immobility of the colossus corresponds to Shakespeare's use of the verb in *Julius Caesar*:

> *Why, man, he doth bestride the narrow world*
> *Like a Colossus, and we petty men*
> *Walk under his huge legs* ... *(I, ii, 135–7)*

'To bestride', however, can also signify movement, as in *OED*, sense (4): 'To stride across, to step across with long strides.' The Oxford English Dictionary, as well as a continuing desire to seek or question the limits of dramaturgic telepathy, would take us to Aufidius's joy at seeing Coriolanus again:

> *more dances my rapt heart*
> *Than when I first my wedded mistress saw*
> *Bestride my threshold.   (IV, v, 116–18)*[12]

But now everything is still. 'Antony' is 'dead'. It is all in the past (tense). Even the crowns and crownets that 'walked' in Antony's livery:

> *His delights*
> *Were dolphin-like, they showed his back above*
> *The element they lived in. In his livery*
> *Walked crowns and crownets; realms and islands were*
> *As plates dropped from his pocket.*[13]

IX

The dolphin-image, which seems to bring 'Antony' into air, is used by Hazlitt in his essay on Shakespeare: 'His genius was his own. He had no objection to float down with the stream of common taste and opinion: he rose above it by his own buoyancy, and an impulse which he could not keep under, in spite of himself or others, and "his delights did shew most dolphin-like".'[14] Shakespeare's 'genius was his own', yet he is identified with Antony. And if Shakespeare is Antony, he is at least equally as much Cleopatra. Hazlitt of course, in his extraordinary reverie on 'the impassioned parts of Shakespeare's language' (p. 55), goes further:

The striking peculiarity of Shakespeare's mind was its generic quality, its power of communication with all other minds. . . . He not only had in himself the germs of every faculty and feeling, but he could follow them by anticipation, intuitively, into all their conceivable ramifications, through every change of fortune or conflict of passion, or turn of thought. . . . He had only to think of any thing in order to become that thing, with all the circumstances belonging to it. . . . Each of his characters is as much itself, and as absolutely independent of the rest, as well as of the author, as if they were living persons, not fictions of the mind. The poet may be said, for the time, to identify himself with the character he wishes

to represent, and to pass from one to another, like the same soul
successively animating different bodies. By an art like that of the
ventriloquist, he throws his imagination out of himself, and makes
every word appear to proceed from the mouth of the person in
whose name it is given. (pp. 47–50)

Following Hazlitt we are drawn to the irresistible hypothesis: Shakespeare *is* telepathy.

But certain qualifications necessarily surround such a formulation. And now the darkness is beginning, or has already begun, to fall. One might, rapidly, try to make out two final shapes, figures, thoughts, perhaps double, perhaps forked. First, in invoking 'Shakespeare' in this context, the name of an author and of a non-living individual, any notion of singularity and self-identity must be displaced. Insofar as a 'subject', a 'Shakespeare himself', is implied, this should be thought on the basis of irreducible multiplicity, dramatically decentred and fragmented, uncontrollably 'telepathic' in accordance with the notion of the subject elaborated out of the earlier reading of Wordsworth and Coleridge. In this respect the text of *Antony and Cleopatra* would constitute a kind of uncanny version, or turning, of 'Shakespeare', 'Shakespeare' as 'telepathy'.

Second, *Antony and Cleopatra* is, lest we forget, a war poem. It is this consideration, perhaps, which puts Shakespeare in eerie contact with, for example, John Keats and Wilfred Owen. But it is becoming difficult to make things out. Shakespeare's play is a war poem not only because it concerns wars in and of the Roman Empire, nor yet because it dramatizes that other war, the undecidably 'tragic' and erotic one between Antony and Cleopatra. It is a war poem in the sense of being at the threshold. It is like utterance confronting the hallucination of itself in the affirmation and fatality of dissolution. It stands on the very verge of the darkness, in the imminence of its own aposiopesis, at the eclipse of suspense, the bestriding of the threshold. It speaks into the air. It recognizes no 'subject', no 'self', no 'body' or 'identity', except as the multiple possibilities of 'air', the dislimning visibility and protean otherness of 'air'.

There 'we' are, we have seen the signs, the pageants that are there, the moonless dark:

Antony: Eros, thou yet behold'st me?
Eros: Ay, noble lord.
Antony: Sometime we see a cloud that's dragonish,
            A vapour sometime like a bear or lion,
            A towered citadel, a pendant rock,
            A forkèd mountain, or blue promontory
            With trees upon't that nod unto the world
            And mock our eyes with air. Thou hast seen these signs:
            They are black vesper's pageants.
Eros: Ay, my lord.
Antony: That which is now a horse, even with a thought
            The rack dislimns, and makes it indistinct
            As water is in water.
Eros: It does, my lord.
Antony: My good knave Eros, now thy captain is
            Even such a body. Here I am, Antony,
            Yet cannot hold   (IV, xiv, 1–14)

9

Raymond Chandler, Telephoning Home

In Raymond Chandler's *Playback* we may read: 'It is like a sudden scream in the night, but there is no sound. Almost always at night, because the dark hours are the hours of danger. But it has happened to me also in broad daylight – that strange, clarified moment when I suddenly know . . .'[1]

LINE 1

There is a certain silence. As Roger Caillois remarked, 'The story opens on a rigged set.'[2] What are the relations between telepathy and detective fiction?

This question immediately raises several others. There are, apparently, numerous leads or lines to follow. How unfold further the logic of *Emma* and its singular status as 'detective story'? How pursue the notion of crypt, the cryptic and cryptaesthetic? What might be made of the intriguing fact that the rise of psychical research and the formal emergence of 'telepathy', in the second half of the nineteenth century, coincided with the rise of detective fiction?[3] What of the undeniably 'magical' quality of detective fiction?[4] Or of the detective as a telepathic figure?[5]

The concerns of the following pages are comparatively narrow. They are confined to the work of Chandler, and to the consideration of one text in particular, namely *The Little Sister* (1949).[6] It is still a matter of a 'new' concept of literature, of a reinscription of the telepathic, of the network or labyrinth of a discursive formation in which any arguably 'ordinary' notion of telepathy will have opened or closed up into another or others. In the present reading, it will be a question of the telephone. The telephone will be my subject.

LINE 2

The Little Sister is the text about the ice-pick murders, about the brother and two sisters from Manhattan, Kansas, all of whom come to Bay City – Orrin Quest, the ostensibly blackmailing photographer; Leila Quest, alias Mavis Weld, the up-and-coming Hollywood filmstar; and Orfamay Quest, the 'little sister' who, perhaps rather bizarrely, comes to Philip Marlowe and initiates his investigations, by asking him to look for her brother. Bizarrely, because she will transpire to have been part of the criminal proceedings, up to and including the murder of Weepy Moyer, alias Steelgrave.[7]

It would be easy enough to show how Chandler's text conforms to the fundamentally cryptic structure described by Dennis Porter: 'In the process of telling one tale a classic detective story uncovers another. It purports to narrate the course of an investigation, but the "open" story of the investigation gradually unravels the "hidden" story of the crime.'[8] Chandler provides a gloss on this, in his 'Twelve Notes on the Mystery Story', when he asserts that 'The most effective way to conceal a simple mystery is behind another mystery', that is to say by 'making [the reader] solve the wrong problem'.[9] It would also be possible to show the extent to which Chandler's narrator, Philip Marlowe, is necessarily omniscient. There is an omniscient reserve of silence which Chandler himself identifies as a kind of formal necessity: 'Regardless of the candor of the first-person narrative there comes a time when the detective has made up his mind and yet does not communicate this to the reader.'[10]

Marlowe seems necessarily to be the one who, all along, knew what was going to happen and, at the same time, to be an *exemplum* or a parody of the participating historian. Todorov's claim, in his essay 'The Typology of Detective Fiction', that 'the author cannot, by definition, be omniscient as he was in the classical novel', is true only within certain limits.[11] It might be more productive to speak of a displaced or occult omniscience. But whose? The relation between Chandler and Marlowe is undecidable, and perhaps unthinkable without some concept or formulation of a double or double-agency. Then again, we may think, in ways which are not reducible to a sense of either author or narrator, that it is as if the text itself has a mind, as if it is the text that is asking, teasing, demanding that you read its mind.

LINE 3

The text 'opens' with a door, or more specifically with the writing or legend on a door, an elliptical legend: 'The pebbled glass door panel is lettered in flaked black paint: "*Philip Marlowe . . . Investigations*"' (*LS*, p. 385). The text 'opens' with two doors, with an invitation, and with a fly:

> *The door is locked, but next to it is another door with the same legend which is not locked. Come on in – there's nobody in here but me and a big bluebottle fly. But not if you're from Manhattan, Kansas. (p. 385)*

This is the opening and the whole strange omniscience of the narrative is inscribed in that reference to Kansas. It is an impossible double time-scheme: impossible because the time of the presence of this fly cannot strictly be amalgamated with the time of the knowledge of a particular person or persons from Manhattan, Kansas. The narrator could only speak of both with the benefit of impossible hindsight. And yet, the two times can *appear* to be amalgamated – in the form of the telephone. For the time of the narrative of *The Little Sister* is that eerie double-time, that two-timing with which only the telephone can connect, or those two temporal perspectives which can be apparently connected only by the telephone.

First the parodically cinematic setting: 'It was one of those clear, bright summer mornings we get in the early spring in California before the high fog sets in. The rains are over. The hills are still green and in the valley across the Hollywood hills you can see snow on the high mountains.' Then back to the fly:

> *I had been stalking the bluebottle fly for five minutes, waiting for him to sit down. He didn't want to sit down. He just wanted to do wing-overs and sing the prologue to* Pagliacci. *I had the fly*

swatter poised in mid-air and I was all set. There was a patch of
bright sunlight on the corner of the desk and I knew that sooner or
later that was where he was going to light. But when he did I
didn't even see him at first. The buzzing stopped and there he was.
And then the phone rang. (p. 385)

After the buzzing of *Pagliacci*, what is a telephone? What is the
time of a telephone? And what relation does the telephone have
to telepathy and literature? *The Little Sister* raises these questions,
like a receiver.

LINE 4

In a manner after which the examples of television and film, and
perhaps of American soap opera in particular, may seem facile,
Chandler's text at once dramatizes and investigates the extent to
which the telephone can structure a narrative. Or rather, the
extent to which the telephone structures and de-structures, orders
and disorders, sets up and upsets. On the one hand, and in
accordance with the most 'commonsensical' notions of reference
and representation, everything in Chandler's text depends on the
telephone: Marlowe has to be in his office in order to receive
phone calls in order for the narrative to have constituted itself and
to carry on; Marlowe has to show himself as the one who is 'right
handy with a pay phone' (p. 510) in order for the narrative to
continue, in order for it to have happened at all.

On the other hand, the text indicates that the telephone has a
much more peculiar character. 'The buzzing stopped and there
he was. And then the phone rang': even in this first allusion the
telephone is connected with death. At the very imminence of the
death of this anthropomorphic fly, 'shining and blue green and
full of sin' (p. 385), precisely when death would have occurred,
the phone rings instead. We may think we know what a telephone is; we may define it, as *Chambers* does, as 'an instrument
for reproducing sound at a distance, esp. by means of electricity'.
But even this definition can scarcely conceal an easily forgotten,
ignored or repressed fact, namely that a telephone re-produces
sound. The telephone does not transmit the voice itself (whatever

that might be). It is not the voice that is transmitted but electronic impulses which reproduce the auditory appearance or effect of a voice. In terms of habitual usage, the telephone is an anthropomorphism. It is anthropomorphic perhaps in a manner exemplary of the Western metaphysical, phonocentric system to which it ostensibly belongs.

Really, we have no idea what a telephone is, of what a voice is, or when or how. Least of all when it is linked up with the question of literature. To read *The Little Sister* in this way is necessarily to call into question the prevailing conception of Chandler's work as phonocentric, as consistently offering us a direct and distinctive transcription of the vitality and energy of 'real, everyday speech', most typically in the form of Marlowe and what Fredric Jameson has described as the 'narrator's voice-over' (p. 141). But whether we are trying to make valid hypotheses about a doubling of author ('Chandler') and narrator ('Marlowe'), or more generally trying to analyse the representation of voice (and silence) in the novel, the following, strange logic could be demonstrated: Where there is voice there is hallucination, hallucination which, because it is double, is also more than double: collective hallucination. Self-presence as a kind of collective hallucination then. For what Derrida (commenting on Rousseau and Saussure) has observed in relation to speech as 'the speculum of writing' involves a logic which could also be shown to affect the operation of hearing-oneself-speak:

> *Representation mingles with what it represents, to the point where one speaks as one writes, one thinks as if the represented were nothing more than the shadow or reflection of the representer. A dangerous promiscuity and a nefarious complicity between the reflection and the reflected which lets itself be seduced narcissistically. In this play of representation, the point of origin becomes ungraspable. There are things like reflecting pools, and images, an infinite reference from one to the other, but no longer a source, a spring. There is no longer a simple origin. For what is reflected is split in itself and not only as an addition to itself of its image. The reflection, the image, the double, splits what it doubles. The origin of the speculation becomes a difference. What can look at itself is not one; and the law of the addition of the origin to its representation, of the thing to its image, is that one plus one makes at least three.*[12]

Who is speaking? Who is listening? Derrida has commented elsewhere on the ' "normal" double hallucination [which] permits me to give myself to hear what I desire to hear'. Double because 'When I speak (to myself) without moving tongue and lips, I believe that I hear myself, although the source is other; or I believe that we are two, although everything is happening "in me" '. We live under what he calls this ' "regime" of normal hallucination'. Hence the paradox that 'To hear oneself is the most normal and the most impossible experience.'[13] This impossibility (which is among other things the impossibility of pure auto-affection) also marks the experience of speaking or listening to someone else.[14] But let us be clear about this: it does not require 'someone else' in order for there to be three; the logic of the more-than-double allows us to consider the notion of 'individual' perception or experience in terms of collective hallucination. To catch, however momently, the collective madness of the voice and of self-presence in so-called solitude; to be 'terrified by the difference within hearing-oneself-speak': more than once *The Little Sister* motions us towards such a thought.[15] It is a thought ineluctably sounded, inevitably exacerbated, by the repeated, haunting representations of telephone calls across the text.

Sometimes it is possible to have the peculiar experience of hearing two voices in one, even though of course there is, strictly, no human, no actual voice. As Marlowe reports of his phone conversation with George W. Hicks, alias Dr G. W. Hambleton: 'I was listening to the voice twice, once when I heard it and once when it echoed in my mind' (p. 414). At other times, off the phone, the human voice is specifically described in telephonic terms. Marlowe has been drugged by Dr Vincent Lagardie: 'A vague but enormously tall figure swung around in front of me and a mule kicked me in the chest. I sat down on the floor. "A little potassium hydrocyanide," a voice said, over the transatlantic telephone. "Not fatal, not even dangerous. Merely relaxing" ' (p. 494). Chandler's description of the voice is not in fact an analogy: there is no 'like' or 'as'. The voice speaks, 'over the transatlantic telephone'. That everyday phrase, 'over the phone', starts to resonate with a certain strangeness. The telephone is represented, or translates itself, as both isolated and single, and simultaneously as mediating and multiple – linking up all over the place. The 'over' seems the index of a certain intra-. There is a strange accumulation of 'trans'-effects ('over', 'transatlantic', 'telephone') within this apparently non-analogical identification of 'voice'. The voice, then, is always 'tele-', and over a distance impossible to decide. We might say that Marlowe (or Chandler) resorts to the metaphor of the telephone in order to convey the hazy, scarcely even semi-conscious perception of a voice. But that would be to valorize too quickly the concept of metaphor itself. It would fail to acknowledge the extent to which such terms as 'metaphor' or 'convey' or 'over' are themselves already telephonic. Where there is telephone there is metaphor, but 'metaphor' is itself telephonic. No metaphor without a telephone, then.

LINE 5

When that anthropomorphic phone rings and Marlowe answers it 'absently', he starts trying to describe it: 'The phone rang before I had quite started to worry about Mr Lester B. Clausen. I reached for it absently. The voice I heard was an abrupt voice, but thick and clogged, as if it was being strained through a curtain or somebody's long white beard' (p. 413). Is it possible here to get put through, put in contact with the celebrated topic of comparative metaphors in Chandler's work? How are those comparative metaphors, which are more or less his signature-effects or signature-tune, connected with the notion of telephone?

What is happening when a voice on the telephone is likened to 'being strained through a curtain or somebody's long white beard'? At least two likenings, two telephonic metaphors here, which together suggest at least two things. First, hilarity: as with other characteristic metaphors in Chandler's writing, the element of hyperbole ensures a certain absurdity, an excess which may find relief in laughter. The absurdity is heightened in this instance by the word 'strained', which (lavatorial homonymy aside) is more suggestive of pouring a cup of tea than of listening to (the hallucination of) a so-called human voice. And by the word 'somebody', which underlines the ever-seductive impression of casual, rapid speech, but which also throws open the comical speculation that the 'long white beard' belongs to 'somebody' else altogether. Second, revelation: whether we imagine the beard as belonging to God, or Moses, or Father Christmas, or some fantastical other, the notion of the 'curtain' inevitably gathers up a certain religious or mystical aura. The telephone is associated with concealment and unveiling, with the apocalyptic, with revelation in a religious sense.

The telephone rings and it could be anybody, or anything. It might be the Queen of Sheba. It might come from anywhere and there's never any knowing how long it might last or how suddenly it might cease. For people are repeatedly hanging up in Chandler's texts and it would certainly be legitimate to read this phenomenon in relation to the rhetorical figure of aposiopesis and connect it with Chandler's entire strategy of generating suspense. Hanging up might almost be called the aposiopesis of aposiopesis in that it can be imposed on the speech-flow of addressor or addressee; or it can be imposed on silence itself. It recurs relentlessly in Chandler's texts, as if punctuating, and puncturing, time itself: the violence of silence. More than once Chandler, or Marlowe, characterizes the violence of hanging up by reference to the face, and consequently to a kind of de-facement. Yet the possibility of such de-facement seems to haunt the very sound of the telephone ringing, whether one answers or not. The phone rings, it is Miss Gonzales:

> '*The hell with you, darling,*' *she said, and hung up in my face.*
> *I turned out the light and left. Halfway down the hall I met a man looking at numbers. He had a special delivery in his hand. So I had to go back to the office and put it in the safe. And the phone rang again while I was doing this.*
> *I let it ring. I had had enough for one day. I just didn't care. It could have been the Queen of Sheba with her cellophane pyjamas on – or off – I was too tired to bother. My brain felt like a bucket of wet sand.* (p. 450)

At what point stop the citation, hang up on the text? Let's at least note that Marlowe here changes his mind, picks up the receiver and gets the 'twittery little voice' (p. 450) of Orfamay Quest who tells him that she has had a telephone call from her brother Orrin and that ' "there's murder in it, Mr Marlowe, and murder is a very nasty word" ' (p. 451). Another illustration, then, of the way in which the structure and movement of the narrative of the text depends on the telephone. The telephone is constitutive. But what is a telephone? Inescapably anthropomorphic, unsettling the very notions of voice and metaphor, it is wired up with uncanny revelation, the fantastical, and death.

LINE 6

Finally *The Little Sister* suggests that the question of the telephone cannot be dissociated from that of telepathy. The telephone plays a kind of partner or accomplice, even a double. The text contains what might be called, in the most 'traditional' respect, telepathic instances, just as it contains apparent denials of the telepathic. And such moments are not necessarily directly identifiable with telephones. But that is not the point: what matters is a certain tele-logic in accordance with which the notions of telephone and telepathy are, however strangely, being put in touch.

Sometimes things just happen. There is no need to read anything into it: ' "... Tramp on it, friend. Make speed," ' concludes the voice behind the curtain. 'The phone clicked in my ear. I hung up. For no reason a pencil rolled off the desk and broke its point on the glass doo-hickey under one of the desk legs' (p. 414). Sometimes you just find yourself saying things and you don't know why; it seems completely crazy, and yet it turns out to be exactly the truth. As, most dramatically, in the case of Marlowe's introduction to Weepy Moyer, alias Steelgrave (see p. 534):

> 'My name's Marlowe, Philip Marlowe. It's extremely unlikely that we've met. And, strange to relate, I never heard of you, Mr Steelgrave. And I wouldn't give a damn, even if your name was Weepy Moyer.' I never knew quite why I said that. There was nothing to make me say it, except that the name had been mentioned. A peculiar stillness came over his face. A peculiar fixed look. (p. 441)

Sometimes you just get a funny feeling. There might be 'no reason' for it, and yet still 'some reason'. This, as *Daniel Deronda* has made clear, is the contradiction that we live, whatever that may mean. There's the nasty little man Marlowe has to deal with at Orrin Quest's old apartment. After relieving him of his 'heater' and a very sharp skiv, Marlowe recounts:

> *He went softly past me and down the wooden steps from the back porch. His footsteps tapped to the street and faded. They sounded very much like Orfamay's heels clicking along the corridor in my office building. And for some reason I had that empty feeling of having miscounted the trumps. No reason for it at all. Maybe it was the steely quality about the little man. No whimper, no bluster, just the smile, the whistling between the teeth, the light voice and the unforgetting eyes. (p. 398)*

If the telephone has an unusual capacity for generating such feelings, there is 'no reason' for it, really. Thus we have another Jane Austen-Jacques Derrida crossing, as Marlowe recalls: 'I pulled the phone towards me. It rang just as I got my hand on it' (p. 457). Something else seems to be crossed up here as well, complicating the chiasmus: does he pull the phone even before his hand touches it? Or as another example, on a later occasion, we encounter Marlowe as if pleading:

> *Let the telephone ring, please. Let there be somebody to call up and plug me into the human race again. Even a cop. Even a Maglashan. Nobody has to like me. I just want to get off this frozen star.*
> *The telephone rang. (p. 517)*

Such instances would perhaps be less provoking, less uncanny, if they did not seem to be participating in a more general telepathic drift or slide. Things intensify markedly from the time when Marlowe goes to Dr Vincent Lagardie's establishment, looking for Orrin Quest. Presentiment begins to pervade: 'Dr Lagardie turned back to me. "Shall we go into my office?" We went across through another door leading to a hallway. I walked on eggs. The atmosphere of the house was charged with foreboding' (p. 487). Marlowe tries to question the doctor, but soon finds himself admitting: 'I'm just talking.... Waiting for something to happen. Something's going to happen in this house. It's leering at

me from corners' (p. 488). Lagardie himself draws attention to it:
'You may have noticed a certain atmosphere and strain about this
house' (p. 489). He explains it, rather enigmatically, by saying
that Lieutenant Maglashan has recently visited, and then, equally
enigmatically, offers to phone him. Marlowe's response resonates
beyond the quick gag: ' "Go ahead, call him," I said. "I just
stopped off here on my way to commit suicide" ' (p. 490).[16]
Marlowe goes on, as he says, 'trying to read [Lagardie's] mind'
(p. 491), until he finds his own mind has 'slowed to a turtle's
gallop' (p. 494) as he falls under the influence of the potassium
hydrocyanide described over the transatlantic telephone.

From then on things become still more explicit. Marlowe
regains consciousness: Dr Vincent Lagardie has evidently
vamoosed. Then he sees a figure slowly coming towards him and,
'for no reason at all' (p. 496), thinks of Orfamay's father, Mr
Quest, whom he has never met, 'back there on the porch in
Manhattan, Kansas'; and it turns out in fact to be the dying figure
of Orrin P. Quest, his son. But this does not dissolve the strange
'atmosphere' of the house: 'the house was still silent and waiting'
(p. 499), we are told. The 'quest' is not yet at an end.[17] Marlowe
leaves but he is being watched as he does so, this time by Orfamay Quest, who later explains herself over the phone, giving rise
to a brief exchange of admissions about 'psychic' experience:

> '. . . I tried to go after you when you came out but I don't know
> the streets down there at all. I lost you. So I went back [to Dr
> Lagardie's].'
> 'What did you go back for?'
> 'I don't really know. I thought you looked kind of funny when
> you came out of the house. Or maybe I just had a feeling. He being
> my brother and all. So I went back and rang the bell. And nobody
> answered the door. I thought that was funny too. Maybe I'm
> psychic or something. All of a sudden I seemed to have to get into
> that house. And I didn't know how to do it, but I had to.'
> 'That's happened to me,' I said. (p. 506)

And then we drive to the climactic scene, in the big house up
at Stillwood Heights. Marlowe is there and it is dark and silent.
The idea of anything 'psychic' or 'telepathic' is apparently to be
treated with wary scepticism: 'I stopped breathing and listened.

Tigers could be in the darkness watching me. Or guys with large guns, standing flatfooted, breathing softly with their mouths open. Or nothing and nobody and too much imagination in the wrong place.' He looks for a light switch but cannot find one, and this leads to a rather different declaration: 'maybe you just spoke and said: "Let there be light," and a mike picked it up and turned the voice vibration into a low-power electrical impulse and a transformer built that up to enough voltage to throw a silent mercury switch. I was psychic that night' (p. 527). Marlowe puts the thought of a bizarre kind of telephone-system directly in touch with the 'psychic'. He calls out and there is only silence. And yet magically it happens, out of the silence: 'And then amber light began to grow high up behind the cornice that circumnavigated the huge room. It brightened very slowly, as if controlled by the rheostat panel in a theatre' (p. 527).

Of course we are given some sort of rationalization of this: Mavis Weld is there; the room is 'Not quite empty' (p. 528) after all. But notions of the 'psychic' and telepathic continue to mark the narrative. Marlowe gets introduced to the corpse of Steelgrave, apparently murdered by Weld whom Marlowe nevertheless tells to 'Get going' (p. 537). He also makes a point of trying to ensure that her friend Miss Gonzales does not get caught up in the murder either. He telephones her and tells her what she should tell the police, if questioned. Their conversation concludes:

> She laughed softly. 'Amigo, you understand me very well.'
> 'Good night,' I said.
> 'One moment, you have not told me what happened.'
> 'I haven't even telephoned you.'
> I hung up and turned. (pp. 536–7)

A silent call, a telephone call which is not a telephone call, which never happened, will have allowed Miss Gonzales to gather information as if telepathically. Then Marlowe telephones the police and as he waits it is as if he is waiting for a future he has already dreamed: 'No siren. But the sound of a car coming up the hill at last. I went out to meet it, me and my beautiful dream' (p. 539).

The police don't seem very pleased with him. As they leave, Marlowe recalls: 'I stared hard at French. He looked at me as if I was the wallpaper. His eyes didn't seem to see me at all' (p. 544). After a night at the station, playing cards with a man whose name is never revealed, there is another uncanny moment:

> *At eight-fifteen Christy French came in and stood with his hat on the back of his head and dark smudges under his eyes.*
>
> *I looked from him to the little man across the table. But he wasn't there any more. The cards weren't there either. Nothing was there but a chair pushed in neatly to the table and the dishes we had eaten off gathered on a tray. For a moment I had that creepy feeling. (p. 546)*

The use of the demonstrative pronoun 'that' gives the uncanniness a twist: it is 'that' creepy feeling, the one we all know, the one that we don't need to talk about, as if we all knew it already. After French leaves, Marlowe observes: 'I could have done the same, but I just sat there and stared across the table at the wall' (p. 548). Strange silence and the identification with a wall, once again. For finally, when the secretary tells him he can go through to the D. A.'s office, it is as if he is still staring at this wall. So the secretary says, 'Hit him in the face with a wet glove', and Marlowe replies:

> *'Who said that?'*
> *'It's the wall,' she said. 'It talks. The voices of the dead men who have passed through on the way to hell.'*
> *I went out of the room walking softly and shut the door against the closer so that it wouldn't make any noise. (p. 549)*

The District Attorney is pragmatic and understanding: he lets Marlowe off. Everything seems to be dealt with. Marlowe goes back to his office and it seems as if we have reached the end. He looks the place over and indulges in some anthropomorphism of the most telephonically-oriented kind: ' "Hello," I said. I was just talking to the office equipment . . . I was talking to the pebbled glass panel and the grimy woodwork and the pen set on the desk and the tired, tired telephone' (pp. 553–4). All of this can be summed up, apparently, as a case of 'talking to the scales on an alligator, the name of the alligator being Marlowe'. And that leads to the last and perhaps most dramatic instance. He decides it is time for a drink:

> *I reached down and put the bottle of Old Forester up on the desk. It was about a third full. Old Forester. Now who gave you that, pal? That's green label stuff. Out of your class entirely. Must have been a client. I had a client once.*
>
> *And that got me thinking about her, and maybe I have stronger thoughts than I know. The telephone rang, and the funny little precise voice sounded just as it had the first time she called me up.* (p. 554)

It is 'the little sister'. It is the uncanny return.

Orfamay Quest's phonecall will be followed by her reappearance in Marlowe's office and the revelation of her involvement in all the proceedings to date, in particular in the murder of Steelgrave. And Chandler's text will rapidly conclude with revelations of the involvement of Miss Gonzales, in particular in the murder of Orrin Quest, and finally with the joint-deaths of Miss Gonzales and her 'discarded' husband (p. 564) (as it evidently transpires), Dr Vincent Lagardie. In terms of narrative complexity, all of this will prove to be 'too complicated' for Marlowe himself properly to be able 'to reason it out' (p. 570).

But it is Orfamay's final telephone call which seems to mark the decisive turning-point in the closing of the narrative. It is an uncanny return in several senses. The text gives special emphasis, for example, to the fact that her 'voice sounded just as it had the first time'. Then, when she comes into the office, she looks as if she is 'right back where she started that first morning' (p. 554). Marlowe further observes: 'She put her bag on the desk and drew a line along the desk with her fingertip. That was just like the first time too' (p. 555). Finally it is an uncanny repetition of the telephone in connection with the telepathic. It reintroduces the notion of the telephone as having some uncanny capacity for organizing narrative itself, for amalgamating the double-time or, better, the irreducibly plural, 'telepathic' time of the narrative. Without needing to call up any further evidence, let us then underscore one of the things which Chandler's text seems to be suggesting: there are no telephones, no voices or transmission, without the telepathic scenario. Orfamay's phonecall is a return not only to the eerily rigged setting of the so-called beginning of the text, but also a return to a moment like the one when Marlowe seems so desperate for the phone to ring. We cited it earlier: 'Let the telephone ring, please. Let there be somebody to call up and plug me into the human race again.... Nobody has to like me. I just want to get off this frozen star. [New paragraph] The telephone rang' (p. 517).

PARTY-LINE

The violence and the silence of a new paragraph. And time perhaps to suggest one or two final lines of thought. First, regarding this notion of uncanny repetition. There is a compulsive (and even compelling) kind of repetitiveness which, as Jameson has intimated, seems to lie at the heart of Chandler's work. Thus he speaks of Chandler's texts as being 'peopled with recurrent phantoms', noting the repetition of a particular 'kind of plot construction in all his books' and the 'persistence' of a certain 'fixed intellectual purpose' (p. 142). Then at a so-called stylistic level, there are the comparative metaphors. These are the metaphors, like telephonic quickfire, which suggest that hyperbole is an almost extinct species, like humanity, and that this may be the last chance to see some. They have a force of absurdity, laughter and truth, producing a sense of familiarity or recognition, as if we knew them before. Like the telephone, they seem marked by death. They can seem 'tired', and with the sort of despair which identifies them with a certain apocalyptic discourse, the tradition of fiction out of which Chandler's texts have been elaborated, where the 'characters lived in a world gone wrong, a world in which, long before the atomic bomb, civilization had created the machinery for its own destruction'.[18]

The Little Sister contains more than its fair share. Given a rather thespian display by his potential new client, Orfamay Quest, Marlowe explains how he 'reacted to that just the way a stuffed fish reacts to cut bait' (p. 391). There's Miss Dolores

Gonzales who, by a provocative synaesthesia, 'smelled the way the Taj Mahal looked by moonlight' (p. 434), who had a 'mouth as red as a new fire engine' (p. 501) and who 'made a couple of drinks in a couple of glasses you could almost have stood umbrellas in' (p. 435). There's the description of the man with 'the sky-blue gaberdine slacks' who 'wore a two-tone leisure jacket which would have been revolting on a zebra' (p. 444). There's Sheridan Ballou whose office 'had everything in it but a swimming pool': 'There was a concert grand Steinway in the corner and a lot of glass and bleached wood furniture and a desk about the size of a badminton court and chairs and couches and tables and a man lying on one of the couches with his coat off and his shirt open over a Charvet scarf you could have found in the dark by listening to it purr' (p. 465). There is Lieutenant Moses Maglashan, a 'big burly man', who 'had a jaw like a park bench' (p. 508). There is the Californian nightlife: 'The Dancers was a blaze of light. The terrace was packed. The parking lot was like ants on a piece of overripe fruit' (p. 520). There is the kitchen at Stillwood Heights which 'was big enough for a dancing class' (p. 526). There is Lee Farrell, 'one of the hottest trouble-shooting lawyers in the country', who 'looked as if it would cost a thousand dollars to shake hands with him' (p. 550). And there is the Château Bercy: 'Its colour scheme was bile green, linseed poultice brown, sidewalk grey and monkey-bottom blue. It was as restful as a split lip' (p. 562).[19]

It is difficult not to feel the force of a certain uncanny repetitiveness in all this; but it is not something which need be identified with 'Chandler' himself, whatever that might mean: as elsewhere, it is a matter of at least the double, right from the start. Indeed it may be that Chandler's texts, in theatricalizing various forms of repetition, are merely exemplary of what is called 'detective fiction'. Following Freud's interlinking of the notions of repetition compulsion and death drive, the popularity of such fiction might then appear in a distinctly unbenign light. And perhaps here too we may be tempted to seek an explanation for the prominence, in *The Little Sister*, of telepathy in its so-called traditional sense. The telepathic or 'psychic' aspects might be seen as corroborating the association, first outlined by Maria Torok, between telepathy and the death drive.

But there are at least two good reasons for hesitating here. First reason: our concern is with the strangeness of literature and fiction, with the uncanniness of *writing* as such. This includes, for example, the question of the intimate (and for Freud in some ways no doubt unrecognized) relations between writing and silence, between representation and death.[20] Thus, even in the most prosaic respect, we might consider the recurrent structure whereby, in Chandler's texts, we are left with a corpse or corpses. Jameson has emphasized the consistency with which Chandler's novels effect a 'very complicated esthetic deception' (p. 147): they 'bring us up short, without warning, against the reality of death itself, stale death' (p. 148). Ending with the assertive and un-expected presentation of the deaths of Miss Gonzales and Dr Lagardie, *The Little Sister* would seem a good example of such a patterning:

> *When they cracked the door he was sitting on the couch holding her pressed against his heart. His eyes were blind and there was bloody foam on his lips. He had bitten through his tongue.*
>
> *Under her left breast and tight against the flame-coloured shirt lay the silver handle of a knife I had seen before. The handle was in the shape of a naked woman. The eyes of Miss Dolores Gonzales were half-open and on her lips there was the dim ghost of a provocative smile. (p. 571)*

Epiphonema of the prosopo-poetic drive: insofar as the text leaves us with a face, it would be this 'dim ghost of a provocative smile' – the 'Hippocrates smile' (p. 571) as the ambulance intern calls it. It recalls the death, the final face, of Orrin P. Quest: 'Something happened to his face and behind his face, the indefin-able thing that happens in that always baffling and inscrutable moment, the smoothing out, the going back over the years to the age of innocence. The face now had a vague inner amusement, an almost roguish lift at the corners of the mouth' (p. 498). As prosopopoeia, the text has this 'lift': it offers a ghostly face at once dead and smiling. The relations between telepathy, writing and death remain undecidable, on the line.

Second reason: our concern is not with the question of 'tele-pathy' in its supposedly ordinary sense. Rather it is with the ways in which Chandler's text permits an altogether different articulation of the telepathic, in particular in terms of the telephone. At this point we might recall, then, that there is no face in *The Little Sister* which is not also affected by the de-facing force of the telephone. In his Manifesto entitled 'Personism', the New York poet Frank O'Hara asserted that he had, in 1959, discovered a new poetry by realizing that it was not necessary for him to write down on paper a poem which he wanted to address to a certain person: he could instead simply telephone him or her.[21] According to this hypothesis, literary texts could be considered as kinds of telephone calls. The apparent phonocentrism of Marlowe's 'voice-over' narration may seem invitingly apt in this context. But our analysis of *The Little Sister* and the telephone would offer no such comfort. Cryptically, as it were beneath the phonocentric soundtrack of the text, there are quite other notions of telephony operating. The telephone is uncanny, connected to apocalypse, nothingness and death, even for 'Marlowe'. Thus, for example, the telephone may never ring again: 'I put my papers away in the drawer, straightened the pen stand, got out a duster and wiped off the glass and then the telephone. It was dark and sleek in the fading light. It wouldn't ring tonight. Nobody would call me again. Not now, not this time. Perhaps not ever' (p. 517).

But who is Marlowe? 'Marlowe' is not only a fictive character and fictive voice, but also a figure of precisely nothing or nobody, even (or especially) when he is supposedly talking to himself: 'I put the duster away folded with the dust in it, leaned back and just sat, not smoking, not even thinking. I was a blank man. I had no face, no meaning, no personality, hardly a name' (p. 517). Reduced to the faceless if ironic terror of the mere cipher of a name, 'Marlowe' rings 'Mavis Weld': 'It rang and rang and rang. . . . I guess there's nobody home. Nobody home to you. I hung up. Who would you like to call now? You got a friend somewhere that might like to hear your voice? No. Nobody' (p. 517). 'Marlowe' has at least two telephones. He has a home number, as he tells Orfamay Quest, early on: 'Call me any time then. My home number is in the phone book, too. Bristol Apartments, Apartment 428' (p. 394). But this is a telephone of which we hear no more. Nor do we ever hear of Marlowe telephoning home. 'Nobody home': rather than guaranteeing the familiar reassurances of communication between two specific individuals, the telephone becomes precisely the unhomely, the *unheimlich* or uncanny. Uncannily, then, it pervades the silence between 'Let the telephone ring, please . . .' and 'The telephone rang' (p. 517). It is Miss Gonzales ringing – in other words what Marlowe gets is the wrong voice, even if this voice speaks of 'she' (p. 517), Mavis Weld. But, in a more radical way, it is always the wrong voice; the telephone is always contaminated with otherness, and contaminating silence. As Roland Barthes observes, in a particularly haunting passage in *A Lover's Discourse*:

> *Freud, apparently, did not like the telephone, however much he may have liked* listening. *Perhaps he felt, perhaps he foresaw that the telephone is always a* cacophony, *and that what it transmits is the ₁wrong voice, the false communication . . . First of all, this [loved] voice, when it reaches me, when it is here, while it (with great difficulty) survives, is a voice I never entirely recognize; as if it emerged from under a mask (thus we are told that the masks used in Greek tragedy had a magical function: to give the voice a chthonic origin, to distort, to alienate the voice, to make it come from somewhere under the earth). Then, too, on the telephone the other is always in a situation of departure; the other departs twice over, by voice and by silence: whose turn is it to speak? We fall silent in unison: crowding of two voids. I'm going to leave you, the voice on the telephone says with each second.*[22]

The Little Sister takes the strange relations between telephones and silence to a kind of limit. It generates the suspense in which, as Chandler stresses, 'Everybody waits while a telephone rings' (p. 487). In this respect, we might say, the novel *is* that telephone. But at the same time it inscribes uncanny silence, inviting us to think of the telephone ringing *in silence*. It may be like the silence of Marlowe's call to Miss Dolores. It may be like the silence of 'nobody home', or between 'Let the telephone ring' and 'The telephone rang'. It may be a buzzing or a ringing in your ears, like the silence before the bluebottle starts again, right back at the beginning. Or it may be a ringing like that of 'Just one bell. . . . Very slow. Tolling is the word' (p. 432).

We might conclude by returning to Frank O'Hara's proposal and attempting to formulate it differently. Literature would be a telephony. Linked up through a kind of intratextual exchange, literary texts would be telephone calls. But to whom? For the notion of telephone here must be understood in accordance with telepathy – with the uncanny and death; with anthropomorphism, collective hallucination and irreducible effects of party-line; with the heterogeneous logic of spacing, strange silences, hanging up and de-facement; with the undecidability of addressor and addressee, and the dissemination of voice as such; with a radical, anostalgic homelessness and the impossibility of telephoning home.[23] It is what is figured, for example, in August Strindberg's *Easter* (1901), when the telephone starts ringing, for 'no reason' at all, and there is no one there.[24] It is the force of literature – the irruption of that telephonic or telepathic network in which, however unthinkably, we must also conceive ourselves.

Notes

Generally speaking, the first reference to any book or article provides full details of publication, together with an indication of any subsequently abbreviated title. Otherwise the chief abbreviations are as follows:

Chambers: *Chambers English Dictionary*, ed. Catherine Schwarz, George Davidson, Anne Seaton and Virginia Tebbit (Cambridge: Chambers and Cambridge University Press, 1988).

OED: *The Oxford English Dictionary*, 2nd edn., prepared by J. A. Simpson and E. S. C. Weiner, 20 vols. (Oxford: Clarendon Press, 1989).

PFL: *The Pelican Freud Library*, trans. James Strachey, Alix Strachey and Alan Tyson, ed. James Strachey, Angela Richards, Alan Tyson and Albert Dickson, 15 vols. (Harmondsworth: Penguin, 1973–86).

1 INTRODUCTION

1 'First Report of the Literary Committee' (9–12–1882) by W. F. Barrett, C. C. Massey, Rev. W. Stainton Moses, Frank Podmore, Edmund Gurney and Frederic W. H. Myers, in *Proceedings of the Society for Psychical Research*, vol. I, pt. 2 (London: Trübner, 1883), 147.

2 See, for example, Michael A. Thalbourne, *A Glossary of Terms Used in Parapsychology* (London: Heinemann, 1982), 81.

3 *Proceedings of the Society for Psychical Research*, vol. I, pt. 2, vi.

4 The development of the word 'empathy' would no doubt provide interesting parallels and connections. Defined in *OED* as 'The power of projecting one's personality into (and so fully comprehending) the object of contemplation', the first use of 'empathy' is given as 1904, based on a translation of the German term *Einfühlung* used by Theodor Lipps. It is striking that the original context is specifically the field of aesthetics. *OED* cites, for example, *The Academy* for 17 August 1912: '[Lipps] propounded the theory that the appreciation of a work of art depended upon the capacity of the spectator to project his personality into the object of contemplation. One had to "feel oneself into it" ... This mental process he called by the name of *Einfühlung*, or, as it has been translated, *Empathy*'. Despite the potential value and significance of tracing its popularization and/or Americanization, for reasons of space a detailed account of the concept of empathy cannot be attempted here. Likewise an analysis of the relations of the historical emergence of 'telepathy' to 'Orientalism'. The notion of telepathy in non-

occidental and colonial literature would certainly merit more than one full-length study; and from the outset it would perhaps be necessary to enquire to what extent indeed one would be possible without the other.

5 Janet Oppenheim, *The Other World: Spiritualism and Psychical Research in England, 1850–1914* (Cambridge: Cambridge University Press, 1985), 1. Further page references are given in the text. It should perhaps be stressed that Oppenheim is not claiming that Christian belief and an involvement in spiritualism or psychical research were incompatible. One of her most memorable counter-examples is Thomas Colley, the 'Beneficed Clergyman of the Church of England' of whom she drily observes: 'Despite his unorthodoxy, Colley remained comfortably settled at Stockton [in Warwickshire] and continued to promote spiritualism on rectory letterhead' (p. 71).

6 Cited by Gordon Claridge, in *Origins of Mental Illness: Temperament, Deviance and Disorder* (Oxford: Blackwell, 1985), 166.

7 See, for instance, *The Other World*, p. 30, and pp. 236–49.

8 See, for example, *The Wolf Man's Magic Word: A Cryptonymy*, by Nicolas Abraham and Maria Torok, trans. Nicholas Rand (Minneapolis: University of Minnesota Press, 1986), especially Torok's 'Afterword: What is Occult in Occultism? Between Sigmund Freud and Sergei Pankeiev Wolf Man' (pp. 84–106), and 'Telepathy' by Jacques Derrida, trans. Nicholas Royle, in *Oxford Literary Review*, vol. 10 (1988), 3–41.

9 I explore this relation in greater detail below, in particular in 'On Second Sight: George Eliot' and 'A Letter on Poetry'. For two stimulating recent studies of the concept of sympathy, see David Marshall's *The Figure of Theater: Shaftesbury, Defoe, Adam Smith, and George Eliot* (New York: Columbia University Press, 1986) and his *The Surprising Effects of Sympathy: Marivaux, Diderot, Rousseau, and Mary Shelley* (London: University of Chicago Press, 1988). Marshall's conception of 'sympathy' is related rather to Adam Smith's *The Theory of Moral Sentiments* (1759), in fact, than to a reading of David Hume's *A Treatise of Human Nature* (1739–40). *The Figure of Theater* contains an extremely good account of 'sympathy' in Smith's work: see his Chapter 7, 'Adam Smith and the Theatricality of Moral Sentiments' (pp. 167–92). At the start of *The Surprising Effects of Sympathy*, he cites Smith's candid expansion of the definition of this term: 'Pity and compassion are words appropriated to signify our fellow-feeling with the sorrow of others. Sympathy, though its meaning was, perhaps, originally the same, may now, however, without much impropriety, be made use of to denote our fellow-feeling with any passion whatever' (p. 3). See Adam Smith, *The Theory of Moral Sentiments*, ed. D. D. Raphael and A. L. Macfie (Oxford: Clarendon Press, 1976), especially Chapter I, 'Of SYMPATHY' (pp. 9–13), and Chapter II, 'Of the Pleasure of Mutual Sympathy' (pp. 13–16). As the editors suggest, his 'unusually wide definition of "sympathy"' (p. 10) is part of the process whereby sympathy becomes what they call, in their Introduction, 'the basis of social behaviour' and 'the core of Smith's explanation of moral *judgement*' (pp. 20–1). For a rather different perspective, see Jonathan Crewe, *Hidden Designs: The*

Critical Profession and Renaissance Literature (London: Methuen, 1986), especially Chapter 2, 'Sympathy' (pp. 35–69). Crewe attempts 'to take the question of sympathy seriously as a phenomenon specific to the Renaissance' (p. 39) and contends that 'if sympathy has its prehistory in the Renaissance, its real emergence and disappearance coincide almost exactly with those of the European Enlightenment' (p. 41). His account usefully emphasizes the earlier, 'occult' associations of this term: 'For the Renaissance, "sympathy" is in the first instance an animistic phenomenon, one that implies the existence of occult powers of attraction joining like to like throughout the cosmos. Bound up with this attraction are natural forms of fellow-feeling, kinship and pity, but beyond these static bonds or forms of identification sympathy must logically entail a kind of harmonic repetition' (p. 40).

10 Henry George Liddell and Robert Scott, *A Greek–English Lexicon*, rev. edn. (Oxford: Oxford University Press, 1968), 1680.

11 Joseph M. Backus, 'Parapsychology and Literature', in *Handbook of Parapsychology*, ed. Benjamin B. Wolman (New York: Van Nostrand Reinhold, 1977), 781, 784.

12 'On Colleges and Philosophy: Jacques Derrida with Geoff Bennington', in *Postmodernism: ICA Documents*, ed. Lisa Appignanesi (London: Free Association Books, 1989), 218.

13 See Derrida's 'The Time of a Thesis: Punctuations', in *Philosophy in France Today*, ed. Alan Montefiore (Cambridge: Cambridge University Press, 1983), 34–50. Around 1957, Derrida says, he registered his thesis topic, entitled 'The ideality of the literary object' (p. 36). He was at this time concerned with 'bending, more or less violently, the techniques of transcendental phenomenology to the needs of elaborating a new theory of literature' (p. 37). He adds: 'For I have to remind you, somewhat bluntly and simply, that my most constant interest, coming even before my philosophical interest I should say, if this is possible, has been directed towards literature, towards that writing which is called literary' (p. 37).

14 This would be most obviously the case with *Glas*, trans. John P. Leavey, Jr., and Richard Rand (Lincoln: University of Nebraska Press, 1986). But, as I hope to make clear, such mutual contamination is very much at work elsewhere, most specifically (in the present context) in his 'Telepathy'.

15 For explorations of the extremely problematic question of speaking on behalf of 'madness', see Michel Foucault, *Madness and Civilization: A History of Insanity in the Age of Reason* (London: Tavistock, 1967), and the celebrated exchange which followed, namely Derrida's 'Cogito and the History of Madness', in *Writing and Difference*, trans. Alan Bass (London: Routledge, Kegan Paul, 1978), 31–63, and Foucault's 'My Body, This Paper, This Fire', trans. Geoff Bennington, in *Oxford Literary Review*, 4: 1 (1979), 9–28. Foucault's response was originally the appendix to the French second edition of *Madness and Civilization* in 1972. A good account of 'madness' in Foucault's work can be found in David Carroll's *Paraesthetics* (London: Methuen, 1987), esp. pp. 107–18. It may be added that Carroll's own project has certain correspondences with what I am attempting in the

present study. His concern is with a notion of 'paraesthetics' as 'something like an aesthetics turned against itself or pushed beyond or beside itself, a faulty, irregular, disordered, improper aesthetics – one not content to remain within the area defined by the aesthetic' (p. xiv). Linking the work of Foucault, Lyotard and Derrida, he seeks to elaborate 'paraesthetics' as what 'has made it possible to begin to develop, if not *a* "critical theory," then at least alternative critical strategies that confront and attempt to undermine and move beyond the closure of theory in its systematic, philosophical form' (p. 3).

16 Philippe Lacoue-Labarthe and Jean-Luc Nancy, *The Literary Absolute: The Theory of Literature in German Romanticism*, trans. Philip Barnard and Cheryl Lester (Albany: State University of New York, 1988), 57. Further page references are given in the text.

17 To adapt a thought concerning psychoanalysis and telepathy put forward by Wladimir Granoff and Jean-Michel Rey in their *L'occulte, objet de la pensée freudienne* (Paris: Presses Universitaires de France, 1983), 198, and to risk a summary proposition, at once no doubt premature and too generalizing, regarding the title of the present study: there is no 'and' between Telepathy and Literature.

18 Paul de Man, Foreword to *The Dissimulating Harmony: The Image of Interpretation in Nietzsche, Rilke, Artaud, and Benjamin*, by Carol Jacobs (Baltimore: Johns Hopkins University Press, 1978), x.

19 See, for example, his 'Collective Cases', Chapter XVIII of *Phantasms of the Living*, by Edmund Gurney, Frederic W. H. Myers, and Frank Podmore (London: Trübner, 1886), vol. 2, 168–270. And cf. the report on 'Collective Hallucinations', by Professor Sidgwick's Committee, in *Proceedings of the Society for Psychical Research*, vol. 10 (1894), 303–30.

20 See Louis Althusser, 'Ideology and Ideological State Apparatuses (Notes towards an Investigation)', in his *Lenin and Philosophy and other Essays*, trans. Ben Brewster (New York: Monthly Review Press, 1971), 127–86; esp. pp. 170–83.

21 Paul Hirst, *On Law and Ideology* (London: Macmillan, 1979), 41–2.

22 *Pace* Gregory Elliott's *Althusser: The Detour of Theory* (London: Verso, 1987), which describes itself as 'anti-anti-Althusserian' [*sic*] (p. 10) and seeks to expound a reading of his work on the basis that 'Althusser is the victim, rather than beneficiary, of philosophical fashion and political circumstance' (p. 1), it is clear that, however paradoxically, the purchase and importance of Althusser's work, at least in Britain, has been weakened in part thanks to the very scrupulosity and vigour of Hirst's critical work: see, for example, his 'Althusser and the Theory of Ideology' in *On Law and Ideology*, pp. 40–74.

2 TELEPATHY: FROM JANE AUSTEN AND HENRY JAMES

1 This text was given as a public lecture at the University of Geneva on 22 May 1987, and first published in *Oxford Literary Review*, vol. 10 (1988),

43–60. In presenting it here in its original form, I seek to preserve its 'tone' of engagement with the notion of the Freudian 'fake lecture'. Some of the following footnotes aim to clarify certain issues which earlier listeners and readers found difficult or opaque: I would like to thank, in particular, Rachel Bowlby, Maud Ellmann and Jonathan Nevitt, as well as those who commented or raised questions at Geneva, at the Theory Group at Keble College, Oxford, and at the Department of Psychology, Helsinki.

2 Jane Austen, *Emma*, ed. and with an introduction by Ronald Blythe (Harmondsworth: Penguin, 1966): page references will be to this edition, preceded by '*E*' where it might otherwise be unclear.

3 See Robert Liddell, *The Novels of Jane Austen* (London: Longmans, 1963), 94.

4 Henry James, *The Turn of the Screw and Other Stories* (Harmondsworth: Penguin, 1969): page references will be to this edition, preceded by '*TS*' where necessary.

5 Shoshana Felman, 'Turning the Screw of Interpretation', in *Literature and Psychoanalysis: The Question of Reading: Otherwise, Yale French Studies*, No. 55/56 (1977), 94–207.

6 'Turning the Screw of Interpretation', pp. 97, 102.

7 Jacques Derrida, 'Telepathy', trans. Nicholas Royle, in *Oxford Literary Review*, vol. 10 (1988), 3–41. Page references will be to this version of the text, preceded by '*T*' where appropriate.

8 *La Carte postale* (Paris: Flammarion, 1980). Pubd. in English as *The Post Card: From Socrates to Freud and Beyond*, trans. Alan Bass (Chicago: University of Chicago Press, 1987). In a note to 'Telepathy', Derrida remarks: 'These cards and letters had become inaccessible to me, materially speaking at least, by a semblance of accident, at some precise moment. They should have appeared, as fragments and in accordance with the plan [*dispositif*] adopted at that time, in "Envois"' (pp. 38–9).

9 These are, primarily, 'Psycho-Analysis and Telepathy', in *The Standard Edition of the Complete Psychological Works of Sigmund Freud*, trans. James Strachey (London: Hogarth Press), vol. XVIII (1955), 173–93; 'Dreams and Telepathy', in vol. XVIII, 195–220; 'Some Additional Notes on Dream Interpretation as a Whole', which includes a section on 'The Occult Significance of Dreams', in vol. XIX (1961), 135–8; and 'Dreams and Occultism', in *New Introductory Lectures*, trans. James Strachey, in *PFL*, 2: 60–87. These texts can also be found collected in *Psychoanalysis and the Occult*, ed. George Devereux (New York: International Universities Press, 1953). A fascinating source of further information, and one on which Derrida's 'Telepathy' closely relies, is the chapter on 'Occultism' in Ernest Jones, *Sigmund Freud: Life and Work* (London: Hogarth Press), vol. 3 (1957), 402–36.

10 See 'Dreams and Occultism': 'For instance, Person A may be the victim of an accident or may die, and Person B, someone nearly attached to him – his mother or daughter or fiancée – learns the fact at about the same time through a visual or auditory perception. In this latter case, then, it is as if

she had been informed by telephone, though such was not the case; it is a
kind of psychical counterpart to wireless telegraphy' (*PFL*, 2: 66).

11 See, for example, Derrida, 'Freud and the Scene of Writing', in *Writing and
Difference*, pp. 196–231; 'To Speculate – on "Freud"', in *The Post Card*,
pp. 257–409; 'Me – Psychoanalysis: An Introduction to the Translation of
"The Shell and the Kernel" by Nicolas Abraham', trans. Richard Klein,
in *Diacritics*, 9: 1 (March 1979), 4–12; and '*Fors*: The Anglish Words of
Nicolas Abraham and Maria Torok', trans. Barbara Johnson, in *The Wolf
Man's Magic Word*, pp. xi–xlviii.

12 Jacques Derrida, 'Of an Apocalyptic Tone Recently Adopted in Philosophy', trans. John P. Leavey, Jr., in *Oxford Literary Review*, 6: 2 (1984), 34.

13 *Letters of Sigmund Freud, 1873–1939*, ed. Ernst L. Freud, trans. Tania and
James Stern (London: Hogarth, 1961), 24.

14 See, in particular, *The Archaeology of Knowledge*, trans. A. M. Sheridan
Smith (London: Tavistock, 1972). For a good critical exposition of the
notion of discursive formation, see *Michel Foucault*, by Mark Cousins and
Athar Hussain (London: Macmillan, 1984), esp. pp. 76–97. Their aim, in
part, is usefully to emphasize that 'The identification of a discursive formation is an irreducibly theoretical decision, it is not an archival discovery'
(p. 91).

15 'What Is an Author?' in *Textual Strategies: Perspectives in Post-Structuralist
Criticism*, ed. and with an introduction by Josué V. Harari (London:
Methuen, 1980), 154.

16 *Totem and Taboo: Some Points of Agreement between the Mental Lives of
Savages and Neurotics*, in *PFL*, 13: 138.

17 See Samuel Taylor Coleridge, *Poems*, ed. John Beer (London: Dent, 1974),
163.

18 *Emma*, Norton Critical Edition, ed. Stephen Maxfield Parrish (New York:
Norton, 1981), 364.

19 Frank Bradbrook, *Jane Austen: Emma* (London: Edward Arnold, 1961), 7.

20 Following Genet, it is Derrida's suggestion in *Glas* that 'The signature is
a wound, and there is no other origin for the work of art' (p. 184).
Signéponge/Signsponge, trans. Richard Rand (New York: Columbia University Press, 1984), in particular, focuses on the ways in which literary
texts (in this case those of Francis Ponge) are concerned with signature-
effects and with the attempt (which need be neither 'conscious' nor even
'unconscious') to monumentalize the artist's name. Derrida stresses the law
which is capable of 'producing *and* prohibiting the signature' (*Signsponge*,
p. 56), and the extent to which any monumentalization is necessarily
marked by otherness, ex-appropriation and death. All of this becomes
distinctly more complex in the case of a woman writer, not least because of
the degree to which 'the desire for the proper' (as Derrida says of Ponge's
texts) is 'joined with the most utterly assumed phallocentrism' (p. 60). See
also Derrida's 'Otobiographies: The Teaching of Nietzsche and the Politics
of the Proper Name', trans. Avital Ronell, in *The Ear of the Other:
Otobiography, Transference, Translation*, ed. Christie V. McDonald (New

York: Schocken Books, 1985), 1–38. This text is concerned with a Nietz-schean notion of the name in terms of 'the dead man and the living feminine' (p. 16) and with a notion of 'the signature of the maternal' (p. 21). There is further treatment of these and related questions in Peggy Kamuf, *Signature Pieces: On the Institution of Authorship* (Ithaca: Cornell University Press, 1988), esp. pp. 95–9, 129–44, 146–73.

21 Paul de Man, *Allegories of Reading: Figural Language in Rousseau, Nietz-sche, Rilke, and Proust* (New Haven: Yale University Press, 1979), 300.

22 *The Post Card*, p. 197.

23 See Torok's 'Afterword' to *The Wolf Man's Magic Word*. p. 86.

24 See, for example, Derrida's 'Of an Apocalyptic Tone', p. 31. There is something of a paradox here, since to say what 'destinerrance' *is* would be, in a way, to presuppose that it does not 'exist'. Tentatively, 'destinerrance' may be said to link the apparently incompatible notions of destination or destiny and erring or wandering, and can be related to the logic of the necessary possibility of non-arrival inscribed in the structure of any des-patch. This necessary possibility, as Geoffrey Bennington has suggested, means that no despatch ever 'completely arrives' ('Deconstruction and the Philosophers (The Very Idea)', in *Oxford Literary Review*, Vol. 10 [1988], 88). For an illuminating (and somewhat idiosyncratic) further account, see John Llewelyn, *Derrida on the Threshold of Sense* (London: Macmillan, 1986), 109–14.

25 This phrase is the title of a collection of essays, *Taking Chances: Derrida, Psychoanalysis, and Literature*, ed. Joseph H. Smith and William Kerrigan (London: Johns Hopkins University Press, 1984). Several of these essays are highly stimulating in this context, in particular Jacques Derrida's 'My Chances/*Mes Chances*: A Rendezvous with Some Epicurean Stereophonies' (pp. 1–32); Samuel Weber's 'The Debts of Deconstruction and Other, Related Assumptions' (pp. 33–65); and Avital Ronell's '*Goethezeit*' (pp. 146–82). Ronell's is specifically concerned with what 'hovers on the frontier between science and its others, be these poetry, superstition, or telepathy' (p. 167). This is also one of the fundamental concerns of her *Dictations*: *On Haunted Writing* (Bloomington: Indiana University Press, 1986), an extended, fascinating and often bizarre treatment of the ghostly, 'remote control' relations between Goethe, Johann Peter Eckermann and Freud, and of Freudian psychoanalysis as a kind of 'Goethe-effect' (p. xiv).

26 This proposal might again be compared with certain aspects of Foucault's work. Foucault characterizes 'literature' in terms of its disruptive and transgressive force, its links with madness, its 'radical intransitivity' and 'precipitous existence' insofar as it is nothing but 'a silent, cautious depo-sition of the word upon the whiteness of a piece of paper, where it can possess neither sound nor interlocutor, where it has nothing to say but itself, nothing to do but shine in the brightness of its being' (*The Order of Things: An Archaeology of the Human Sciences* [London: Tavistock, 1970], p. 300). In this last respect it must appear that he brackets off 'literature' from other kinds of discourse. Yet Foucault's own work on the 'silence' and 'policing' of discourses – formulated most succinctly perhaps in 'The

Order of Discourse' (trans. Ian McLeod, in *Untying the Text: A Post-Structuralist Reader*, ed. Robert Young (London: Routledge, Kegan Paul, 1981), 48–78) – has taught us to be alert to precisely such bracketing-gestures. At least one question is then raised: in what ways is Foucault's bracketing off of 'literature' necessary to the coherence and efficacy of his 'own' discourse? There is a very good discussion of this issue in Chapter 5 of David Carroll's *Paraesthetics* ('Disruptive Discourse and Critical Power: Foucault', pp. 107–29). He emphasizes an important paradox: Foucault not only identifies 'literature' as 'a sort of "counter-discourse"' (*The Order of Things*, p. 44), he also identifies *with* it (see *Paraesthetics*, p. 118). Carroll notes: Foucault's 'own critical perspective is posited in such a way as to be so marginal, so disrespectful of tradition, that it cannot be situated, in its turn, by anything – by any history, ideology, or language – by anything, that is, but itself and the "disruptive discourses" with which it identifies itself and from which it takes its bearings' (p. 108). Foucault's position involves what Carroll calls a 'contradictory and impossible task': 'To speak without speaking, to interpret without interpreting' (p. 127). Carroll persuasively argues that 'the force of Foucault's critique would be more powerful, more disruptive, if it were less subjugated by these texts; if the disruptive beauty of texts such as Rivière's, Sade's, Artaud's, Bataille's, etc., were not "revered," but analyzed more critically; if those approaches he opposes were not ridiculed or dismissed, but were more carefully considered in terms of their relation to his own' (p. 128). The present study, then, confronts a doubly impossible task: it is an attempt to be both more critical *and* more literary than Foucault. What may, I hope, facilitate such an attempt is a refusal to bracket off 'literature' in the way he does, and at the same time a willingness to see how the elaboration of 'telepathy' both links and disorganizes 'literature' and 'criticism'. To give an example: in 'What Is an Author?' (in *Textual Strategies*, pp. 141–60), Foucault proposes that the author is 'the ideological figure by which one marks the manner in which we fear the proliferation of meaning' (p. 159). The privileging of the figure of the author is primarily a means of reducing 'the great peril, the great danger with which fiction threatens our world' (p. 158). Foucault goes on to say: 'It would be pure romanticism, however, to imagine a culture in which the fictive would operate in an absolutely free state, in which fiction would be put at the disposal of everyone and would develop without passing through something like a necessary or constraining figure' (p. 159). At least since the eighteenth century, notes Foucault, this figure has been that of the author. The present study would then show two necessarily linked concerns. First, a concern to displace further the notion of the author and, with it, notions of proper name and signature, subject and self. Second, a concern to impose 'telepathy' as the 'necessary or constraining figure' through which 'literature' (the novel, short story, drama and poetry) might be thought. It would be in this context, and in giving an additional stress to the militaristic connotations of the phrase, that we might begin to conceive of literature as a 'discursive formation'.

27 'Theory of the Text', trans. Ian McLeod, in *Untying the Text*, p. 44.

3 CRYPTAESTHESIA: THE CASE OF *WUTHERING HEIGHTS*

1 Page references to Abraham and Torok will be given in the text, preceded by '*WM*' where appropriate; roman numeral references are to Derrida's Foreword (pp. xi–xlviii) and Rand's Introduction (pp. li–lxix). All quotations from *Wuthering Heights* are taken from the Norton Critical Edition, ed. William M. Sale, Jr., 2nd edn. (New York: W. W. Norton, 1972), hereafter '*WH*' where clarity dictates.

2 For some recent publications in this context, see *Diacritics*, 18: 4 (Winter 1988), which contains Nicolas Abraham's 'The Phantom of Hamlet or The Sixth Act: Preceded by The Intermission of "Truth"', trans. Nicholas Rand, pp. 2–19; Nicholas Rand's 'Family Romance or Family History? Psychoanalysis and Dramatic Invention in Nicolas Abraham's "The Phantom of Hamlet"', pp. 20–30; and Esther Rashkin's 'Tools for a New Psychoanalytic Literary Criticism: The Work of Abraham and Torok', pp. 31–52. Rashkin, who provides a clear and very stimulating account, consistently represents the work of Abraham and Torok as a 'tool', even though she specifically acknowledges aspects of that work which 'lie beyond the scope of any hermeneutic theory or tool previously offered by psychoanalysis' (p. 40). The publication of Nicholas Rand's translation of Abraham and Torok's *L'écorce et le noyau* is forthcoming from University of Chicago Press.

3 'Introjection/Incorporation: *Mourning* or *Melancholia*', in *Psychoanalysis in France*, ed. S. Lebovici and D. Widlöcher (New York: International Universities Press, 1980), 5.

4 Nicolas Abraham, 'The Shell and the Kernel', in *Diacritics*, 9: 1 (Spring 1979), 19. Cited by Derrida in his 'Me – Psychoanalysis: An Introduction to the Translation of "The Shell and the Kernel" by Nicolas Abraham', in the same issue of *Diacritics*, p. 6. The next sentence of Abraham's text reads: 'If non-presence, the kernel and ultimate ground of all discourse, is made to speak [*se fait parole*], can it – must it – make itself heard in and through presence to self?' (p. 19).

5 *The Ear of the Other*, p. 109. Further page references will be given in the text, preceded by '*EO*' where appropriate.

6 Nicolas Abraham, 'Notes on the Phantom: A Complement to Freud's Metapsychology', trans. Nicholas Rand, in *Critical Inquiry*, 13: 2 (Winter 1987), 287–92: see p. 291.

7 Winifred Gérin's *Emily Brontë: A Biography* (Oxford: Oxford University Press, repr. 1972) observes of the Brontë sisters that 'To keep their own initials was a natural [*sic*] wish' (p. 185). Otherwise, Gérin contends, 'There appears to be no clue to the origin of Emily's choice of name, Ellis' (p. 186). Despite its somewhat paradoxical characterization of Emily Brontë as 'a very real [*sic*] and inflexible individual' (p. 227) who liked to take 'refuge from reality' (p. 195), Gérin's biography does have the merit of underlining both the extent to which 'For her there had never been in any case a separation between the imagined and the real life' (p. 205) and the extent to

which 'Emily Brontë' might (especially in the context of the present study) more accurately and more productively be conceived in terms of multiplicity and heterogeneity. Thus along with other supposedly 'impersonated' (p. 195) characters, 'Ellis Bell' is a demonic, different identity. Gérin notes, for example: 'the longer Emily lived with Ellis Bell, the greater the freedom "he" enjoyed. Not only on paper, but in daily life, Ellis Bell very often "took over" when vigorous action was required' (p. 196).

8 J. Hillis Miller, '*Wuthering Heights*: Repetition and the "Uncanny"', in his *Fiction and Repetition: Seven English Novels* (Oxford: Basil Blackwell, 1982), 57.

9 Nicholas Rand's 'Family Romance or Family History?' and Esther Rashkin's 'Tools for a New Psychoanalytic Criticism' both draw attention to the importance of the notions of 'crypt' and 'ghost' as trans-generational. The familiar (and perhaps insuperable) problems of attributing an 'unconscious' to a putatively fictional character are not specifically addressed. Rashkin, however, at one point seems to be implying a non-psychologistic notion of 'motive': 'The idea that the speech and behavior of fictional characters may be generated by hidden dramas inscribed within a text implies that some texts carry within them the motive force of their own production' (p. 51). This might usefully be linked to Derrida's observations about 'what effectively produces *both* the effect of arbitrariness *and* the effect of motivation' in language (See 'Fors', esp. pp. xlvi–xlvii).

10 David Cecil, 'Emily Brontë and Wuthering Heights', in *WH*, p. 304.

11 See 'Notes on the Phantom', where Abraham concludes that 'it is reasonable to maintain that the "phantom effect" progressively fades during its transmission from one generation to the next and that, finally, it disappears' (p. 292); and cf. Abraham and Torok, 'A Poetics of Psychoanalysis: "The Lost Object – Me"', trans. Nicholas Rand, in *SubStance*, 13: 2 (1984), 17, n. l: 'The buried speech of the parent becomes (a) dead (gap), without a burial place, in the child. The unknown phantom comes back from the unconscious to haunt and leads to phobias, madness, and obsessions. Its effect can persist through several generations and determine the fate of an entire family line.'

12 'Notes on the Phantom', pp. 287, 291.

13 Dream-like memories of reading *Wuthering Heights* would accord with Lockwood's 'own' experience when, adding yet another frame to the narrative, he returns to the locality of Wuthering Heights, in September 1802: '"Gimmerton?" I repeated – my residence in that locality had already grown dim and dreamy' (p. 241).

14 For a recent discussion of naming and magic in literature, see, for example, Michael Ragussis, *Acts of Naming* (Oxford: Oxford University Press, 1988), pp. 166–8, 198–208, 215–29.

15 Cf. *The Post Card*, pp. 152–3, 160.

16 Thalbourne, p. 33.

17 See, for instance, Thomas Moser, 'What Is the Matter with Emily Jane? Conflicting Impulses in *Wuthering Heights*', in *Nineteenth-Century*

Fiction, 17: 1 (1962), 1–19; Carol Jacobs, '*Wuthering Heights*: At the Threshold of Interpretation', in *Boundary 2*, 7: 3 (Spring 1979), 49–71; and Patricia Parker, 'Anagogic Metaphor: Breaking Down the Wall of Partition', in *Centre and Labyrinth: Essays in Honour of Northrop Frye*, ed. Eleanor Cook, Chaviva Hošek, Jay Macpherson, Patricia Parker, and Julian Patrick (Toronto: University of Toronto Press, 1983), 38–58, Moser's is a piece of ostensibly straightforward 'Freudian' literary criticism, proposing that 'Each scene dramatizes a dispute of some sort over entrance through a door or window. Heathcliff always wins, and the images suggest that the victory is a sexual conquest' (p. 5). (Actually, Freud's own remarks are more equivocal than this. Indeed, it could be argued that his apparent theoretical hesitation or uncertainty, in relation to the notion of 'threshold symbolism', marks the site of a more serious and more general disruption: see *The Interpretation of Dreams* (*PFL*, 4), esp. the shifting of positions expressed on pp. 647–8 and 712.) Carol Jacobs, on the other hand, proceeds from the recognition that, 'Like the entrance to Wonderland, the entrance to *Wuthering Heights* is marked by the metaphor of the doorway. Passage through that threshold will generate a crisis both in the voice of the self and in the logic of the good text' (p. 50). Patricia Parker stresses the extent to which Brontë's novel is concerned with 'the question of boundaries or "partitions"' (p. 55), and in particular with the 'sense of something threatening to break down all such partitions' (p. 56).

18   Giving 1923 as the first appearance of this word, *OED* cites S. de Brath's translation of Richet: 'A single phenomenon which the magnetizers of a past age called "lucidity" or "clairvoyance" (*hellsehen*); which is now called telepathy ... I propose to name it cryptesthesia.'

19   In this respect the strategy of paleonymy or paleonymics may be illustrated by the quotation from Derrida's 'The Time of a Thesis: Punctuations', which served as an epigraph to our Introduction. But it is important to recognize that we are not dealing here with the apparently simple matter of a chronological shift from 'old' to 'new'. 'Paleonymy' is itself, in a sense, cryptaesthetic: it is concerned with the perception of what is hidden, of what was always already there. As Derrida explains in his talk at the ICA 'On Colleges and Philosophy': 'I use the word "palaeonomy" to explain the way we should use an old word; not simply to give up the word, but to analyse what in the old word has been buried or hidden or forgotten. And what has been hidden or forgotten may be totally heterogeneous to what has been kept' (*Postmodernism: ICA Documents*, p. 224). See also Derrida's *Positions*, trans. Alan Bass (Chicago: University of Chicago Press, 1981), 71.

20   As for 'telepathy' in the so-called traditional sense, *Wuthering Heights* presupposes or inscribes an acceptance of it. The text is also pervaded by apparent instances of the death drive: Nelly, Isabella, Catherine and Heathcliff, among others, manifest explicit desires for oblivion or self-obliteration. This might seem to corroborate Torok's linking of the two. But if this too signifies a crypt, *where* would it be? and *whose*?

21 Samuel Beckett, *The Unnamable*, in *The Beckett Trilogy* (London: Picador, 1979), 381–2.

5   ON SECOND SIGHT: GEORGE ELIOT

1 George Eliot, *The Lifted Veil*, With a new afterword by Beryl Gray (London: Virago, 1985), 49. Further page references will be to this text, preceded by '*LV*' where appropriate.
2 George Eliot, *Daniel Deronda*, ed. Barbara Hardy (Harmondsworth: Penguin, 1967), 35. Further page references will be given in the text, preceded by '*DD*' where appropriate.
3 This is not to say that there has not been valuable and exciting work on *Daniel Deronda*. The final chapter of Gillian Beer's *George Eliot* (Brighton: Harvester, 1986), for example, admirably emphasizes that this text is Eliot's 'most experimental' (p. 214): it is a 'singularly dark and glittering work' (p. 228) which leaves us, suspended and estranged, with 'the dangerous power of the uncharted future' (p. 223). Neil Hertz has some provoking pages in the 'Afterword' to his *The End of the Line* (New York: Columbia University Press, 1985), 217–39, in which he considers the 'end-of-the-line structure' of the 'uncertain relation' between Deronda and his author (p. 227), while specifically highlighting Eliot's representation and treatment of Deronda's mother. Cynthia Chase provides a subtle and stimulating reading in 'The Decomposition of the Elephants: Double-Reading *Daniel Deronda*', in her *Decomposing Figures: Rhetorical Readings in the Romantic Tradition* (Baltimore: Johns Hopkins University Press, 1986), 157–74. Chase argues deconstructively against what she calls 'one of the main ostensible meanings of the novel: seriousness and idealism triumph over parody and the ironic spirit' (p. 158). But reducing Eliot's text to this dualistic tension has its disadvantages. Her assertion that 'The narrative is relentlessly referential' (p. 166) perhaps says more about Chase's critical approach than about Eliot's text. The formal, dualistic framework – however subversively treated – points to a more general characteristic of even the best of recent writing on *Daniel Deronda*, namely its assumption that Eliot's text is 'a novel' and should therefore be approached from a more or less conventional 'literary critical' stance. Hence, for example, an essay in literary criticism such as Timothy Pace's 'Who Killed Gwendolen Harleth? *Daniel Deronda* and Keats's "Lamia"', in the *Journal of English and Germanic Philology*, 87: 1 (January 1988), 35–48, which stresses the Nietzschean and disruptive potentiality of Gwendolen and contends that 'Eliot withdraws from associating Gwendolen with potentiality and thereby creates the major source of the novel's impression of unfulfilled imaginative power' (p. 44). Pace carefully illuminates the notion that 'It is the sense that Eliot herself imposes an inappropriate certitude on her final picture of Gwendolen that mars the novel's ending' (p. 48). But for all its discreet attention to 'potentiality', the essay remains very firmly within a conven-

tional mode of 'representing literature'. The critical work which seems to
me most forcefully to disengage from such assumptions is Jacqueline Rose's
essay 'George Eliot and the Spectacle of the Woman', in her *Sexuality and
the Field of Vision* (London: Verso, 1986), 105–22. Rose's work is directed
in terms of the crucial double perspectives of feminism and psychoanalysis.
In particular through its concentration on questions of hysteria and sexual
difference, her essay is able to unfold some of the kind of 'potentiality' Pace
writes about. (Hysteria and sexual difference form, in part, the subject of 'A
Letter on Poetry'.) In the present piece, considerations of character, plot
and theme are to a high degree secondary: I am concerned rather with a text
(*Daniel Deronda*) as it works at and over the limits of what conventionally
governs the classification of 'the novel' (and, as an inevitable corollary, the
classification of 'criticism').

4 The same goes for the (telepathic) notion of being able to read the future: 'if
the whole future were laid bare to us beyond to-day, the interest of all
mankind would be bent on the hours that lie between; we should pant after
the uncertainties of our one morning and our one afternoon' (*LV*, p. 43).

5 'The Facts in the Case of M. Valdemar', in the *Complete Stories and Poems
of Edgar Allan Poe* (New York: Doubleday, 1966), 276–83. Beryl Gray, in
fact, regards *The Lifted Veil* as having only 'a superficial affinity' (*LV*, p.
87) with Poe's text: the latter is dismissed on account of having mere
'*frisson*' as its 'main objective', whereas *The Lifted Veil* has a 'serious end'
in view (p. 88), namely to recount the story of what Gray sees as 'essentially a moral journey' (p. 72).

6 Roland Barthes, 'Textual Analysis of Poe's "Valdemar" ', trans. Geoff Bennington, in *Untying the Text*, p. 140.

7 See, for example, Gillian Beer, 'Myth and the single consciousness: *Middle-
march* and *The Lifted Veil*', in *This Particular Web: Essays on 'Middle-
march'*, ed. Ian Adam (Toronto: Toronto University Press, 1975), 91–115;
Ruby V. Redinger, *George Eliot: The Emergent Self* (London: Bodley
Head, 1976), 400–5, 418, 434; Charles Swann, 'Déjà Vu: Déjà Lu: "The
Lifted Veil" as an Experiment in Art', in *Literature and History*, 5: 1
(Spring 1979), 40–57, 86; Sandra M. Gilbert and Susan Gubar, *The Mad-
woman in the Attic: The Woman Writer and the Nineteenth-century Liter-
ary Imagination* (New Haven: Yale University Press, 1979), 443–77; and
Mary Jacobus, *Reading Woman: Essays in Feminist Criticism* (London:
Methuen, 1986), 254–74.

8 *The George Eliot Letters*, ed. Gordon S. Haight (New Haven: Yale University Press, 1955), Vol. V, 380; cited by Gray, *LV*, p. 71. *The Lifted Veil*
was first published alongside *Silas Marner* and *Brother Jacob* in the Cabinet
edition of 1878, a fate which, as Beryl Gray puts it, 'has perhaps helped to
hide rather than to "harness" it' (*LV*, p. 71). Gray's concern is to 'harness'
it in terms of Eliot's 'moral philosophy' (*LV*, p. 77): the present reading is
concerned with something rather different.

9 George Eliot, *Silas Marner: The Weaver of Raveloe*, ed. Q. D. Leavis

(Harmondsworth: Penguin, 1967), 113, Further page references will be given in the text.

10 George Eliot, *The Mill on the Floss*, with an introduction and notes by Walter Allen (London: Pan Books, 1973). (On the 'interruption', see for example *LV*, pp. 77–8, and Redinger, p. 404.) Above all one might become flooded or enmeshed by the apocalypticism of this text, especially the 'Come!' interwoven through its closing pages. Like other Eliot texts, *The Mill on the Floss* is deeply absorbed with notions of sound, music and voice in relation to the materiality of writing. This is evident not only in Stephen's letter to Maggie, with the 'strange power' of its voicing of the demand to 'Come!' (p. 488). It also marks Philip Wakem's letter to her, declaring from an uncanny sense of distance: 'But I shall not go away. The place where you are is the one where my mind must live, wherever I might travel. And remember that I am unchangeably yours: yours – not with selfish wishes – but with a devotion that excludes such wishes' (p. 478). One might hear, then, what Derrida has referred to as the apocalypticism and 'insupportable vibration' of a 'Come' (see his essay 'Of an Apocalyptic Tone Recently Adopted In Philosophy', esp. pp. 31–5) across these letters and these final pages, and go on to consider ways in which *The Mill on the Floss* and *The Lifted Veil* might seem, from before the beginning, to say 'Come!' to one another.

11 Gillian Beer, *George Eliot* (Brighton: Harvester, 1986); Simon Dentith, *George Eliot* (Brighton: Harvester, 1986).

12 See Maurice Blanchot, 'The Narrative Voice (the "he," the neuter)', in his *The Gaze of Orpheus and Other Literary Essays*, trans. Lydia Davis (Barrytown, NY: Station Hill, 1981), 133–43.

13 George Eliot, *Middlemarch*, ed. W. J. Harvey (Harmondsworth: Penguin, 1965), hereafter '*M*' where appropriate. For another account of *Middlemarch* in this context, see Michal Peled Ginsburg, 'Pseudonym, Epigraphs, and Narrative Voices', in *ELH* [*Journal of English Literary History*], 47: 3 (1980), 542–58.

14 For two recent accounts which highlight the crucial importance of this concept in Eliot's work, see Simon Dentith's *George Eliot* (esp. pp. 27–55), and David Marshall's '*Daniel Deronda* and the Wisest Beholder', in his *The Figure of Theater*, 193–240. Dentith's concern is to analyse the project of what Eliot called 'the extension of our sympathies' primarily in terms of class relations. This leads him to conclude that 'The attempt to bind people together in society, to gain recognition for people on the strength of their moral rather than their social worth, obscures these real material [as well as other class] differences that will continue to divide people no matter with what sympathy "we" regard our "more heavily-laden fellow-men"' (p. 53). Marshall, on the other hand, is concerned with reading *Daniel Deronda* as 'a dramatization of Smith's *Theory of Moral Sentiments*' (p. 194). Thus he argues that 'Gwendolen and Deronda can be seen to act out a theory of moral sentiments that amounts to a serious investigation of the epistemolo-

gical conditions of sympathy as much as a romantic lesson in the failings of solipsism and the virtues of identifying with others' (p. 195). Cf. also Neil Hertz's exploration of the question of the 'validity of the novelist's imagination of others' (p. 94), in his essay 'Recognizing Casaubon', in *The End of the Line.*

15 The verb 'gambol' occurs at least once, in the context of Gwendolen: 'Gwendolen felt as if her heart were making a sudden gambol, and her fingers, which tried to keep a firm hold on her work, got cold' (p. 374).

16 Beer, *George Eliot*, p. 214.

17 A haunting link between 'grass' and (absence of) hearing is also made in *Silas Marner*, where we are told that Nancy Lammeter 'carried these decided judgements within her in the most unobtrusive way: they rooted themselves in her mind, and grew there as quietly as grass' (p. 216).

18 Wordsworth's poem, concerned with the demonic breaking up of 'bower' and 'bough', concludes: 'Then, dearest Maiden, move along these shades/In gentleness of heart; with gentle hand/Touch – for there is a spirit in the woods' ('Nutting', in *Romantic Poetry and Prose*, ed. Harold Bloom and Lionel Trilling [New York: Oxford Unviersity Press, 1973], 150–2).

19 Thus, for example, of the second half of the nineteenth century Oppenheim notes: 'The varied records of spiritualism during these decades amply illustrate the use of the term "psychological" as synonymous with "spiritualist" and the application of the word "psychology" to the pursuit of evidence supporting human immortality' (*The Other World*, p. 239).

20 See, for example, *DD*, pp. 98, 100, 112, 126, 431, 480, 481, 525, 570, 571, 602, 622, 660, 670, 713.

21 And this allows Gwendolen, and Eliot, to play upon the apparent banality of spiritualism. Rex tells Gwendolen what Anna said. '"Did she?" said Gwendolen, laughingly. "What a little clairvoyante she is!" "Shall you [want to ride after the hounds this morning]?" said Rex, who had not believed in her intending to do it if the elders objected, but confided in her having good reasons. "I don't know. I can't tell what I shall do till I get there. Clairvoyantes are often wrong: they foresee what is likely. I am not fond of what is likely; it is always dull. I do what is unlikely"' (p. 100). Eliot does not merely 'thematize' clairvoyance, whatever that might mean: even in the above example, there is a work of double-bind going on – a denial which is also a participation; a 'thematic' reference (old style) which is also a constitutive necessity of the narrative itself.

22 Ludwig Wittgenstein, *Philosophical Investigations*, trans. G. E. M. Anscombe (Oxford: Blackwell, repr. 1984), § 18.

23 See *LV*, p. 33.

24 See *Beyond the Pleasure Principle*, in *PFL*, 11: 332. And cf. his remarks for example in 'Dreams and Occultism': 'Permit me now … to proceed as though I believed in the objective reality of telepathy. But bear firmly in mind that that is not the case and that I have committed myself to no conviction' (*PFL*, 2: 66).

25 For Derrida's observation about Freud's playing with a notion of 'acredibility' in *Beyond the Pleasure Principle* and elsewhere, see his 'Telepathy', p.
21.

26 See *DD*, p. 362, and *Beyond the Pleasure Principle*, in *PFL*, 11: 332, 292.
For an account of various uncanny aspects of *Beyond the Pleasure Principle*,
see Derrida's 'To Speculate – on "Freud"', in *The Post Card*, pp. 257–409.
Concerning the '*advocatus diaboli*' reference, for example, Derrida wonders: 'why compare to a diabolical operation that which is presented here as
a suspensive procedure, a concern of curiosity, or even scientific curiosity?'
(p. 379) And cf. Hélène Cixous's celebrated analysis of 'Fiction and its
Phantoms: A Reading of Freud's Das Unheimliche (The "Uncanny")',
trans. Robert Denommé, in *New Literary History*, 7: 3 (Spring 1976),
525–48. Cixous's characterization of 'The "Uncanny"' might also be
applied to *Beyond the Pleasure Principle*: it is, she argues, 'less a discourse
than a strange theoretical novel' (p. 525). In both texts, moreover, we might
see Freud being represented as 'in some way a *ghost*' (p. 541).

27 Cf. Mirah's presentiments on the journey (again calling up *The Lifted Veil*)
to Prague: 'You will think I had not enough reason for my suspicions, and
perhaps I had not, outside my own feeling; but it seemed to me that my
mind had been lit up, and all that might be stood out clear and sharp. If I
slept, it was only to see the same sort of things, and I could hardly sleep at
all. Through our journey I was everywhere on the watch. I don't know
why, but it came before me like a real event, that my father would suddenly
leave me' (p. 260).

28 This has a weird correspondence to an anecdote recounted by Ernest Jones
in his chapter on 'Occultism', in *Sigmund Freud: Life and Work*: '. . .
Ferenczi was now getting venturesome. Seeing a soldier in a tramcar he made
a guess at his name and as they got out asked him, 'Are you Herr Kohn?'
The astonished man answered in the affirmative. Freud found the story
"uncannily beautiful", but could not attribute it to telepathy because the
man could hardly be expected to carry a visual picture of his name about
with him. He said afterwards, however, that he was impressed by Ferenczi's
argument that a man's name was a sensitive area and thus could more easily
be communicated to a stranger' (p. 415).

29 Cf. the strange dimension of 'forecasting imagination' when Deronda brings
Mordecai news of Mirah: 'As Mordecai rose to greet him, Deronda was
struck with the air of solemn expectation in his face, such as would have
seemed perfectly natural if his letter had declared [though it had not] that
some revelation was to be made about the lost sister' (p. 631).

30 *DD*, p. 548. A link between the moon and sympathy is made earlier, in the
epigraph to Chapter 29, where Eliot cites Walt Whitman:

> Surely whoever speaks to me in the right voice,
> him or her I shall follow,
> As the water follows the moon, silently,
> with fluid steps anywhere around the globe. (p. 371)

31 To give, here in passing, just three examples, three strands one might follow out of psychoanalytic discourse: first, the context established by Gregory Ulmer, in *Applied Grammatology: Post(e)-Pedagogy from Jacques Derrida to Joseph Beuys* (Baltimore: Johns Hopkins University Press, 1985): 'The superego, according to Freud, is constructed "on the model not of its parents but of its parents' superego; the contents which fill it are the same and it becomes the vehicle of tradition and of all the time-resisting judgments of value which have propagated themselves in this manner from generation to generation" [citing J. Laplanche and J.-B. Pontalis, *The Language of Psycho-Analysis*, trans. Donald Nicholson-Smith (London: Hogarth Press and Institute of Psycho-Analysis, 1973), 437]. Here is the question of "telepathy"' (p. 135). Second, there is the more maternally oriented work of Abraham and Torok, as described by Esther Rashkin in her 'Tools for a New Psychoanalytic Literary Criticism': 'Everyone creates being for herself or himself. Every child's emergence as an individual is distinctive, constituted by repressions of uniquely charged pieces-of-the-mother, each bearing affects specifically related to the singular circumstances and psychic traumas of the mother's life. Moreover, since every mother is also the child of another mother, she must herself be understood as always carrying the contents of another's unconscious' (p. 35). Finally, in a less specifically generational context, there is Lacan's observation in 'The Circuit' about 'those striking coincidences Freud noted in the sphere of what he calls telepathy': 'it is through being links, supports, rings in the same circle of discourse, agents integrated in the same circle of discourse, that the subjects simultaneously experience such and such a symptomatic act, or discover such and such a memory' (*The Seminar of Jacques Lacan. Book II: The Ego in Freud's Theory and in the Technique of Psychoanalysis 1954–1955*, trans. Sylvana Tomaselli [Cambridge: Cambridge University Press, 1988], 89).

32 See de Man's 'Autobiography as De-Facement', in his *The Rhetoric of Romanticism* (New York: Columbia University Press, 1984), 75–7.

33 One way of pursuing this question might be in terms of what Jacqueline Rose suggests – 'at the risk of troubling the concept of an *écriture feminine*' – about 'suspending [a] relation to the very fact of sexual difference' and using writing 'to *masquerade*': see 'George Eliot and the Spectacle of the Woman', p. 120.

34 Cf. Derrida's reading of Levinas, in 'Violence and Metaphysics: An Essay on the Thought of Emmanuel Levinas' (in *Writing and Difference*, pp. 79–153), with its emphasis on the notion that 'The visage is a face only in the face-to-face' (p. 98).

35 On spirit photography, see for example Oppenheim's *The Other World*, pp. 70–1, 351–2. We are certainly not proposing here a concurrence with Virginia Woolf's thesis, evocative as it may be, concerning Eliot's 'own' face. Woolf writes: '. . . one cannot escape the conviction that the long, heavy face with its expression of serious and sullen and almost equine power has stamped itself depressingly upon the minds of people who

remember George Eliot, so that it looks out upon them from her pages' ('George Eliot', in Woolf's *Collected Essays*, vol. 1 [London: Hogarth Press, 1966], 196–7). Likewise it should be stressed that the use of the term 'physiognomy' here is to be distinguished from any traditionally 'spiritual-ist' determination: if anything we might again speak of a *paleonymic*, more radically *textual* 'physiognomy'. For another account of Eliot and physi-ognomy, see David Marshall's *The Figure of Theater*, pp. 229ff.

36 An indeterminacy of the living and the dead is attributed to the face of Grandcourt from the beginning, as when we read: 'It was not possible for a human aspect to be freer from grimace or solicitous wrigglings; also it was perhaps not possible for a breathing man wide awake to look less animated' (p. 145). Cf. the later, mortifying comparison between a lacertian Grand-court and a prawn, while he and his wife are breakfasting: ' "I like frank-ness: that seems to me a husband's great charm," said Gwendolen, with her little upward movement of her chin, as she turned her eyes away from his, and lifting a prawn before her, looked at the boiled ingenuousness of its eyes as preferable to the lizard's' (p. 649). The text goes on to suggest that, in more than a simple sense, Gwendolen then 'devour[s] her mortification'.

37 'Dreams and Occultism', in *PFL*, 2: 86. Cited by Torok, in her 'Afterword' to *The Wolf Man's Magic Word*, p. 100. It is also cited by Mikkel Borch-Jacobsen, in *The Freudian Subject*, trans. Catherine Porter (London: Mac-millan, 1989), a study which, in its clarity and rigour, may illuminate and lend support to some of the arguments and conclusions of the present work. In an analysis of Freud's 'Group Psychology and the Analysis of the Ego' (*PFL*, 12: 93–178) and one of its precursor-texts, Gustave Le Bon's *The Crowd* (1895), Borch-Jacobsen argues that Le Bon's notion of the 'unconscious ... is indissolubly nonsubjectal and "social," to the extent that he never designates anything but immediate communion with others (their representations, desires, affects) prior to any consciousness of self, and thus also prior to any consciousness of others. Taken to the extreme, it is thought transmission, telepathy ... [T]he members of the crowd are merely *mediums* controlled (entranced, possessed) by suggestion' (p. 140). In a footnote, he then draws attention to a contemporary synonymity of 'telepathy' and 'mental suggestion', before adding: 'This dream of direct communication – or sociality – without intermediaries comes up again in Freud's text; Freud then quite oddly concedes to the telepathy thesis all that he denied the thesis of suggestion: "If only one accustoms oneself to the idea of telepathy, one can accomplish a great deal with it – for the time being, it is true, only in imagination. It is a familiar fact that we do not know how the common purpose comes about in the great insect commun-ities: possibly it is done by means of a direct psychical transference of this kind. One is led to a suspicion that this is the original, archaic method of communication between individuals and that in the course of phylogenetic evolution it has been replaced by the better method of giving information with the help of signals which are picked up by the sense organs. But the older method might have persisted in the background and still be able to

put itself into effect under certain conditions – for instance, in passionately excited mobs" [*PFL*, 2: 86]. Thus the mass bond may have to be thought of as a telepathic umbilical cord' (*The Freudian Subject*, p. 266, n. 12). While emphasizing the continuing and unavoidably disturbing significance of notions of hypnosis, suggestibility and 'thought transmission' for the theory and institution of psychoanalysis (see, for example, p. 150), Borch-Jacobsen does not further theorize the specifically telepathic dimensions of this 'extreme'.

38 See *LV*, pp. 84ff.
39 This formulation is indebted but obviously not reducible to Virginia Woolf's celebrated remark about Eliot's heroines: 'The ancient consciousness of woman, charged with suffering and sensibility, and for so many ages dumb, seems in them to have brimmed and overflowed and uttered a demand for something – they scarcely know what – for something that is perhaps incompatible with the facts of human existence' ('George Eliot', p. 204).
40 Cf. Derrida's outline of a 'foresight saga' for 'Sigi' (i.e., Freud), in 'Telepathy', pp. 36–7.
41 'Determinism, Belief in Chance and Superstition – Some Points of View', in *PFL*, 5: 300–44. See also Derrida's extremely stimulating account of these aspects of Freud's thought, in 'My Chances/*Mes Chances*', esp. pp. 20ff.

6   A WALK IN 'KEW GARDENS'

1 'Kew Gardens', in *The Complete Shorter Fiction*, ed. Susan Dick (London: Triad Grafton, 1987), 119–27. Further page references are to this edition.
2 *The Letters of Virginia Woolf*, vol. III *(1923–28)*, ed. Nigel Nicolson and Joanne Trautmann (New York: Harcourt Brace Jovanovich, 1978), 54.
3 Woolf uses 'Wall' in her letters to Violet Dickinson, at least initially as an abbreviated form of 'Wallaby'. See *The Letters of Virginia Woolf*, vol. I *(1888–1912)*, ed. Nicolson and Trautmann (New York; Harcourt Brace Jovanovich, 1975), 242, 245–8, 254, 266.
4 Cf. 'The Mark on the Wall' (in *The Complete Shorter Fiction*, pp. 109–18), which concludes by identifying the subject, or object, of its title and of its narrative: 'Ah, the mark on the wall! It was a snail' (p. 118).
5 In a letter to Vanessa Bell in July 1918, Woolf describes 'Kew Gardens' as 'a case of atmosphere', adding 'I dont [sic] think I've got it quite': see *Letters*, vol. II *(1912–22)*, ed. Nicolson and Trautmann (New York: Harcourt Brace Jovanovich, 1976), 257. She goes on to make some rather elliptical references to her 'aesthetic philosophy', suggesting that 'Its [sic] a question of half developed aesthetic emotions, constantly checked by others of a literary nature – in fact its [sic] all very interesting and intense' (p. 257).
6 *Letters*, vol. II, p. 96.
7 *Collected Essays*, vol. I (London: Hogarth Press, 1966), 296.

8   In his seminar on 'The Split between the Eye and the Gaze', Lacan speaks of Choang-tsu who dreams he is a butterfly: 'he is a captive butterfly, but captured by nothing, for, in the dream, he is a butterfly for nobody. It is when he is awake that he is Choang-tsu for others, and is caught in their butterfly net': see *The Four Fundamental Concepts of Psycho-Analysis*, ed. Jacques-Alain Miller, trans. Alan Sheridan (London: Hogarth Press and the Institute of Psycho-Analysis, 1977), 76.

9   *Collected Essays*, vol. I, p. 294.

10   *Collected Essays*, vol. I, p. 291.

11   See, for example, *The Anxiety of Influence* (New York: Oxford University Press, 1973), 139–55.

12   Some measure of the force of these relations is suggested by the fact that Janet Oppenheim's study, for instance, stops at 1914: to have extended it beyond the outbreak of the Great War would have involved a considerably larger body of research material. The popularity of 'telepathy' during war-time can no doubt partly be explained by the phenomenon of suffering (pathos) in the distance (tele-): by the huge numbers of soldiers away from their families and loved ones, at a distance and possibly (or actually) dying. Perhaps then it is not surprising to find the telepathic invocation, the call from the distance in the name of a telepathic exchange, even in as traditional a poem as Rupert Brooke's 'The Soldier': 'If I should die, think only this of me: / That there's some corner of a foreign land / That is for ever England.' Then the start of the concluding sestet: 'And think, this heart, all evil shed away, / A pulse in the eternal mind, no less / Gives somewhere back the thoughts of England given' ('The Soldier', in *The Oxford Book of War Poetry*, ed. Jon Stallworthy [Oxford: Oxford University Press, 1984], 163). Doubtless this poem also broaches the complex but fascinating question of the relationship between telepathy and nationality or nationalism.

13   Walter Pater, *The Renaissance* (New York: Modern Library, 1919), 198. For an account which is in certain fundamental respects Bloomian, see Perry Meisel, *The Absent Father: Virginia Woolf and Walter Pater* (New Haven: Yale University Press, 1980). Meisel observes: 'my working assumption throughout is that Woolf betrays her indebtedness to Pater by the recurrent and habitual use of particular figures of speech borrowed from the decisive moments in Pater's own vision, and that such borrowed figures betoken her capture by Pater on the level of stance as well' (p. xiv).

14   *The Renaissance*, p. 197.

15   See, for example, *Letters*, vol. II, p. 282.

16   Maurice Blanchot, *The Madness of the Day*, trans. Lydia Davis (Barrytown, NY: Station Hill, 1981), 18.

17   For a more extended account of the notion of destination in Woolf's work, see Rachel Bowlby, *Virginia Woolf: Feminist Destinations* (Oxford: Blackwell, 1988). Shelley's 'The Question' (*Poetical Works*, ed. Hutchinson, corrected by G. M. Matthews [Oxford: Oxford University Press, 1970], 614–15) describes a dream in which the narrator 'wandered by the way', seeing myriads of flowers, before concluding:

Methought that of these visionary flowers
I made a nosegay, bound in such a way
That the same hues, which in their natural bowers
Were mingled or opposed, the like array
Kept these imprisoned children of the Hours
Within my hand, – and then, elate and gay,
I hastened to the spot whence I had come,
That I might there present it! – Oh! to whom?

It is important to set this phantom nosegay adrift from any simple notion of Romantic solipsism. The nosegay is just as much the description of its constituent flowers as it is any 'flowers-in-themselves'. In this way, the final rhetorical question is addressed to the impossibility of its being read: there is no reader to whom this textual nosegay can be presented. Shelley's question, which is specifically cited and re-cited in *The Waves* (London: Granada, 1977) (see, for example, pp. 38, 139, 187, 194), can be regarded as characteristic of Virginia Woolf's texts in general, but on two conditions. First, that 'Virginia Woolf' is here conceived in terms of the ghostly, multiple and heterogeneous. Second, that this state of affairs also applies to the reader.

7 A LETTER ON POETRY

1 Coleridge, 'Frost at Midnight', in *Poems*, ed. John Beer (London: Dent, 1974), 137–9. Line numbers will refer to this text. Page references to other Coleridge poems will be to Beer's edition.

2 'S. T. C.' adds his celebratedly odd footnote regarding that 'thin blue flame' or 'film': 'In all parts of the kingdom these films are called *strangers* and supposed to portend the arrival of some absent friend' (*Poems*, p. 138). For a highly stimulating and rather different reading of the 'stranger' here, see Richard A. Rand's 'Geraldine', in *Untying the Text*, pp. 280–316.

3 'Kubla Khan, Or, A Vision in a Dream: A Fragment' (*Poems*, pp. 167–8) closes with an expressed desire to 'build that dome' and 'those caves of ice' (ll. 46–7) which, after all, owe their existence to the vision with which the poem opens (ll. 1–36).

4 'Only connect', the epigraph to E. M. Forster's *Howards End* (Harmondsworth: Penguin, repr. 1976), occurs three times on one page of this novel, alongside the injunction to 'Live in fragments no longer' (p. 188). In saying that Forster is 'wrong again' I am not referring so much to his fiction, and certainly not to *A Passage to India* (1924), a text potentially very exciting in relation to the concerns of the present study. His critical prose, however, is different. To give only one example – the chapter on 'Prophecy' in his *Aspects of the Novel*, ed. Oliver Stallybrass (Harmondsworth: Penguin, repr. 1977), 116–33. This chapter is by no means without interest, not least in its attention to 'prophecy' as 'a tone of voice' (p. 116). This leads to at least one haunting evocation of Emily Brontë's novel: '*Wuthering Heights*

is filled with sound – storm and rushing wind – a sound more important than words and thoughts' (p. 131). But there is much to question in any event: for instance, Forster's hoodwinking rejection of the claims of 'common sense' (p. 117); his representation of George Eliot as (merely) 'a preacher', without 'prophetic' qualities (pp. 122–4); his assertion that 'Hardy's novels are surveys; they do not give out sounds' (p. 125) (scarcely clear, say, from that passage of *The Mayor of Casterbridge* [Harmondsworth: Penguin, 1978] which treats of the 'regal power' of music, mixing the figure of the double with 'a very fugue of sounds' [p. 371]); his assertion that the work of Joyce 'is talk, talk, never song' (p. 126); and his absurd characterization of D. H. Lawrence as a writer 'who has the rapt bardic quality, and whom it is idle to criticize' (p. 130).

5 See *Feminine Sexuality: Jacques Lacan and the école freudienne*, ed. Juliet Mitchell and Jacqueline Rose, trans. Jacqueline Rose (London: Macmillan, 1982), 154.

6 *Feminine Sexuality*, p. 154.

7 Wallace Stevens, *Opus Posthumous*, ed. Samuel French Morse (New York: Alfred A. Knopf, 1957), p. 158.

8 See A. Walton Litz, 'Particles of Order: The Unpublished "Adagia"', in *Wallace Stevens: A Celebration*, ed. Frank Doggett and Robert Buttel (Princeton: Princeton University Press, 1980), 68.

9 'Living On / Border Lines', in *Deconstruction and Criticism*, by Harold Bloom et al. (New York: Seabury Press, 1979), 107.

10 See the Index entry for 'hysterical symptoms' in Sigmund Freud and Joseph Breuer, *Studies on Hysteria*, in *PFL*, 3: 415–16.

11 David Carroll, *Paraesthetics*, 109; and see pp. 125ff for his valuable discussion of distinguishing between what he calls 'a transgressive aesthetics of the sublime' and 'the literary-aesthetic trap'.

12 *Studies on Hysteria*, in *PFL*, 3: 295–6.

13 On Freud's 'conversion' see Derrida's 'Telepathy', p. 33, and Ernest Jones's chapter on 'Occultism', III, p. 422.

14 See her 'Jeffrey Masson and Alice James', in the 'Sexual Difference' special issue of *Oxford Literary Review*, 8 (1986), 189. Cf. also Lacan's characterization of psychoanalysis as the 'hysterisation of discourse' (cited in *Feminine Sexuality*, p. 161, n. 6).

15 Thomas Hobbes, *Leviathan*, ed. C. B. Macpherson (Harmondsworth: Penguin, repr. 1981), 88. For a very stimulating general account of this and related notions, see Michael V. DePorte's *Nightmares and Hobbyhorses: Swift, Sterne, and Augustan Ideas of Madness* (San Marino: Huntington Library, 1974), esp. Chapter 1, 'Abnormal Psychology in England 1660–1760', pp. 3–53.

16 Cf. Derrida's comments in the discussion following his presentation of 'Structure, Sign, and Play in the Discourse of the Human Sciences' (in *The Structuralist Controversy: The Languages of Criticism and the Sciences of Man*, ed. Richard Macksey and Eugenio Donato [Baltimore: Johns Hopkins University Press, 1972], 247–72): 'Perception is precisely a concept, a

concept of an intuition or of a given originating from the thing itself, present itself in its meaning, independently from language, from the system of reference. And I believe that perception is interdependent with the concept of origin and of center and consequently whatever strikes at the metaphysics of which I have spoken strikes also at the very concept of perception. I don't believe that there is any perception' (p. 272).

17 See de Man's 'Review of Harold Bloom's *Anxiety of Influence*', in his *Blindness and Insight: Essays in the Rhetoric of Contemporary Criticism*, 2nd edn. (London: Methuen, 1983), 271, and Derrida's 'Living On / Border Lines', p. 147.

18 Paul de Man, Foreword to *The Dissimulating Harmony*, p. xi.

19 See Dalia Judovitz, *Subjectivity and Representation in Descartes: The Origins of Modernity* (Cambridge: Cambridge University Press, 1988), 142. Judovitz's excellent study is concerned to show how Descartes 'redefines the subject in such a way as to exclude its necessary relation to language' (p. 158) and to argue for the value and importance of 'forays into thought that recognize its tentative that is, representational character' (p. 198).

20 William Wordsworth, *The Prelude 1799, 1805, 1850*, ed. Jonathan Wordsworth, M. H. Abrams, and Stephen Gill (New York: Norton, 1979): hereafter 'Norton' when referring to editorial notes in this volume. Quotations from *The Prelude*, unless otherwise specified, will be from the 1805 text.

21 Hirst and Woolley, *Social Relations and Human Attributes* (London: Tavistock, 1982), p. 116, n. 2. Our own notion of 'trance' here corresponds more closely with the account of hypnosis furnished by Borch-Jacobsen in his *The Freudian Subject*: see esp. pp. 140ff and 225ff. Roughly, we might suggest, there would be no 'state of self-obliteration' for Borch-Jacobsen, because there is no 'self' to be obliterated.

22 See Norton, p. 42, n. 5.

23 See Lucy Newlyn's *Coleridge, Wordsworth and the Language of Allusion* (New York: Oxford University Press, 1986), esp. Chapter 6, ' "A Strong Confusion": Coleridge's Presence in *The Prelude*', pp. 165–94. Newlyn's study is concerned with the notion of a double bond which is generated through allusion. This bond is subject-centred: it is 'with the initiated reader, who is allowed access to hidden meanings, and with the other writer, whose words are being quoted, appropriated, or misused'. For Wordsworth and Coleridge, she claims, 'allusion becomes dialogue': this then becomes a matter of interpreting 'what amounts to a private language' (p. vii). Our own interest here is rather with everything (for example in the logic of quotation and iterability) which contaminates or overruns, rendering such notions of 'dialogue' and 'private language' problematic or indeed impossible. (For a detailed account of iterability, see Derrida's 'Signature Event Context', in *Margins of Philosophy*, trans. Alan Bass [Chicago: University of Chicago Press, 1982], esp. pp. 315ff.)

24 See David Hume, *A Treatise of Human Nature*, ed. L. A. Selby-Bigge, 2nd

edn., rev. P. H. Nidditch (Oxford: Clarendon Press, 1978), 363, 316, 253, 259. For a useful account of identity in Hume, see Wade L. Robison, 'Hume on Personal Identity', in *Journal of the History of Philosophy*, 12 (1974), 181–93.

25 Smith writes: 'We sympathize even with the dead, and overlooking what is of real importance in their situation, that awful futurity which awaits them, we are chiefly affected by those circumstances which strike our senses, but can have no influence upon their happiness. It is miserable, we think, to be deprived of the light of the sun; to be shut out from life and conversation; to be laid in the cold grave ... The happiness of the dead, however, most assuredly, is affected by none of these circumstances; nor is it the thought of these things which can ever disturb the profound security of their repose. The idea of that dreary and endless melancholy, which the fancy naturally ascribes to their condition, arises altogether from our joining to the change which has been produced upon them, our own consciousness of that change, from our putting ourselves in their situation, and from our lodging, if I may be allowed to say so, our own living souls in their inanimated bodies, and thence conceiving what would be our emotions in this case. It is from this very illusion of the imagination, that the foresight of our own dissolution is so terrible to us, and that the idea of those circumstances, which undoubtedly can give us no pain when we are dead, makes us miserable while we are alive' (*The Theory of Moral Sentiments*, pp. 12–13). For a fuller account of the 'dream' or 'fiction of sympathy' in Smith, see David Marshall's *The Figure of Theater*, pp. 167–92. Marshall emphasizes an important paradox. On the one hand, Smith 'takes as a presupposition the separateness of other minds, the limitations of our ability to share other people's feelings'. Yet at the same time he 'imagines the possibility of sympathy enacting identification, transfer, transport, presence; *The Theory of Moral Sentiments* represents acts of the imagination that would deny the distance and difference that divide people from each other and themselves' (p. 180). Our own concern lies partly in a further exploration of this paradox – especially insofar as 'sympathy' may be seen always already to involve a specifically literary scenario, and insofar as it involves a kind of *a priori* disturbance of presence, proximity or distance, or the necessity of what we might call a certain telesthetics. In his more recent study, *The Surprising Effects of Sympathy*, Marshall also focuses on the relations between sympathy and the aesthetic. Thus he observes, for example: 'Our sympathy, like the work of art that moves us, takes place within the realm of fiction, mimesis, representation, and reproduction. If the success of a novel, play, or painting depends on acts of sympathy, our experience of sympathy depends on an aesthetic experience. Sympathy in this sense is always already an aesthetic experience' (*Surprising Effects*, p. 21).

26 See Norton, p. 152, n. 3; and the synaesthetic 'one Life' of Coleridge's 'The Eolian Harp', in *Poems*, p. 52. The phrase 'shapes and sounds' is of course from 'Frost at Midnight':

> so shalt thou see and hear
> The lovely shapes and sounds intelligible
> Of that eternal language, which thy God
> Utters, who from eternity doth teach
> Himself in all, and all things in himself.
> Great universal Teacher! he shall mould
> Thy spirit, and by giving make it ask. (57–64)

27 Alan J. Bewell, 'A "Word Scarce Said": Hysteria and Witchcraft in Words-worth's "Experimental" Poetry of 1797–1798', in *ELH*, 53: 2 (Summer 1986), 357–90: see p. 363. Further page references to this article are given in the text.

28 Karen Swann, ' "Christabel": The Wandering Mother and the Enigma of Form', in *Studies in Romanticism*, 23 (Winter 1984), 533–53: see p. 535.

29 See Parveen Adams, 'Symptoms and Hysteria', in *Oxford Literary Review*, 8 (1986), 182–3. Adams's clear and extremely helpful account of Freud's formulations of 'hysteria' can be complemented by her more recent essay, 'Per Os/cillation', in *Thresholds: Psychoanalysis and Cultural Theory*, ed. James Donald (London: Macmillan, 1990), a collection of essays which also includes John Forrester's 'Psychoanalysis: Telepathy, Gossip And/or Science'. 'Per Os/cillation' offers an important reconsideration of notions of hysterical identification in the light of the work of Borch-Jacobsen.

30 Yet, in accordance with the characteristic capacity of Wordsworth's poetry for suspending the logic of non-contradiction, this frailty may be set off against a later reference in the same Book, where 'A little yellow canvass-covered book, / A slender abstract of the *Arabian Tales*' is described as 'but a block / Hewn from a mighty quarry' (see V, 482–91). It constitutes, says Wordsworth, 'A promise scarcely earthly' (491). More extravagant, perhaps, might be the claim made by Hardy in his 1913 poem 'At Castle Boterel':

> Primaeval rocks form the road's steep border,
>   And much have they faced there, first and last,
> Of the transitory in Earth's long order;
>   But what they record in colour and cast
>   Is – that we two passed

(*The Complete Poems*, ed. James Gibson [London: Macmillan, 1976], 352). At the same time, however, it is clear that the hysterical force, the dramatic terror and anxiety of the dream incorporates a recognition of rock or stone as likewise 'frail'. Thus J. Hillis Miller, in 'The Stone and the Shell: The Problem of Poetic Form in Wordsworth's Dream of the Arab' (in *Untying the Text*, pp. 244–65), emphasizes 'those tiny, pulverized stones, the sands which in the dream passage form the environment of the "Arab phantom's" solitude and of his crazy quest' (p. 262, n. 18).

31 Michel Foucault, 'The Order of Discourse', in *Untying the Text*, p. 52.

32 For another account of the death drive in this respect, see Samuel Weber's

The Legend of Freud (Minneapolis: University of Minnesota Press, 1982). Weber argues that 'In the final analysis, "im letzten Grunde," what the drives repeat is neither a ground nor an abyss, but a violent process of in-scription, alteration, and perhaps above all: narration' (p. 139). He goes on to suggest that 'The "death drive" would then be merely another name for a story that seeks to organize the other, precisely by naming it' (p. 145).

33 For an identification between 'apocalypse' and 'contemplation', see Derrida's 'Of an Apocalyptic Tone Recently Adopted in Philosophy', p. 4. 'Contemplation' is also, of course, the word which Wordsworth uses (see V, 157, and 1850: V, 1).

34 *The Interpretation of Dreams*, in *PFL*, 4: 756 (cited by Adams, 'Symptoms and Hysteria', 180); *PFL*, 4: 694. See also 'Some General Remarks on Hysterical Attacks', *PFL*, 10: 97.

35 'A Note on the Unconscious in Psychoanalysis', in *Proceedings of the Society for Psychical Research*, 26 (Part 66) (1912), 312–18; and in *PFL*, 11: 45–57. See p. 53, and Editor's Note in *PFL* 11: 47–9.

36 J. Hillis Miller, 'The Stone and the Shell', p. 253. There is in fact a striking correspondence between Miller's description here and what Norman Kemp Smith says about Descartes's three dreams, or 'threefold dream', in *New Studies in the Philosophy of Descartes: Descartes as Pioneer* (London: Macmillan, 1953). Norman Kemp Smith observes in a footnote that Freud considered Descartes' dreams to be 'of the "von oben" type, i.e., as consisting in idea-formations due to what has been happening in the preceding waking-consciousness, and drawing their substance only in certain of their parts from more deeply hidden states of mind' (p. 33, n. 1). Miller's account of the 'hypnagogic' may be compared with the definition of 'hypnagogic state' provided by Michael Thalbourne in his *Glossary of Terms Used in Parapsychology*: 'the transitional state of consciousness experienced while falling asleep, sometimes characterized by vivid *hallucinations* or imagery of varying degrees of bizarreness' (p. 33). Miller's stress on the subject ('a man') and the experiential ('perceiving and thinking') is in keeping with a reading of the dream of the Arab necessarily reliant on the 1850 text.

37 Cf. Cynthia Chase's 'The Accidents of Disfiguration: Limits to Literal and Figurative Reading of Wordsworth's "Books"', in her *Decomposing Figures: Rhetorical Readings in the Romantic Tradition* (Baltimore: Johns Hopkins University Press, 1986), 13–31. Her reading of Book V shows how, for example, Wordsworth 'predicts the interpretive retrievals of the critical reader' (p. 24). Chase contends that 'It is as true to say that Wordsworth's text reads its interpretation literally as to say that the interpretation literally reads Wordsworth's text' (p. 28). Cf. also Timothy Bahti, 'Figures of Interpretation, The Interpretation of Figures: A Reading of Wordsworth's "Dream of the Arab"', in *Studies in Romanticism*, 18 (Winter 1979), 601–27. Like Chase, Bahti emphasizes the 'Dream of the Arab' as a text which 'exhibits Wordsworth's confrontation and interpretation of rhetorical figures, and also offers its own writing of their reading or interpretation, the reading of its own writing' (p. 607).

38 *Studies on Hysteria*, in *PFL*, 3: 64.
39 Norton, p. 158, n. 4. For an English translation of the account given of Descartes' 'threefold dream' in Baillet's *Vie de Descartes* (1691), see Norman Kemp Smith's *New Studies in the Philosophy of Descartes*, pp. 33–9. The standard account of Descartes' dreams and Wordsworth's 'dream of the Arab' is Jane Worthington Smyser's 'Wordsworth's Dream of Poetry and Science', in *PMLA* [*Publications of the Modern Language Association of America*], 71: 1 (1956), 269–75. As to why Wordsworth in 1839 decided to 'make the dream his own' for the later (1850) version, Smyser argues that it was 'solely for the sake of dramatic credibility' (p. 274).
40 See Norton, p. 157, n. 1. The 1850 text describes the Arab as 'an uncouth shape' (1850: V, 75) and thus identifies him with the 'uncouth shape' of the Discharged Soldier (IV, 402). It may be noted, in passing, that the soldier is another figure, another stranger last seen in a doorway (see IV, 496–504).
41 Cf. Borch-Jacobsen's account of the 'birthplace' of a subject, in *The Freudian Subject*. The subject, he concludes, is 'born in myth, in fantasy, in art': 'This birth will have been merely mythical, fantasmatic, fictive, and doubtless nothing (no Father, no Narcissus, no Master) has preceded the situation of *Dichter* – that is, of actor, mime' (pp. 238–9).
42 Cf. Judovitz's account of hyperbolic doubt which necessarily involves 'Descartes' in 'a theatre with a cast of feigned characters: Morpheus, God the deceiver, and the evil genius' (*Subjectivity and Representation in Descartes*, p. 140). It may be of interest to note that the 'evil genius' also comes up in the first part of Descartes' 'threefold dream'. It would appear, moreover, to be hysterically concerned with disturbances of walking. In Baillet's account we learn that there was 'a great weakness in [Descartes'] right side which disabled him from leaning on it. Ashamed of walking in that manner he made an effort to straighten himself, but felt an impetuous wind which, catching him up in a kind of whirlwind, made him revolve three or four times on his left foot ... [He assumed that] all this was the work of some evil genius bent on seducing him' (see *New Studies in the Philosophy of Descartes*, pp. 33–4). All of this might give a new force to Pierre Gassendi's already ironic version of Descartes' most famous formula, 'I walk, therefore I am': see *Subjectivity and Representation in Descartes*, p. 114.
43 See *Phantasms of the Living*, I, 496–518, which includes consideration of 'a group of arrival-cases where the impending arrival was unknown or unexpected by the percipient; or where the phantasm has included some special detail of appearance which points to a telepathic origin' (p. xxxii).
44 See *Phantasms of the Living*, I, xxxii.
45 Cf. one of the most curious of the marginalia in 'The Rime of the Ancient Mariner', regarding the moon: 'In his loneliness and fixedness he yearneth towards the journeying Moon, and the stars that still sojourn, yet still move onward; and every where the blue sky belongs to them, and is their appointed rest, and their native country and their own natural homes,

which they enter unannounced, as lords that are certainly expected and yet there is a silent joy at their arrival' (*Poems*, p. 180).

46 Cited by David S. Miall, in 'The Meaning of Dreams: Coleridge's Ambivalence', in *Studies in Romanticism*, 21 (Spring 1982), 60.

47 The phrase 'speak into the air' is taken from I Corinthians 14. Hillis Miller has perceptively remarked on the ways in which this Biblical passage *informs* the 'dream of the Arab': see 'The Stone and the Shell', pp. 262–3, n. 21. He quotes: 'Now, brethren, if I come unto you speaking with tongues, what shall I profit you, except I shall speak to you either by revelation, or by knowledge, or by prophesying, or by doctrine? And even things without life giving sound, whether pipe or harp, except they give a distinction in the sounds, how shall it be known what is piped or harped? For if the trumpet give an uncertain sound, who shall prepare himself to the battle? So likewise ye, except ye utter by the tongue words easy to be understood, how shall it be known what is spoken? for ye shall speak into the air. There are, it may be, so many kinds of voices in the world, and none of them is without signification' (I Corinthians 14: 6–10).

48 See 'Of an Apocalyptic Tone Recently Adopted in Philosophy', in particular its proposition that 'as soon as one no longer knows very well who speaks or who writes, the text becomes apocalyptic' (p. 27). This is not to be read as some veiled egotism on the part of some presupposed, putatively unique and self-identical signatory ('Derrida', for instance), but rather it is characteristic of what he refers to, in the same essay, as 'the language of writing, this given trace that always comes from the other, even if it is no one' (p. 4).

49 See 'The Stone and the Shell', pp. 257–9.

50 *Opus Posthumous*, p. 62.

51 See Jacqueline Rose, 'Introduction: Feminism and the Psychic', in *Sexuality in the Field of Vision*, pp. 20, 15. Rose attributes this notion of 'an endless dispersal of subjectivity' to Derrida, in what is evidently a serious misreading: cf. Geoffrey Bennington, 'Deconstruction and the Philosophers (The Very Idea)', p. 117, n. 8. A remark made by Derrida in a discussion in *The Ear of the Other* is perhaps more characteristic and more apt: '... this is not to say that one has to turn oneself over, bound hand and foot, to the *Unheimliche*, because I don't believe in that. In other words, I don't believe in seeking out absolute risk, absolute nonreappropriation, alienation, and madness for their own sake, and, besides, I don't want to have anything to do with that. I'm too afraid of it' (p. 156).

8 SOME THOUGHTS ON *ANTONY AND CLEOPATRA* BY MOONLIGHT

1 All references are to William Shakespeare's *Antony and Cleopatra*, ed. John Ingledew (Harlow, Essex: Longman, 1971). References to other plays are

taken from *The Riverside Shakespeare*, ed. G. Blakemore Evans et al. (Boston: Houghton Mifflin, 1974).

2 Kirby Farrell, 'Prophetic Behavior in Shakespeare's Histories,' in *Shakespeare Studies*, XIX (1987), ed. J. Leeds Barroll, 17–40: see p. 21.

3 K. M. Briggs, *Pale Hecate's Team: An Examination of the Beliefs on Witchcraft and Magic among Shakespeare's Contemporaries and His Immediate Successors* (London: Routledge, Kegan Paul, 1962), 186.

4 Here, as elsewhere, I am indebted in particular to Ingledew's explanatory notes in the New Swan (Longman's) edition: see *Antony and Cleopatra*, p. 128.

5 The notion of dramaturgic telepathy would necessarily have disruptive or transformative implications for the concepts of 'theme', 'imagery', 'motif', not to mention 'character', 'plot' and assorted other traditional terms of criticism. It is in part for this very reason that I am proposing here to leave open to further inquiry and discussion a possible typology of 'dramaturgic telepathy' and the question of its limits.

6 In his note on the word 'arm-gaunt', John Ingledew observes: 'The meaning of this word, which occurs nowhere else, is uncertain. It has been variously conjectured to mean "worn thin with hard service in armour", "hungry for battle", "looking fierce in armour", "ready for conflict". Many scholars have considered the word textually corrupt and have proposed such emendations as "arm-girt", "arrogant", "termagant", "war-gaunt"' (*Antony and Cleopatra*, p. 30). See also Appendix I ('An arm-gaunt steed') to the Arden *Antony and Cleopatra*, ed. M. R. Ridley (London: Methuen, 1954), 235–6. Corrupt or not, coincidental or not, we may add that the repetition of 'arm' ('the arm / And burgonet', 'arm-gaunt') might be taken to illustrate another oddly 'telepathic' instance.

7 'Hop' is the word used by Enobarbus in the context of attributing to Cleopatra a 'power' beyond life or breath:

> *I saw her once*
> *Hop forty paces through the public street,*
> *And having lost her breath, she spoke, and panted,*
> *That she did make defect perfection,*
> *And, breathless, power breathe forth. (II, ii, 231–5)*

8 The verb 'to stay' is also associated with eroticism and death when Antony, in characteristically (or recurrently) valedictory fashion, tells his followers, 'I look on you / As one that takes his leave. Mine honest friends, / I turn you not away, but like a master / Married to your good service, stay till death' (IV, ii, 28–31).

9 'Toil', as Ingledew points out, here has the sense of 'snare'. If the word unavoidably (and as it were deceptively, in the manner of a snare) carries with or within itself the more 'primary' connotation of 'labour', this would only further highlight the dramaturgic telepathy linking Caesar's description to Antony's earlier soliloquy: 'Since the torch is out, / Lie down and

stray no farther. Now all labour / Mars what it does: yea, very force entangles / Itself with strength' (IV, xiv, 46–9). Ingledew provides the following gloss: 'strength itself only gets more firmly tied up when it exerts itself. – The image is apparently that of an animal struggling in the nets which have trapped it' (*Antony and Cleopatra*, p. 164).

10 See Jacques Derrida's account of 'The Colossal', in *The Truth in Painting*, trans. Geoff Bennington and Ian McLeod (Chicago: University of Chicago Press, 1987), 119–47. Following Kant's 'Analytic of the Sublime', Derrida notes that the colossal derives from the sublime, and that 'the sublime is not in nature but only in ourselves' (p. 132). What is the size or measure of the colossal? Exploring Kant's emphasis on the notion of the colossal as the 'almost too large' or the *'almost unpresentable'* (p. 125), Derrida attempts to 'consider magnitude anew' (p. 135). Among other things, he introduces the crucial and fascinating question of 'narrative' and 'voice'. In order to sense the colossal, for instance in viewing the Egyptian pyramids (and we may remember that only a few moments earlier, in Shakespeare's play, Cleopatra has conjured up her 'country's high pyrámides' as the 'gibbet' where she might be hung up in chains [see V, ii, 60–2]), it is necessary 'to find a middle place, a correct distance for uniting the maximum of comprehension to the maximum of apprehension, to take sight of the maximum of what one cannot take and to imagine the maximum of what one cannot see'. Stressing that this account is based on a narrative, namely Savary's *Letters from Egypt*, Derrida wonders: 'But does not the distance required for the experience of the sublime open up perception to the space of narrative? Does not the divergence between apprehension and comprehension already appeal to a narrative voice? Does it not already call itself, with a narrative voice, the colossal?' (p. 142) Besides elsewhere showing an attentiveness to the question of 'size' and of its reproduction or projection (for instance when she declares 'Our size of sorrow, / Proportioned to our cause, must be as great / As that which makes it' [IV, xv, 4–6]), Cleopatra's allusion to 'the hearing of the gods' confirms the extent to which Shakespeare's text likewise acknowledges the uncanny role, in relation to the colossal, of narrative and voice. We may also here note what appears, in the passage in question, to be a particularly provoking signature-effect: 'voice' itself is identified in terms of 'shak[ing]' and 'spheres' (V, ii, 83ff).

11 Jean Pierre Vernant, 'The Representation of the Invisible and the Psychological Category of the Double', in his *Myth and Thought among the Greeks* (London: Routledge, Kegan Paul, 1983), 305–20. Further page references are given in the text. Vernant stresses that in later Greek history the colossos became merely 'a sign whose purpose was to recall the memory of someone dead to those still living', then goes on to note: 'Yet a different attitude can sometimes be glimpsed' (p. 314). In other words, there still seems to remain something of the older, more uncanny character of the colossos. Vernant observes that originally the colossos 'is not an image; it is a "double"' (p. 306). It is, he says, 'not a "natural" object, but nor is it simply a product of the mind.... The double is something separate from

the person who sees it, something whose peculiar character sets it in opposition, even in appearance, to familiar objects in life's ordinary setting' (p. 308). How is this 'glimpsed' in later forms? He concludes that 'In effect the colossos's function is to establish a real contact with the beyond and to bring about its presence in this earthly world. Yet, in so doing, it at the same time emphasizes all the elements of the inaccessible, the mysterious, and the fundamentally foreign that the world beyond death holds for the living.' The colossos, then, is aimed at establishing 'a bridge with the divine', yet 'it must at the same time emphasize the gap' (p. 315).

12   Finally, it is tempting to sense in this verb 'to bestride' a kind of cryptaes-thetic reference back to the 'demi-Atlas' (I, v, 23) Antony on his horse. As *OED* states, of sense (1): 'To sit upon with the legs astride. *a.* To ride, mount (a horse, etc.). The original use. *b.* To sit across (other things) as on a horse.'

13   What or who walked? Ingledew proffers: 'Kings and princes wore his colours (*livery*) – i.e., were his servants' (*Antony and Cleopatra*, p. 188). But the word 'crownet' (i.e., coronet) would also telepathize its only other appearance in the play, namely in Antony's anguished expression of betrayal:

> *Betrayed I am.*
> *O this false soul of Egypt! This grave charm,*
> *Whose eye becked forth my wars, and called them home,*
> *Whose bosom was my crownet, my chief end,*
> *Like a right gipsy hath at fast and loose*
> *Beguiled me, to the very heart of loss. (IV, xii, 24–9)*

14   William Hazlitt, 'On Shakespeare and Milton' in his *Lectures on the English Poets and The Spirit of the Age* (London: Dent, 1910), 44–68: see p. 56. Further page references are given in the text.

9   RAYMOND CHANDLER, TELEPHONING HOME

1   Raymond Chandler, *Playback*, in *The Second Chandler Omnibus* (London: Hamish Hamilton, 1973), 531.

2   Roger Caillois, 'The Detective Novel as Game' (1941), trans. William W. Stowe, in *The Poetics of Murder: Detective Fiction and Literary Theory*, ed. Glenn W. Most and William W. Stowe (New York: Harcourt Brace Jovanovich, 1983), 4.

3   Besides the well-known parallels between Freud's case histories and detective fiction, there is also for example his almost lifelong preoccupation with the so-called Bacon–Shakespeare controversy. As I argue in an essay in *Oxford Literary Review*, vol. 12 (1990), this preoccupation is itself not unrelated to the question of telepathy.

4   As Roger Caillois has noted: 'The pleasure one gets from a detective novel is not that of listening to a story, but rather that of watching a "magic" trick which the magician immediately explains' ('The Detective Novel as Game', p. 4). Actually this antithesis between 'story' and 'trick' is deceptive, since it inevitably draws attention away from what it is in 'story' which empowers the 'magic'.

5   This is what F. R. Jameson starts to highlight, when he evokes the weird web in which a Chandler narrative begins: 'It is as if the world of the beginning of the book, the imaginary Chandler Southern California, lay in a kind of uneasy balance, an equilibrium of large and small systems of corruption, in a tense silence as of people straining to listen.... The upshot is a whole series of murders and beatings: it is as though they existed already in a latent state, the acts that had merited them having already been committed, like chemical substances juxtaposed, waiting for a single element to be withdrawn or added in order to complete a reaction which nothing can stop. The appearance of the detective is this element' ('On Raymond Chandler', in *The Poetics of Murder*, 143–4: further page references to Jameson will be to this essay). In Jameson's quietly impassioned account, then, the detective becomes a figure of telepathy: he is nothing less than the agent whereby Americans can come to see and thus genuinely be themselves, to see themselves as linked to one another, as part of a single society: 'the form of Chandler's books reflects an initial American separation of people from each other, their need to be linked by some external force (in this case the detective) if they are ever to be fitted together as parts of the same picture puzzle' (p. 131).

6   *The Little Sister*, in *The Chandler Collection*, vol. 1 (London: Picador, 1983), 383–571: further page references will be to this text, preceded by '*LS*' where it might otherwise be unclear.

7   Cf. Jameson's observation that 'it seems to make little sense that a criminal would go to a detective in the first place and ask him to solve a murder of which he or she was, in reality, guilty' (p. 145).

8   Dennis Porter, 'Backward Construction and the Art of Suspense', in *Poetics of Murder*, 328.

9   Raymond Chandler, 'Twelve Notes on the Mystery Story', in *The Note-books of Raymond Chandler and 'English Summer: A Gothic Romance'*, ed. Frank MacShane (New York: Ecco Press, 1976), 38.

10 'Twelve Notes on the Mystery Story', p. 39.

11 Tzvetan Todorov, 'The Typology of Detective Fiction', in *Modern Criticism and Theory: A Reader*, ed. David Lodge (London: Longman, 1988), 161.

12 *Of Grammatology*, trans. Gayatri Chakravorty Spivak (Baltimore: Johns Hopkins University Press, 1976), 36. See also Derrida's *Speech and Phenomena: And Other Essays on Husserl's Theory of Signs*, trans. David B. Allison (Evanston: Northwestern University Press, 1973), especially Chapter 6, 'The Voice That Keeps Silence', pp. 70–87.

13 'Qual Quelle: Valéry's Sources', in *Margins of Philosophy*, p. 297.

14 See 'The Voice That Keeps Silence': 'To speak to someone is doubtless to hear oneself speak, to be heard by oneself; but, at the same time, if one is heard by another, to speak is to make him *repeat immediately* in himself the hearing-oneself-speak in the very form in which I effectuated it' (p. 80).

15 'Qual Quelle', p. 291.

16 For another example of what appears to be a predisposition towards death on Marlowe's part, see his response to the advances of Dolores Gonzales: ' "Just for half an hour," I said, "let's leave the sex to one side. It's great stuff, like chocolate sundaes. But there comes a time you would rather cut your throat. I guess maybe I'd better cut mine" ' (p. 519).

17 See also Marlowe's play on 'Quest' as acronym: 'Quest. Q as in quintessential, U as in uninhibited, E as in Extrasensory, S as in Subliminal, T as in Toots' (p. 486).

18 'Raymond Chandler Introduces "The Simple Art of Murder" ', in *The Midnight Raymond Chandler* (Boston: Houghton Mifflin, 1971), 1.

19 Perhaps the most hyperbolic accumulation comes in Marlowe's description of his condition shortly after the potassium hydrocyanide: 'I wet my lips and made some kind of a vague noise to which nobody paid any attention. I got up on my feet. I was as dizzy as a dervish, as weak as a worn-out washer, as low as a badger's belly, as timid as a titmouse, and as unlikely to succeed as a ballet dancer with a wooden leg' (p. 496).

20 For detailed discussion of these notions in relation to Freud's work, see, in particular, Derrida's 'Freud and the Scene of Writing', in *Writing and Difference*, pp. 196–231; 'To Speculate – on "Freud" ', in *The Post Card*, pp. 257–409, esp. 353ff; and Samuel Weber's *The Legend of Freud* (Minneapolis: University of Minnesota Press, 1982). Weber presents, among other things, an important reading of the 'silence' Freud attributes to the death drive (see, for instance, *PFL*, 15: 157, 241, 381), showing that 'if we listen closely, or rather, if we read attentively, we may remark that the very *Stummheit* of the death drive precludes it from ever speaking for itself; it is inevitably dependent on another discourse to be seen or heard. And that discourse, however much it may seek to efface itself before the "silence" it seeks to articulate, is anything but innocent or neutral. The death drive may be dumb, but its articulation in a theoretical and speculative discourse is not' (p. 129).

21 See 'Personism: A Manifesto', in *The Collected Poems of Frank O'Hara*, ed. Donald Allen, with an Introduction by John Ashbery (New York: Alfred A. Knopf, 1971), 498–9.

22 *A Lover's Discourse: Fragments*, trans. Richard Howard (London: Jonathan Cape, 1979), 114–15. See also Ned Lukacher, *Primal Scenes: Literature, Philosophy, Psychoanalysis* (Ithaca: Cornell University Press, 1986), who regards this as 'one of the most brilliant and important passages in all of [Barthes's] work' (p. 80). Lukacher in fact cites it in connection with 'uncanniness' in Heidegger, adding the claim that 'Freud's explorations of

the "uncanny" in the experience of hypnosis, suggestion, thought transference, and telepathy, and in the transference generally, should likewise be regarded as extreme or marginal instances of what is a fundamental ontological experience of the subject' (pp. 79–80).

23 'Telephoning Home'. The rain nonstop, nearly dawn, it doesn't seem possible, every time I go to sleep, when I'm just nodding off, when the pictures are coming, or the words, a word like 'rape' in its sense of seizure, and hurry, and turnip, or a picture like of the British Telecom people finally arriving to instal my phone, just then, when I'm nodding off, I wake up again. It must be connected with what happened.

Every time I wake up it's nearly dawn and, more cases than not, pouring with rain, in this dingy little place I've been living three months now, but not a short story, don't get me wrong, it's just I had a friend who used to write them, until one day, dead of night, there was this car-chase, him and me, most of it on the ring-road, and neither of us was drunk, looking back it was madness, a car-chase, a double mega-burn-up, that's what he called it, a mega-burn-up, on the ring-road, all over an argument about short whatever-the-name-is, stories, and minus a happy ending let me add. His name was Terry, Tel to his friends, and what an argument, more like a pitched battle, and that's what it turned into, him in his jumped-up Ford Escort and me in the Chevette I'd borrowed off a friend. Doing eighty we were, and ninety, side by side, swerving in and out, across the lanes of the dual, missing each other by a whisker, blaring our horns at each other and, certainly in my case but I expect Tel was doing the same, screaming at the top of my voice, absolute murder. I think even if the police had been around, and seen us, they'd have kept clear, it was so hairy. Didn't see another car the entire time, but then I wasn't really looking, nor was he, we were both more interested in flashing our lights and thumping our horns and yelling our heads off. Dazzling it was, and all because I couldn't stick it anymore, couldn't stick Tel telling me about his whatever-you-call-thems, short stories. I told him, in no uneasy words, that it was over, caput, 'No more, Tel, they're over, you're living in a dream world if you think otherwise,' I told him, 'You need your brain seen to.'

Well, Terry wasn't very pleased. So we had the car-chase, the mega-job, and it ended in tears, not surprisingly. It was a collaboration, so to speak. I mean, we agreed, if you took the aitch out of car-chase you had a proper carcase, one of us was saying something irrational like that, but we agreed, that one car took the form of what Tel would have called you know what, while the other took the form of another you know what, and that we'd run them both, simultaneous-like, and see how it turned out. It was nearly dawn when we shook on it and got into our vehicles and went tearing off south, down to join the ring-road, I could have died, blood everywhere, and both of us raving to establish our positions, and, needless to remark, Tel ending it, sixty feet through the windscreen after sailing through the central reserve. No one's fault, though I must admit to varying the account a bit, faced with the law, but I fooled them into understanding. After all we were neither of us drunk, we were sober as judges, I don't remember how I told it, what there was to tell.

About the telephone, and why I'm talking to you, if you can call it that. But then if I started explaining about that now, it would only be for the purpose of putting off the business about the rape. What rape? Ask me what I've done, what I do, you'd be asking more than they did, down at the dole office, that's for sure. I don't do anything, why should I do anything, I live in this bedsit, I walk around a bit, I borrowed someone's Chevette one time, I sit in the park don't I, and at bus-stops watching the traffic, I'm on the dole, I do that, what else, redundant, nice word, do us a favour.

Nearly dawn, the rain pouring down as usual. The little shop where I get my fags in the morning, and my food, I reckon he knows, I'm convinced of it. Sometimes I don't hear right, I'll admit, but last week, it was Tuesday, and I needed to get some shopping, I got some tins of soup, minestrone, tomato, oxtail, plus some baked beans, and a loaf of bread, and twenty Benson and a box of matches, and I had this plastic carrier bag with me, and I'd put the cans and things in it, and Derek, that's his name, was adding it all up on his little pad, when I thought to myself, I fancy a couple of apples. 'I'll have a couple of a apples as well, if you don't mind, Derek,' I said, and he looked up, straight in the eye, and said to me, 'Certainly, Jim,' he said. I could tell, from the way he looked at me so straight, I'm convinced of it. He put them in a small white paper bag and then, very helpful, went to put it in my carrier.

Well, in those situations you don't think do you, you just open the bag. I said, 'Thanks mate' to him, but only after he said, and this is where I should have begun really, only after he said to me, looking down into my carrier, 'Uncanny how similar tins look innit?' Of course I might be wrong, in the normal run of things I'd reckon I must have misheard him, or else I was daydreaming. After all, it wasn't exactly your typical sort of remark. Still I'm convinced that's what he said and that's why I'm sure that he knows. I should have said so earlier, should have explained how those words, to do with what was in my carrier, passed the lips of Derek down at the shop.

Nearly dawn, I keep dropping off, the rain nonstop, it's the problem of getting to speak to the right person, it can take hours, it took me weeks, to get a telephone fitted, I couldn't be without a phone, and I had a couple of hundred pounds stashed away, when I came here, this dingy little bedsit. So the process started, of finding out where the nearest telephone box was, getting put through to the operator, at the exchange, explaining the situation, so as to get put through to someone else, some other voice, which tells you that you need yet another one, and so on endlessly, you get through to somewhere and you get a voice, only to discover you haven't got through yet, you're still on your way. I nearly hung up, about a dozen times, what could be more tedious, more totally aggravating, it was too much, I kept on hanging up, in the middle of the day, rain streaming down the glass.

That was when I first saw Derek, outside his shop I mean, off of the premises. He was standing on the other side of the street, and talking to some geezer, a friend I thought, though now I wouldn't swear to it. I didn't suspect him then, I just noticed it was him, Derek from the cornershop, standing chatting with some other bloke, opposite the phone-box. Looking back on it, I realize he must have heard every word, everything I said, because the box had been done over and there was no glass, or there was glass everywhere, all over the ground, and leaning against the fence, and standing on the pavement, I've forgotten, what was there to tell, you couldn't see for glass, and I don't know why I did it, and did it so many times, I'd lost count before I started.

Pissing with rain and I can't sleep, I'm tempted to start describing all the voices I had to put up with. It was a good fortnight or three weeks before they came, whoever they were, the people from the DHSS, or the people from British Telecom, if you can call them people, they looked more like a troupe of doctors and nurses to me, I don't mean that doctors and nurses aren't people, just it was difficult to tell, because they arrived in what I'm convinced was the middle of the night and when I was fast asleep. And then I woke up with all this knocking on the door, hammering fit to wake the dead it was. I was furious, I can tell you. It was nearly dawn and I staggered down the stairs and I'd opened the door and in they all marched without the slightest attention to what I was saying, I was screaming mad what in Christ's name did they think they were doing, coming round like this and hammering at the door in the dead of night, just because I'm unemployed did they think I'd got nothing better to do than sit up all night waiting on the offchance they'd turn up, and have nothing better to do all day either, than merely sitting waiting?

They said something like just, 'Well, Mr Robson, we've tried to contact you more times than we care to remember. We've called round here a hundred times if we've called once, and you're never in, or never answer, whichever the case may be.' Maybe it was true, I spend a lot of time on the streets, sitting in the park or at bus-stops eyeing the traffic as I said, I can't stick being cooped up, especially in a room like this one, for more than a couple of hours at a stretch. Or maybe I was having a nap, that's different, sound asleep every time they called round, I've forgotten, how should I be expected to remember?

I said none of this, and showed them up. The bulb had blown a couple of days before, so it was pitch dark on the stairs. I couldn't make any of them out, I couldn't even begin to guess how many of them there were, it could have been hundreds, because there were still people, if you can call them that, coming in through the front door of the building, while I was at the top of the stairs showing the first arrivals into my room. When I managed to get a light on, there were seven of them. Two of them started speaking at once. One was saying they were from the DHSS, and the other that they were telephone people, from BT. I'm not sure, as I said I don't always hear right, and I decided to concentrate on listening to the second one, even although it was perfectly obvious to me that they were a bunch of medical people, you could see that plain as day from what they were wearing.

Fitting the phone was not going to be particularly easy, they said, and would I please take off all my clothes. I had a towel wrapped round me, and just stared at them. 'Towel then,' said one of the women wearing a nurse's uniform, and smiled. 'Would you please lie on the table?' I just did what she said, you know, what else could I do, you put yourself into their hands completely in situations like that, I could have killed her, I could have killed all of them, waking me up like that, and coming in like a herd of stormtroopers, and telling me to undress and lie down on the table, and I reckon on another occasion I would have, for instance pushed them all through the window. I'm on the first floor here and it's quite high up really, and there's steps and an old basement you'd land quite nastily in, if you fell.

But I wanted my bloody telephone installed and wasn't going to miss this opportunity, not for the world, I couldn't afford to, it had been three weeks of hell already.

As it turned out I must have fallen asleep, or they gave me an anaesthetic, something pretty knockout anyhow because I don't remember anything about the operation. I'd read about getting a pacemaker fitted, but that was nothing compared with this. The operation alone lasted forty-eight hours and I was conscious throughout. But I didn't let on about the fact that I was conscious and I'm quite sure I felt no pain, just the agony of looking with my screwed up eyes at all those faces, and the pincers, and the screwdrivers and wirecutters, and listening to all the engineer's little requests like 'Could you give me a line on ...?', I thought it would never end. Even now maybe I'm wrong, and it's still being fitted, how are you supposed to know?

The first person I called was Tel, but his line was engaged and then, much worse than that, I remembered that he was dead. Why do people call me Jim, or James, when my name's Barry, that's what I want to know. It's the newspapers and the TV that does it, giving you widescale coverage of the most sensational crimes and acts of violence and expect you to take a merely academical interest, month in month out, and then small mentions of things like multiple personalities and personality disorders, it's enough to make your flesh creep, is that what I mean? And it's not easy to see what the alternative is either.

I keep dozing off, then on again, backwards and forwards like a yo-yo, and I still don't know how I did it, if I did do it at all, sometimes I'm not sure, and it's the furthest thing from my mind, other times I'm absolutely positive, it's a dead cert.

The cornershop's also a newsagent, of course, and I buy a paper once in a while. You should've seen my face the morning I went in, a couple of months ago now thank God, and there it was, splashed all over the fronts of the tabloids, what a nightmare, that's when my suspicions of Derek began, just because he must have seen my face, I mean when I saw the frontpages. I could only buy a pint of milk, I don't even know how I managed to do that, my voice was all over the place, and I couldn't for the life of me hand over the 23 pence without dropping all the coins on the floor. As I walked out my body felt like it was just turning to ice, or stone, I couldn't move fast enough, whereas in fact the sweat must have been pouring off like a sauna.

I had to really brace up courage and walk up the street to another newsagent, where I think I managed to pick up a copy of *The Sun* and *Daily Express* without getting noticed. I don't have to tell you how long I spent that day looking in the mirror, and scouting round my room, looking for shreds of evidence. It was no surprise not finding any trace of the knife, or the dark blue balaclava, or the green anorak, but I did genuinely believe there might be some more minor detail, like grazes, cuts or bruises on my body, or a bit of torn clothing, a couple of strands of hair, something small but significant like that. And then the more I couldn't find anything, the more crazy I got. Again and again I came to the conclusion that the best place to look was my own body, and I used both the mirrors, to make certain I covered everything in as much detail as possible. I checked the lot, every hair, mole and freckle, every single inch of me. Of course the telephone kept getting in the way and I had to go careful because they're delicate things and it's easy to make a real mess of the transmission, the reception and everything. Never seen so many wires. There was this terrible moment I was convinced I was being bugged, you know like in a 'police film', what else, but I forgot about it, there were more important things to worry about. I was becoming frantic, and in the end I just took the whole carpet up and then wrenched up all the floorboards, and to my horror I discovered, I've forgotten, who cares? By this time the room was looking like a what-dyou-call-it, ouija-mi-flip, archeological dig, and I decided to give up. How many times I did it, if I did, I don't know, who cares, it was like having a seizure, an epileptic fit, or else it wasn't, but it was nearly dawn, and I was falling asleep.

When is this going to be investigated, that's what I want to know, when's the DHSS or BT, and who by, it's hard to say, the voices keep coming, maybe Derek, I've had my suspicions, you can be sure I've kept a close watch on that man. You wouldn't have thought it was illegal, to have a little patch down at the local allotment, and grow turnips and everything, on the other side of town, by the ring road, what else, hardly headline news. Jesus, the things people dig up, I don't know, you wouldn't believe it, I've forgotten, what else is there to tell?

The rain nonstop and it's virtually dawn, I just can't get any sleep, it's too late now, you'd have thought at least there'd be an operator to answer calls at this hour, but no, so it's this. Tel came over in the evening and he's stayed all night, I can hear all the voices now, we had this huge argument, more like a pitched battle as a matter of fact, and then I've forgotten, nearly daybreak or it might have been, once. Tel's gone downstairs and out into the street, fuming mad, we're going for a spin, if that's the word, he'll be standing waiting now, really furious, by his Ford Escort. I'm borrowing Derek's Chevette.

24 See August Strindberg, *Three Plays*, trans. Peter Watts (Harmondsworth: Penguin Books, 1958), 154. For link-ups between the telephone and Strindberg see also Avital Ronell's recent and admirable study *The Telephone Book: Technology, Schizophrenia, Electric Speech* (Lincoln, Nebraska: University of Nebraska Press, 1989), 113, 124. Although it appeared too late for consideration here and although it does not deal with the work of Chandler, the white and yellow pages of Ronell's book offer numerous and engaging interconnections with the present reading.

Index